INNERKINETICS

Your Blueprint
To
Excellence and Happiness

Ray W. Lincoln

INNERKINETICS
Your Blueprint to Excellence and Happiness

International Standard Book Numbers
Softcover: 978-0-9842633-7-0

Library of Congress Control Number: 2010917996
Printed in the United States of America

Cover design by Bookcovers.com

Apex Publications
Littleton, CO USA

Dedication

Dedicated to the memory of:

Charlie Bennett
Who fired my spirit when I was young

John Deane
Who taught me to dream and live with love

Professor E. M. Blaiklock
Who still stands in constant memory as my model and most noble
influence

The people I have coached
Who have enlightened me about the intricacies of human nature and
still do

Understanding Is Underrated
~ Ray W. Lincoln

Contents

Introduce Yourself To Your Strengths   153

Releasing and Developing Your Innerkinetics   333

Appendix   373

Selected Bibliography

Preface

The passion for this book was ignited by the hopes and achievements of successful clients who discovered their best by the use and development of their strengths. Also, there were the pains and cries of many others who fell short of their best only to find it (like the successful ones) in the discovery of themselves and the direction their lives were intended to go.

"From heaven descended the precept 'Know yourself,'" wrote Juvenal. "Die to 'missing the mark,'" mused Paul. Philosophers, saints, gurus and thinkers in all ages have pondered the way to reach our potential and settle for nothing less. Therefore, climb to the peak of your powers by finding yourself and in doing so discover a fulfillment and satisfaction that breeds a happiness you will never give up once you have found it.

Years of personal study, following the urges inside of me, started and then fueled my journey. I am a philosopher of human nature by choice, experience, and training. The most complicated organism is the human system and it creates a complexity in living that no one will ever fully understand or analyze. I propose to take from the learning of hundreds of people in the fields of temperament, neuroscience, personal growth, and faith and, together with the struggles of hundreds more (my clients), help you find your inner journey to the top, whatever that peak of success may be for you.

First (as I indicated) I had to find, identify, and learn about the powers living in me that I felt were demanding to be liberated. Their thirst for release and full expression also created an incessant hankering for me to try to reach my potential. The two urges were closely related. Having discovered my strengths by means of a temperament assessment, the task of understanding them correctly began. I had affirmed the results of the assessment I had taken but still struggled to release those strengths, to develop them, and feel their rewarding fulfillment. I had yet to discover that a correct understanding of them held the secret to what I was made to be and to how my fulfillment and happiness would be reached. It took me years to map my path. I was going it alone.

My hope is to shorten your search dramatically. This book explains how to discover and release your temperament's powers, your *Innerkinetics*, not just to define them.

Failure lives on every street and in every home, but failure can teach some very positive lessons. Failure is spelled "o-p-p-o-r-t-u-n-i-t-y." Don't misspell it! People don't want to fail, but it pulls with gravitational constancy and prophesies its own success all too often. Decades of dealing with searching and unfulfilled people, whose failure to find their strengths had led them to defeat, despair, and sometimes deep depression, has shown me that the path to success is a matter of rising to our greatness by the opportunity the use of our temperament's strengths provides. Failure might also be defined as "not using your strengths." The book will explain.

The many books that urge set principles of success on all of us as though there is only one path for all of us to follow made me urgently want to tell you that there is a unique path for each of us. Your path is written inside of you: your own individual, successful way to your very best. Find it with me.

Many books have been written about these universal principles of success, but few start with understanding ourselves and with the power of self-discovery. Temperament, or what I like to also call our *Innerkinetics*, leads us to a profitable and accurate discovery of ourselves and describes our path to our potential greatness. This is the path best traveled and, unfortunately, least traveled. In these pages you will find your dream.

I am indebted to all those who have given of their wisdom and knowledge to me over the years. The bibliography will reveal a few of these sources. In the field of temperament, my debt is acknowledged to people like Jung, Myers-Briggs, Keirsey, Montgomery (whose book makes the complex simple) and many others who stand out, having made significant contributions.

To Professor Ernest Blaiklock I owe more than I can tell. His scholarly mind and kind encouragement given to me years ago have influenced me greatly and returned many times to light the way in times of struggle.

Also, I am thankful to my wife, whose love, devotion, and superb work has literally made this book possible, along with a team of helpers who have aided this project with skill and professionalism. To all, a deeply felt thank you!

INNERKINETICS

Introduction

Who would not want to rise unfailingly to the dizzy heights of success, to be all they can possibly be since only have one life to live and we feel that incessant inner call to our own greatness? This book is about a blueprint for success that is located inside of each of us, and it isn't the same for everyone.

Here is the exciting journey I invite you to take in these pages:

- Should you want to be the best *(the very best)* you can be, travel with me.

- Should you long to know how you have been made (on the inside) and what powers are the formative, fantastic, forces in your inner "DNA," read on.

- Should you want to discover your real purpose in life, a plan for which you have been gifted and intricately designed, commit to the journey.

- Should you want to learn the path to your success, the path that is written in your *innerkinetics* (your temperament) and what it will mean to feel completely fulfilled, happy, and satisfied with your life, you must release and use your powers.

- Should you **want to follow a unique blueprint to your potential**, look inside of you with the guidance you will be given.

- Should you desire to learn how to release your strengths, how to maximize them, and how to get rid of your weaknesses, follow the signs.

- Should you crave to know yourself better, to understand why you do what you do and how to reinforce the good things and change what you want to change, read on.

These wonderful advantages of discovering *the real you* and having her or him stand up will, I promise you, change your personal perspective and set you on your unique path where the real you stands up boldly, confident and strong.

To read about *the real you* and not all the other people out there:

- Read the first four chapters

- Complete the temperament key in Chapter Five

- Read Chapter Six

- Read the chapter that describes your temperament as identified by the results of your temperament key (choose from Chapters Seven through Ten).

- Read Chapter Eleven

- Read the chapter on your temperament from chapters twelve through fifteen

- Finally, read Section Five.

You can read the entire book, of course, and if you do it will give you the advantage of knowing how other people are made as well. It will brighten the image of your own self to see yourself in contrast to others. I recommend you read the entire book!

What Is Different About this Book?
Ever been to your favorite bookstore and browsed the self-improvement section? It's full of books that are avidly selling you the idea that all you have to do is follow a set of "tried-and-true" principles to find success. It's the same path for everyone and was also mine, as I told you in the preface, until I found a better way. Because I've traveled those roads, I understand how following set principles, however great they may be (and they usually are great), does not address our differences. We are not all the same. We don't respond to things, people, or pressures the same way. All of us have different preferred ways of thinking and doing. Using the same path for everyone can lead to frustrating struggles and disappointments.

Now, this is important. How do I, for example, persevere or believe with greater conviction? Do I follow how someone else does it, or is there a path for me? The "how" is also not the same for everyone! We will find the how for you. That will make this book a handy personal manual to your becoming the best you can be.

Helping people discover themselves first and then discover the individual path to their success that is written inside their strengths, I have found, transforms their actual success. There is no one way for everyone — can't say that enough. Your own path is much more successful than traveling a public highway to an average goal. No, this is not a rehashing of those so-called universal principles I mentioned. People are different but, at the same time, share similarities. You will be led by your own inner path that takes both your differences and similarities into account!

This is also different from other studies on temperament because it will take you beyond the knowledge of how you are made. It will take you to an understanding of your strengths and weaknesses and how to release your strengths in a powerful way. It will also show you how to develop those strengths. Temperament is not made up of both strengths and weaknesses. That fact will lead you to find the way to deal immediately with those pesky weaknesses — yet another discovery.

What's Not Different About this Book?
We will use the 2,500-year-old "secret" of temperament to help you find your distinct path to your very best. The discovery of temperament is not new. There are many studies on temperament and many different "tests," so which one should you use? Stay in the mainstream is my advice after years of searching.

For two and one half millenniums the basic four temperaments observed by Hippocrates have been used by scholars, philosophers, novelists, researchers, and the medical world (to name a few sectors of society) to aid us in understanding ourselves. Knowing ourselves is the first step in understanding who we are and in what direction we are intended to go. That advice is very old. So is this part of the journey. The thesis of this book is based solidly on a very compelling history of temperament's usefulness.

This long history of human studies passes through the works of well-known names such as Hippocrates, Jung, and then Myers-Briggs, who created the first assessment that enabled us to discover our true preferences and that lead to enlightening self-knowledge. This was a breakthrough.   Keirsey followed, showing us how this kind of assessment can identify which of the four temperaments we are. He streamlined the Myers-Briggs Type Indicator and added to the vast research that has helped solidify this as the mainstream of temperament study. It has been used by many millions of people just in the last few decades alone.   I will stay with this mainstream of temperament psychology since it makes no sense to me to abandon such immense research and attempt to unnecessarily recreate the wheel. And why, when it is so accurate?   I owe a debt of gratitude to these brilliant minds and can benefit greatly from all the research that has been done by them and others.

If you wish a more detailed history of temperament you will find one of many in my book, *I'm a Keeper.*   In the bibliography of *INNERKINETICS* you will also find works by the authors I have just mentioned and others that are highlighted as particularly helpful for further study if you so desire.

Where this Book Will Take You
In the first four chapters we will discuss how important it is to uncover what is inside you (how you are made), to define success correctly, to discover the direction your life is intended to go, to follow your blueprint to success that is written into your strengths and etched into your *innerkinetics,* and to feel the rewards of your possible dream. *(For those who did not read the preface I have coined the word "innerkinetics" and use it, where not otherwise defined, as a synonym for temperament. I will explain its more precise meaning in Chapter Two.)*

In Chapter Five you will be invited to complete the Adult Temperament Key, a tool that will help you discover your temperament and much more. This will give you a code with four letters. You may have already taken this kind of assessment, such as the MBTI or Keirsey's Temperament Sorter II, or something else built on the same principles. The two I just named are excellent. The Temperament Key in this book will indicate your inbuilt temperament and you will be the final judge, verifying the results. You will use the code the assessment will provide as you read the chapters that follow to delve into the complexity and wonder of your makeup and set you on the path to your greatness.

In chapters six through ten, *the real you* stands up. This is your first understanding of how you are made on the inside, using two of the letters in your code. You will be introduced to some "Keys to Developing Your Potential" and you will then receive a fine-tuning of your path to success, using not just two but the four letters.

Chapter 11 is most important since it will help you understand the part your strengths and weaknesses play in your life and how to get rid of your weaknesses. Wouldn't that be great?

Chapters 12 through 15 will introduce you to your strengths and you will be asked to choose one of your strengths to begin a process of further development. Suggestions and guidelines for developing each of the strengths will slake your thirst for "how-tos."

In Chapters 16 through 19, the tools to release and develop your strengths to their maximum power are laid out in some detail. You will be encouraged to use these tools according to your temperament's preferences — personalize them, in other words.

Your journey will restart, not end, with the plea to chart your course and follow your blueprint to your highest potential and act on your knowledge with a daily plan. From there, it's on to be the best that you can be!

Section One

Find the Real You

You're In Control —
Determine Your Future

Men are born to succeed, not fail.
~ Henry David Thoreau

For what is the best choice for each individual is the highest it is possible for him to achieve.
~ Aristotle

Does the word success make you feel queasy? Has it been contaminated with the idea that it's all about money or social status, fame or even dishonest practices? Has it become trite?

How about rescuing the word and filling it with your own meaning? What is your idea of success? Is it reaching your personal potential in a chosen field? Is it creating loving, harmonious relationships? Is it making a difference in the world for yourself and others? Perhaps, achieving a dream? Is it simply being the best you can be? Whatever it is, you must know what success is for you before you set out on the road to find it.

The very word *succeed* (or *success*) may kick-start your efforts at defining it personally for you. It's a great word and comes to us from the Latin and French words that mean "to go after, to go up, or to follow." Go after your passions; go up to the summit of your potential; and follow your beliefs, values, and heart, and you will define your success more effectively and optimistically.

The Wrong Definition

Maybe you've been trying to succeed by following your friend's advice, not that doing so is all bad. However, embedded in your friend's advice is *your friend's* goals and *our friend's* paths, not *yours*. Make sure to define the word *success* for yourself. You must deliberately carve the shape of your destiny and not let circumstances or others do it for you.

At one time, my success was being dictated by others. I was answering every call for help and my own goals and needs were shunted to the back burner. I had to learn to take control of my schedule and, as a result, to take control of my life. You take control of your destiny by first defining success for yourself and then making room in your busy life for it to happen.

Your Definition of Success Must Fit

Success goals must feel as though they fit. Get rid of all the goals that you know in your heart are not yours: goals you have chosen because you are copying someone else. Perhaps you have read how someone has succeeded and you want to succeed like them, so you adopt their goal. That's a common cause of failure. Goals that fit will arise from within you, not from some other person's experience.

Maybe you've read many books on success but still nothing has happened for you — nothing really significant, that is — or worse, you have become frustrated and wondered what it is that others seem to have that you don't have. They succeed and you don't. The fact stares at you. Perhaps you've agonized over why you can't seem to succeed like others? You seem to be different. The reason could well be that you are chasing after a hazy goal of success. If your definition of success is not clearly defined, you will not reach it. You would not know you had reached it even if you had. Clarity sharpens not only the goal, but also our motivation.

Too many of those frustrating experiences increase our feelings of worthlessness. That's a real shame, since it damages our self-worth and lessens our chances to achieve our goals. The attempts become increasingly counterproductive if our goals are not clear and they don't arise from within. Could following someone else's path be wrong? I think so, and I'll show you why. Each of us has an individual road to an individual goal. That's what this book is about.

Answering "Who Am I?" Leads to Better Goals

Philosophers have pondered this deep, personal question of identity from the days of Plato and even before. "Who are we?" they have asked. We are all asking for the same reason. How can we know what is the real goal is for our lives if we have no idea who we are or whether defining of who we are is adequate?

Defining success for yourself from within means defining it from the knowledge of self. For one of my clients, his goal was found by listening to his inner longing to bring healing and wholeness to the world. The Temperament Key confirmed his desire. Starting with the identification of this powerful drive in his temperament, he began to sculpt a goal that would be realized in stages and bring him to his highest feelings of fulfillment as he made a significant difference in healing the woes of others. He found his path.

The success for those who have discovered themselves has been remarkable, and people keep expressing happiness and relief at finding how they were made in the hidden corners of their inner being. Both finding who they are and then discovering the goal that fits this discovery is what motivates them.

This self-knowledge that you will gain is accurate too. I always hear from those I have coached, "How do you know this about me?" People are always amazed when they understand themselves and feel the relief it brings. The accuracy of the Temperament Key even surprised me early on in my practice.

Self-Verification

As we follow this proven way of self-discovery, you will see for yourself whether it fits. I promise, this book will not try to force upon you some explanation of who you are or the goal you should adopt. Rather, you must verify all conclusions for yourself, and you *can* do this. If you conclude that you have discovered your inner strengths after completing the Adult Temperament Key and verifying its result, read on, because I will teach you how to release those "God-given powers" within you and follow the purpose for which you were made all the way to your self-defined success.   You will discover not only if your temperament fits, but whether your ideas of success fit, and how and why they fit.

To be the best person, parent, leader, helper, or whatever you generally desire to be, you must take this journey deep inside. As machines take over more of what we did with our hands and feet, it becomes more important to develop the strengths of our inner lives and define our goals more precisely to find success at anything.   Our success in *all* things lies with an inner self-understanding.

If no drum beats relentlessly within your spirit, thumping out the passion that says, "Oh, to God that I could be successful as I define success, cease to be derailed by my own weaknesses, find the power within me that drives my desires, discover and live in my own strengths, and be the best that I can be," this book is not for you — not yet.

Desires Can Help Define Success
If you are still saying, "Honestly, I don't know who I am, and that bothers me. I need to find myself before I find my goal," your are right. You will find yourself as you discover the *real you* in Chapters five through ten.   Then your goals will come into sharp focus and your definition of success will be further refined by your temperament's strengths and urges.

However, for now, consult your desires, some of which are a direct result of your inner drives — your strengths. Your desires are more *you* than the success others want for you. You will need to know your real desires anyhow. They are one important pointer to your goals and an indicator of your true inner drives.   Your *innerkinetics* produce the desires that motivate you, so there is a direct cause and effect connection.

Begin your awareness now of what your true goal in life should be by consulting your desires, and later we will test them against the real indicator: your temperament.

No doubt you have dreamed of being successful, perhaps even daydreamed about it. Your desires as expressed in these dreams indicate something about what you define as success for you. Do you dream of rewarding relationships or being significant or creating a perfect family? Ponder your desires and your personal definition of success — even if they seem unrealistic — and ask what it is that these dreams are telling you about your goals and the direction of your life.

Let's Start Defining Success YOUR Way

Success for one is failure for another. My ideas of success should not be forced on you, nor yours on me. So go ahead and write down what you define as your goal for success now. It will be instructive to see the changes to your definition, if any, as we go along.

Consider the following as you define success for yourself:

- Is my definition of success one I got from someone else?

- Is it formed to satisfy me or someone else?

- Does it make me feel as though I will have to become someone else to achieve it?

- Does it feel as though it fits?

- Does it inspire me?

- Is it too hazy, lacking sharply-defined boundaries?

- Is it an adequate goal?

- Does it support my values?

My initial goal or definition of success is:

_____

_____

_____

Can I Do Anything — Anything At All?

When I was young, I was told I could do anything I wanted to with my life. They didn't lie, but they did deceive me. "Can I do anything?" is the wrong question to ask. Some use this question to avoid facing the tough task of defining their goals of success. The attitude that you can do anything can lead to doing "anything." "Just follow your desires," is the "in-fashion" cry. However, to reach your potential you must do the homework and consult more than your desires because, when misunderstood, they can seriously deceive you.

The *wrong question* means you will get the *wrong answer*. Yes, of course, you can do anything you want. However, that's not the answer that will lead you to personal success. What if you want to do something for which you are not gifted? Will you be able to do it? Probably, but not to the same degree of success as someone who is truly gifted to accomplish that goal. Why would you want to fashion your life around something for which you are not designed to excel?

So your questions should be:

- What's inside me?

- What am I built for?

- In what direction does my greatest potential lie?

- Would *the real me* please stand up?"

Your Blueprint to Your Success — Your Innerkinetics

"Philosophy...is our individual way of just seeing and feeling the total push and pressure of the cosmos."
~ William James

Unlock your powers and you transform the future.
~ Ray W. Lincoln

We need a blueprint to be able to build our lives successfully. It will direct us individually (not just anyone) on our own path. Our greatest future lives in that blueprint. However we define our success, this blueprint will be our dependable road map to all of our achievements. We find this road map in our *innerkinetics* (or temperament), our inner blueprint, and it does not lie.

Having begun to define our goals, we also need to define the terms we will use and learn a little more about temperament. This chapter is more technical but is included here to increase understanding.

What Is *Innerkinetics?*

Temperament! That's the short answer.

> *Innerkinetics* is the package of strengths (powers or drives) inside of us that has been traditionally called our temperament.

Here's the long answer.

> *Innerkinetics* is:
> The understanding that temperament is made up of strengths, *not* strengths *and weaknesses.* Weaknesses are self-made and not given, nor are they an automatic accompaniment to our strengths. All our weaknesses are negative reflections of our strengths and are created when we either don't use, overuse, or misuse our strengths. This distinguishes my understanding of temperament from those who see it as describing both our strengths and weaknesses.
> *Inner kinetics* means *inner powers.*

Therefore, our strengths (not both our strengths and weaknesses) form our *innerkinetics* and are the blueprint for all of our successes.

Temperament (or *innerkinetics*) is how we have been "wired" with these strengths from birth. They are the driving powers and basic patterns of our inner make up. Each of us finds that we prefer certain ways of doing things or not doing things, and these preferences are an expression of our inner drives. Preferring one thing over another is something we are familiar with.

Although we are all different, we can observe that we have similarities in our "wiring" or temperament. These patterns or similarities help us identify and understand ourselves and each other and that's why they are so important to our success. They are the beginning of self-understanding. Our *innerkinetics* will be our most helpful tool in coming to a knowledge of the path to success that each of us must follow.

Reliable patterns are a necessary structure for success. We usually rely on principles of success, our understanding of others, and our knowledge of some product or service. If there were nothing to rely on, success would be too difficult to achieve. However, having a reliable knowledge of ourselves is much more important than a reliable product or a reliable work force. Success is not limited to a commercial model. Success starts with us.

Traditionally, Hippocrates' four different types of people have been called the "four humours" or the four temperaments, and I will use the four temperaments in this book as defined by the recent, erudite work of David Keirsey with, of course, a few observations of my own. The work of Keirsey is widely used and he is perhaps the defining figure in the definition of the four temperaments today.

Each of the four temperaments has been seen to have four distinct variations, creating 16 types.

The similarities among us that are seen in the descriptions of the temperaments, I would argue, tell us a lot more about ourselves than our differences tell us. Therefore, we should not focus on the details of each person without reference to the larger picture. The meaning given to our lives is found in the large, functioning patterns of our human systems, not in the small differences that make each of us unique.

Additionally, when we focus on differences we soon find that the differences among us are infinite. We are like snowflakes — one of a kind — and there is no end to the study of human differences. Although focusing on our differences can tell us a lot about the details, it doesn't help us see the overall patterns that drive us and define us.

These four patterns make us readily understandable. Their names have varied from being given letters (SP, SJ, NT, and NF) to being given names like those Keirsey uses: Artisan, Guardian, Rational, and Idealist, respectively. They have served us well as a user-friendly guide to understanding ourselves for all these years and still are the best tools available for self understanding today. They will effectively lead you to success.

The word *temperament* today is also used to indicate any feature of personality that someone thinks deserves to be called a part of temperament. The word temperament has become a catchall. There are as many temperaments talked about now as the researcher desires. This does not help us identify patterns or groupings in personality. It is not a user-friendly tool for our purposes.

Therefore, since there is confusion over what the word *temperament* means today, I have coined this new word, *innerkinetics*, to help remove the confusion about my meaning.

Our Individual Powers

Our *innerkinetics* are our powers or drives. Deep inside us there are urges that direct our lives every moment of every day. I call them strengths, drives, or urges; and since our *innerkinetics* display the meanings of all three of these words, I need to define their use for you. (Mostly, these three words are used synonymously in this book.)

Strengths
When I talk about having strengths, I refer to our nonmaterial "muscles" that empower us and enable us to succeed. They play a part in our physical, mental, and emotional actions. The strengths we possess determine the nature and direction of our natural potential. Therefore, whatever strengths we have indicate what we can do best.

Urges
The word *urges* emphasizes how they work. They prod, stimulate, even impel us to act in certain ways. This prodding is consistent so that we reliably prefer to act in certain ways. The consistency in each temperament can be easily observed. It helps us know who we are and who we can be.

Drives

Drives speak of directional energies that motivate us or push or pull us in their direction. We feel the pressure generated by these drives and when we don't feel their motivation, we know that we are not operating according to our natural drives. Without their power driving us we falter and fail, becoming apathetic.

The powers, the prodding, the motivations inside of us are the distinguishing qualities and actions of our *innerkinetics*. Understanding what is inside of us is the key to our personal success — I can't say that enough! So, reading this book will help you invest time and effort in understanding how you are designed to function, who you are, and what is the path to your very best. The more we understand and become aware of when our strengths are in use, the easier it is to live in our strengths.

Strengths, Not Weaknesses

Our *innerkinetics* are made up of our strengths, not our weaknesses. **This is very important to understand.** That's why you will read it often. We will explore the relationship of strengths and weaknesses in full in Chapter Eleven, but for now we need to have a basic knowledge of what this means.

The strengths, urges, or drives that make up our *innerkinetics* are positive, not negative. We can be thankful we have positive forces to drive our lives rather than negative ones. To be given negative forces (weaknesses) as inborn drives at the core of our being that would determine our lives and our achievements would be damaging and frustrating to us, to say the least.

We make our own negativity or weaknesses — too much and too many, at times. Weaknesses, therefore, do not belong to who we are and are not inbuilt, hard-wired constituents of our temperament.

Because of this we *can* get rid of our weaknesses. The shaping of our lives is always, at any age or under any set of circumstances, in our control. Thinking our weaknesses are an unavoidable part of us can even negatively affect the way we complete the Adult Temperament Key, so I want you to know this now.

Maybe this will help your understanding: **We cannot be given weaknesses,** so they can't constitute our temperament. A weakness is a negative, and we cannot be given a negative. A negative force in our lives is created by the nonuse or misuse of some force. This is great news because, if our temperament were made up of strengths and weaknesses, we would be hard-wired with both from birth and we would not be able to get rid of our weaknesses! They would be an inseparable part of us. I'll explain the great news and how to get rid of our weaknesses later. For now, become aware of this important reality that shapes our lives.

Powers or Strengths Come in Packages

Our inner powers or strengths form a "power package" inside of us, our *innerkinetics*.

Nobody has only one strength. We know this by simple observation. We have many strengths, usually related in some way to each other. The similar characteristics that some of our strengths share with other strengths interrelate them. For example, responsibility shares common characteristics with reliability, which in turn is aided by caution. The SJ temperament, which you will learn about later, has all three strengths — responsible, reliable, and cautious.

The similarity of certain strengths increases their individual power when used together. One fuels the other and multiplies the power of each. Therefore, you will learn as you study your strengths how to use more than one strength and develop supporting strengths to multiply their power to become super successful. The *real you* is the maximum power of our unified strengths.

We will need to combine our strengths to make our larger dreams happen. Read your blueprint carefully and use all the relevant strengths that maximize your powers together. Your full blueprint is in the chapter that applies to your temperament titled "Introduce Yourself to Your Strengths."

Strengths Are Not the Same As Abilities

We can't find the strengths in our blueprint by testing for our abilities. Strengths are not the same as abilities. Abilities can be native to our strengths or something we learn to do. So many tests that aim at discovering our strengths are really aimed at discovering our strengths and our abilities, which means both our natural and learned abilities. The problem is that the tests don't differentiate between the two.

We often become good at what we have practiced most. That may be the skills our job demanded of us or skills others thought we would be good at — nothing to do with who we really are. Abilities will not lead to our real and highest potential, nor our satisfaction. Learned abilities produce only limited feelings of fulfillment and limited success. Our drives trump any learned ability.

We can even use a drive that is part of our *innerkinetics* but that is not the one relevant to our goals of success as the following illustrates.

"How did you become a teacher," I asked?

"My parents were teachers and I guess they encouraged me, told me I would be good at it, and I thought that since I was their child, I was cut out to be a teacher too — you know, genes and all. It felt right too, since I had a desire to be what my parents expected I would be and it pleased them. I now know that it was not far off from what I really love to do, and so I guess I was lulled into the feeling that it was my purpose in life. It sort of felt right, you see."

What Marie had found was that her drives were, in part, fulfilled in bringing knowledge to others and, particularly, in making a needed contribution to society. She wasn't really fulfilled, though, and although she was a good teacher, she felt something was missing. She had not seen the difference between her native strengths and her learned skills. This is an example of someone who was exercising a given strength but not the right one to reach real fulfillment.

It was in the profession of law that she found the opportunity to use her strengths to their maximum. Her introversion, along with major strengths, found its comfort in law. Once her right drives for reaching her success goals were energizing her life, she found her true fulfillment and her performance at its best.

Many people are caught in this trap. How disappointing when you are so near to a great life and yet not there — using a well-learned ability (but not the right native strength) or even an unrelated strength. Find the relevant drives to your goals and hopes and you will find the blueprint to your real power and happiness.

Moods

To think that temperament is only another word for our moods is an oversimplification and very misleading. All temperaments are capable of any mood: happy, ecstatic, sad, morose, depressive, gloomy, whatever. Moods, therefore, can't be a defining characteristic of a particular temperament.

The Greeks wondered if temperament was an expression of bodily fluids, which seemed to them with their limited knowledge to cause four distinct moods. They, therefore, thought of the four temperaments as four different moods that affect a person's behavior. Yet, on the other hand, as they pondered about the four temperaments they realized it was more than a mood. Temperament was made of distinct powers that fashioned the person and fitted them for different functions and purposes in society. This is why Plato describes his perfect society by having the four temperaments perform their naturally gifted functions in that society — nothing to do with mood.

Thinking of temperament as the moods that we display has led some to identify the optimistic mood of an SP as a clear indication of that temperament. However, the NF, when the future is bright, is very optimistic too. If you think of *innerkinetics* as a mood it will confuse your identification of temperaments. For instance, a pessimistic mood often is not a sign of an SJ living in their weaknesses but the result of depression, which always displays a negative frame of mind and can be seen in any temperament.

The right attitude or mood is necessary to succeed but, on its own, will not lead you to success or indicate your temperament.

Not Produced by Environment

Our blueprint to success is not constructed from our experiences or formed by our environment. Environment and what it does to us may modify our use of our temperament's preferences but will not change them into the preferences of another temperament. It can, however, cause us to deny our preferences and even lose sight of them. We can also act in opposition to our temperament's urges, but even that does not change our temperament. It simply masks them or puts them on hold.

Our preferences determine how we see our environment. Once we see it, we then choose how to react to it. To imagine that we are controlled by our circumstances is to picture a creature who is a robot and has no will to oppose or alter the effects circumstances have on it. The opposite is what humans have demonstrated they can do.

Environment or circumstances will not make you a success either, so don't let them mold you or your future. Their power is limited, even though on occasions they can hand you material success. They can't even withhold your success if you are determined to turn the trash you were given into gold. Your *innerkinetics* hold the secret powers that can overcome any circumstance. The path to success, you will be happy to know, is not in "fortunate circumstances." True success always incorporates more than the material things of life and often doesn't include them at all.

Are All People of the Same Temperament Alike?

Are the four temperaments and their four blueprints four cookie-cutter patterns, stamping out four different temperaments that are all rigidly alike? Thank goodness, no! The world does not need another me. Each of us is a unique creation and here are some of the reasons why two people of the same temperament are not identical twins.

- Each is likely to have some of the strengths of the same temperament but not all the same ones.

- If they have the same combination of strengths that belong to the same temperament, they will most likely not possess them to the same degree. Therefore, they will look and be different.

- Each may have very different secondary strengths they have borrowed from other temperaments and are using quite effectively or ineffectively. (Yes, we can "borrow" strengths that belong to another temperament, and we often do.)

- If they are living in their weaknesses rather than their strengths, two people of the same temperament can even appear as opposites, and who of us does not drop into our weaknesses at times.

- Each brings his own twists (modifications) from their environment and culture into the use of his strengths.

- Temperament is not the only factor that defines us. Features of personality go beyond temperament.

We could go on, but you get the drift. We are all as individual as the snowflakes, yet we share commonalities that reveal an overall pattern.

"I can't find myself," this young woman complained. She was successful and lacked very little in the eyes of our culture, but she was empty and crumbling inside. Kay's own standards that would bring her satisfaction were still somewhere out there but not in what she was doing, not in her plans. "What are my powers, my strengths, the purpose for which I am made," she agonized? She had a personal faith in a Divine Being and knew her spiritual purpose in life, so she told me, but not how she had been made.

How had she been made on the inside? Kay's innerkinetics were lying idle, waiting to be aroused and used. That's the difference between living in our own strengths and living in borrowed strengths (i.e. between following our own blueprint or one that belongs to another).

Although Kay's *innerkinetics* were what we call the NF temperament, she looked like anything but an NF at times. Only her hidden preferences truly identified her when she completed the Adult Temperament Key and verified the results.

Your journey of understanding is continuing. You have a blueprint to success, whatever that is for you, written in the power package of your inborn strengths, and in the use of that package lies your greatest potential.

The One and Only Road to Your Greatest Potential

It is possible to fail in many ways while to succeed is possible in only one way.
~ Aristotle

We have examined how our personal blueprint to success is hidden in our *innerkinetics*. Now, to the questions:

- Tell me how to translate my blueprint into real success and about the road that will take me there.

- How complicated is this journey?

- What traps lie on its path?

- Is the destination guaranteed, or would it be better for me to follow a few principles, like work hard; be honest; don't give up, and have faith, while I hope for the best?

- Life is unfair anyhow, so why not just settle for whatever comes?"

Follow the principles of hard work, honesty, perseverance, and faith (which are wonderful and needed rules; don't get me wrong) and you still will not be guaranteed a successful, rewarding life. There is more to success, in whatever form it takes, than general concepts.

The true road to success for each of us should be an enjoyable one too, because using and developing our natural strengths pays well. For many, to be rewarded and fulfilled would be regarded as successful anyway you look at it. The "wages" are the subject of the next chapter. How we get to that payback is the subject of this one.

The Road to Success Made Very Simple

The road should be enjoyable *and* simple. I applaud the statement of Ludwig Wittgenstein (1889-1951), the Cambridge professor and philosopher, "Why is philosophy so complicated? It ought to be entirely simple!" I agree passionately, and the great minds are capable of saying profound things in simple language. So let's try to express ourselves and our journey to success simply, even though we humans are the most complicated operating system in our universe. Here is the road to success in language as simple as I can adequately state it.

One: We are born with urges or strengths that enable us to fulfill the purpose for which we were designed.

Two: We need to use these strengths, and if we choose the relevant strengths of our *innerkinetics* for the accomplishment of our goals and use them, they will take us on our best successful journey to our goals.

Three: Our strengths produce desires or preferences within us. We prefer one thing over another, one way over another, and we must follow these preferences that arise out of our natural inner drives, our *innerkinetics*, wherever possible.

Four: The actions that result from following the preferences of our *innerkinetics* are the actions that will lead to our success because they are the actions we can execute superbly.

Five: To attain ultimate success, the potential for which we were created, we must develop and train these strengths — not just use them — and make them our way of life.

These are not five steps to take one at a time, although they do have a usable sequence to them. First, discover your *innerkinetics* and its strengths. Second, follow the preferences that these strengths produce. Third, develop them using all the great principles, like work hard; be honest with yourself and others; persevere; and believe in yourself, your goals, and your helpers (both human and divine).

This is the road from discovering your blueprint to your most successful building project called "you at your greatest."

Now, let's understand some of the contingencies along the way to a successful building project.

Remove Unnecessary Guilt

Understanding our temperament will give us an explanation of why we do the things we do and feel the way we feel. When most people complete the Adult Temperament Key and understand their temperament, they invariably say something like this: "Wow, that explains why I feel 'such and such,' and I always have worried about that. I have felt guilty for years and now I see that I don't need to. What a relief!"

For example: An NF person, who is very sensitive to people's actions, to the mood of a place, to the fact that others don't seem to care about people's feelings, and who reacts strongly internally (if not also externally) to all these feelings, can for the first time realize that their troubling sensitivity is, rather than a curse, a gift they were born with. What a relief it is to see a troubling strength as a gift. They discover it is really a strength (not a weakness), one they can use to succeed in life, something they can develop as a gift.

They must, however, learn how to use it helpfully and productively without damage to themselves or others. I have seen many NFs who use their sensitivity to become the best ever at people skills. Only a person with such sensitivity to the feelings of others and their surroundings can excel at winning people to the extent they do.

Often we are puzzled at why we feel we have to act this way or that. When, for example, we say "We want to be free to be ourselves," we could be expressing an inner urge for self-expression that is part of our makeup, not a rebellious attitude. Of course, there is a place for fulfilling this urge and a place for holding it back, but when we follow our temperament's urges we feel empowered. When we don't, we feel depressed and somehow guilty. All people of the SP temperament can avow to this example.

Some people are more familiar with these feelings of guilt than others. They are horribly confused when they feel relieved from the guilt, because they have been told they should not engage in good feelings about themselves. It usually turns out that the person who wants us not to think well of ourselves is of a temperament that is cautious and expects all people to be responsible and behave the way they do. They see everyone through their own temperament's eyes, and self renunciation is, to them, an across-the-board policy.

Mostly we choose to act the way our inner urges pressure us to act. We then tend to defend that way of doing things and resist when we are asked to change and act the way other people act: in other words, to follow someone else's preferences. This causes many angry confrontations and subsequent guilt for some. Each thinks he is right because his way makes sense to him and confirms his inner desires. The path to success lies in understanding our own temperament and then understanding others. Respecting the way other people are made is a sure path to happily incorporate others on your road to success.

Although change is happening faster in our decade than ever before and we have made so much progress in technology and science in general, people still know little more about themselves than they did thousands of years ago. The focus of this century is on technology and understanding our world, not ourselves. As a result, our individual success is forfeited because we don't focus on self-knowledge to understand ourselves and others. Our focus should be on people, who ultimately command technology. "Know yourself," said a number of the Greek philosophers and it carries more urgency in our world today than in theirs. The theme runs through the major religions of the world too.

Struggling with Disconnects

Our actions sometimes don't express our *innerkinetics,* and here's where most of the traps are set that cause us to fail or get sidetracked on the road to success. Our choices can create a disconnect between our preferences and the way we behave. If we follow our temperament's urges and don't overuse or misuse our strengths, it's hard to miss the correct turns and wander off in alien territory. By now you are almost tired of me saying that the blueprint inside us is the journey to success, not some side road to distracting choices that have nothing to do with our purpose, but it is the key.

Are all of us slaves to our preferences? Can we disengage from our preferences and drives and act contrary to their urgings? Yes! Do we? Yes, unfortunately. The reality for most of us is something like this: Most of the time we do what our inner urges tell us to do and that's where consistency of character and personality come from, but occasionally we make bad choices and leave the road. This is particularly true when we are stressed, hurried or, conversely, laid back and relaxed — either. At times when we are not feeling pressured to act another way (that is, not pressured by people or circumstances) we follow our preferences and no disconnect occurs. Our natural preferences form a kind of default mechanism that activates at all times unless we deliberately override it. Pressure of some sort is what derails us.

Let's take a look at what might cause us to override our preferences and create a disconnect, since we are not slaves to our preferences and this disengagement can and does happen.

Circumstances. If I am following the urge of my introversion, let's say, and enjoying some downtime, happily recharging in my backyard when a fierce dog hops the fence, I might want to override my preference for engaging in some pleasurable recharging. It might occur to me that a fast retreat would be a better choice. In this case, for me, it would become my first choice! Note the change in circumstances (a fierce dog is now with me in the backyard) which can cause me to choose actions other than what I preferred. It's the pressure of circumstances.

Perhaps we are pursuing a fulfilling career when suddenly we are laid off and must move to another city to find work to pay our bills. Circumstances are then forcing choices upon us that may upset, at least temporarily, the pursuit of our chosen path. We can still, however, make choices that will lead us back to do the thing that fulfills us or to another job that equally fulfills the urges of our strengths. Circumstances can cause disconnects in our choice of job.

People. Our best friends often feel they know what is best for us, but they can be wrong. Sometimes it is the old misunderstanding of suggesting to us things that would be best for them, given their temperament. If we feel we don't know what to do and then trust our friend's judgments out of ignorance or desperation, we can override our true preferences in favor of a choice foreign to the "real me," but natural to them. Following the advice or wishes of our friends can cause disconnects. Pressure again causes us to abandon our blueprint.

Bad choices. We can also deliberately choose to do what we know is wrong and, as a consequence, make a disastrous choice. Perhaps some voice inside us is shouting "Don't!" but we choose in opposition to that voice anyway, and soon we are feeling the misery of the consequences. Don't tell me you haven't done this; we all have. Following our blueprint will require right choices if we want to avoid the side trips that disconnects create. If we do venture off course, we will require choices that will lead us back.

Disconnects Arise Out of the Freedom to Choose

Freedom is the name of the game of life. We are free to make any choice we want and in the exercise of our freedom we are all tested.

Ultimately, we make our own lives — for good or ill — by our choices. For example: If we are normally cautious, conservative, and somewhat timid, we can still, if we so choose, throw caution to the winds and go sky diving just for the heck of it. (Nothing wrong with giving these things a try, whatever our *innerkinetics*.) Just don't pin your hopes on real happiness from the experience if you are of an overly cautious, nervous temperament.) You will feel a contrary current within yourself and the flags of fear will be waving. Perhaps you should conclude that you were not born to be a sky diver and settle for terrestrial pleasures! Choose the opposite of your drives and you become inwardly fragmented.

Such denial of our preferences will cause us considerable inner tension, but there is nothing to stop us acting any way we want or any way we feel, whether we are forced to or not. All of us are free to be whomever we choose to be — even not to be ourselves. The freedom we prize can turn out to be our nemesis.

Sandra made that choice even though she was made in a very conservative mold. Her mother had always overprotected her and she never had to make the big choices. Out on her own in a world she had not experienced, she chose to live wildly and feel the "excitement" of fear. It wasn't long before she was enmeshed with a gang who lived on the edge of danger and risk. That was too much. Constantly resisting her inner urges to play it safe and cautious, she plunged ahead, becoming more nervous and insecure with each denial of who she was. Finally, she was overcome with this feeling of disconnectedness and was feeling increasingly guilty every day — an inner feeling she couldn't really explain — while she plunged uncomprehendingly ahead. (Whenever we live contrary to our best urges we sacrifice inner integrity and that causes a feeling of guilt.)

She soon fell apart emotionally and had to be committed to a mental health institution. Denying our urges can be costly. It was only after successful medical treatment and the discovery of who she really was and where her true happiness was to be found that she began a new rewarding life.

Freedom to Choose Operates Within the Laws of Cause and Effect

None of us want to be a robot and be forced to perform to the demands of others, but when we choose wrongly we create a complex inner picture. There is a structure within each of us whose job it is to protect our feelings of security. When we choose in a way that threatens our safeguards, we create cross currents, turbulent feelings that go into action with the intent of offsetting the threat. We find ourselves at odds with ourselves. Our system is objecting to the wrong choice.

We really cannot blame our temperament for wrong choices, whether we act according to its preferences or not. We are responsible for the choice of acting, waiting till another time to act, or simply choosing not to act no matter what that choice is. Therefore, temperamental urges do not relieve us of individual responsibility for our actions. The path our blueprint describes that leads to our success is narrowly one of personal responsibility in all situations and decisions — no escape clause.

Every reaction to the circumstances of life passes through the filter of human freedom. To follow our temperament is a responsible choice, even if, for us, it is a likely to be an almost automatic choice. Our *innerkinetics* will lead us to the path of our success, but it will not absolve us from the responsibility of our choices, whether ignorant or just plain bad. When things go against us, they call for a right choice; that is all.

Perhaps this has flagged us to the main distractions, diversions, or failures that cause us to depart from our blueprint.

Living Your Dream and Enjoying the Paybacks

What if you slept? And what if, in your sleep, you dreamed?
And what if, in your dream, you went to heaven
And there plucked a strange and beautiful flower?
And what if, when you awoke, you had the flower in your hand?
Ah, what then?
~ Samuel Taylor Coleridge

There's a possible dream out there for you. No, it is not some reduction of your goals that you or someone else thinks might be attainable. The possible dream is the greatest you can be, the achieving of impressive success in whatever way your strengths are pointing and to a goal you have carefully defined. Your possible dream is your greatest dream.

Dreams are the wishes of our hearts and when we put goals, steps and actions to those wishes, they soon become realities. But our dreams will never become real if we struggle to achieve them with strengths we do not possess. Nor will we pursue them for long if they lack the fulfillment that brings true happiness. There has to be payback for all of us. Your blueprint carries a guarantee of wonderful wages.

Dream with me for a moment before we go on. Select which of these four dreams fits you best.

Dream One
"I long to be someone who makes a contribution to this world and to leave it a better world for my loved ones. I want to feel worthwhile and appreciated, to feel people can depend on me and that I have made my family and society proud of me. I want to be known as responsible and reliable, someone the world can depend on."

Or...

Dream Two
"I want to grow strong and courageous and be admired, making an impact on people. I want to feel that I have lived a free and expressive life, to be a unique individual, not a copy of others. "Free indeed," those words taste like honey to me. Give me a life of adventure and excitement where the adrenaline flows unabated with abandon, and let me express the potent urges in my spirit."

Or...

Dream Three
"I want to be loved because I have loved and to frolic in the wonders of loving and harmonious relationships. I want harmony, not just for myself, but for all people. I want to know myself better and keep learning, because in learning I expand and feel complete. I feel called to influence the world and mentor it for good and touch the beat of its soul. I want to be significant and feel that my life is deeply meaningful."

Or...

Dream Four
"I feel I am intelligent and capable, and when discovering the secrets and wonders of this world, I feel my ingenuity growing and satisfying me. Discovery is my passion and my dream. Strategy is my method of penetrating the future and forming the theories that guide my discoveries. I want to fill my days with finding new and better ways for people to live."

If you respond to one of these dreams, you are already discovering something about your *innerkinetics* and the direction your life is intended to go. And if you respond to more than one, that too will inform you and lead you to a more insightful knowledge of yourself. If you can't choose, simply wait until you have discovered your temperament and then it will sort itself out.

Give Yourself Permission to Fly!

"Yes! I want to dream and live my dreams, to be the best that I can be. I want to soar above my depressing, self-made limitations, look fear in the face, and scorn it as I defeat its threat. I want to test the impossible and feel it crumble before me. I want to be maximized in all areas of my life."

"The boldness of a possible dream that I once thought impossible is empowering and refreshing to me. I long to be reborn with a red-blooded hope. I will give myself permission to fly."

Is this you?

Your possible dream is what you were born to be and achieve. It is what you long for and imagine in the rich moments of a pregnant intuition. It is all that you can be, and it brings with it some wonderful paybacks that I have already alluded to and which are the subject of this chapter.

The Payback of Achievement

Why is success and achievement so appealing? Because our feelings of worth are fed. Our self-image is built to varying degrees and in subtly different ways by success, and this is true for each of the temperaments. That self-image seeks different expressions and goals according to our temperament.

If we have a different package of strengths from those of another person, our feelings of personal worth will be felt in a different way. The feelings of worth in one temperament may be in being appreciated for reliable and faithful service and in another, recognition of our ingenious discoveries. A high self-esteem, regardless of what creates it, is essential to high achievement in all areas of life.

We are all built in an image that calls us to higher things, to feel as though we can do anything. The human system craves to distinguish itself and to do this by exercising its inner powers. This drive to be something or someone is latent in all of us. A spiritual belief can add significantly to this urge for many. If, as some believe, they are made in the image of a Divine Creator and are to spend their lives living in that image, this belief impels them to be the best they can be and struggle to be better and better. Whatever your spiritual belief, or none at all, a higher call will aid you on your search for your best and beyond — your possible dream. It's simply more motivation, and who has enough motivation to be their best?

The direction your life is intended to go is not a downhill slide but an uphill climb. It is reaching or stretching for the stars with the excitement of achievement and success. Even the little successes on the way empower us more than a stubborn resolve.

To live healthily, our drives must be propelling us to excel. When we cease to live in the thrust of our drives, our brain sends a message to our body that our body is no longer needed, and we begin to decay and fall apart, physically as well as mentally.

Achievement Is for All Temperaments
A perfectionist who ceases to care any longer about perfection loses her edge and begins to fade into life's sunset. A passionate person who is no longer passionate becomes an insignificant blip in the moving landscape of humanity. An ingenious wizard who ceases to pursue the drive of his temperament wilts, losing the strength and power that kept him vital to himself and others. A person with the drive to be reliable and responsible but who fails to succeed to the point of being appreciated, feels of no use to society and soon his life force vanishes. A brave, daring, lion of a person who becomes timid forfeits his confidence and command and inwardly dies. To achieve is human.

Achievement Is for All Ages

Watch children respond to their urges to succeed. In their early years they struggle to use their strengths and often overuse them or wrongly use them as they seek to discover their proper and powerful place in life. If they do not exercise these inborn temperamental drives they lose self-esteem and can fall into depression because they lose the forward and upward thrust of their *innerkinetics* — the drive to achieve. Our lives, from the earliest of days, are one long urge to achieve. When we finally reach retirement age, the call to achieve is still a monitor of health and a way to rejuvenate any dying soul. Achieve to the end.

Why do we struggle to live and fight to stay alive when all seems lost? If there is not some kind of inner force demanding we be more, then what is it that causes that drive? Our blueprint never ages and it keeps forcing us on to the fullness of our dreams?

The Compensation of Direction

There's nothing like being out on the high seas and enveloped in a fog to teach you the essential nature of direction. Being lost is simply having no knowledge of which direction to take. The path to success that is written within us gives us the comfort, peace, and certainty of knowing our direction when landmarks are invisible. Lost? Find yourself.

Panic is debilitating and scary in itself. The compensation of being born into this world and finding the directions for our journey through life inside ourselves is a death blow to fear and a nervous system that is paralyzing us.

Not having to rely on the opinions and suggestions of others, and being able to verify with our own intuition (our sixth sense) what really fits us and is us, releases a confidence that we discover we can't live without. We are designed to follow these deep acknowledgments of how we are uniquely made. When you complete the Adult Temperament Key you will be asked to verify the results. To verify means to sense and feel if they are right or not. The realization may come slowly, but it will come. After completing the key, your temperament will be known to you and you will verify it or not when

31

you consult your feelings and intuition (which all of us have to some degree).

When you find your direction, you will feel empowered, relieved, released, excited — the kind of feeling the sailor feels when he has at last identified a direction in which he has confidence.

"I have no idea of where I am going, but I'm making good progress," is the hopeless cry of many people who have not found their life's bearings.

The Enticement of Potential

Why would potential reward us?   Potential is something that hasn't happened yet; it isn't real.   But it can be real.   It has not yet come into being; it is only latent, possible.

It's the lure of the possible that makes it rewarding.   Potential pulls at us and keeps us motivated.   It's the carrot held out to the donkey, the candy that entices the child, the chocolate that creates a powerful obsession in the chocoholic.   Simply, it's the check at the end of the week.

Without potentials in a human's life we would lose desire and eventually all satisfaction.   Potential is built around another potent inner power called expectation.   Expectation, too, feeds us and calls us with the promise of fulfillment.

Success is a vague hope to many, the call of "wolf" to others.   But potential is hope that lives on.   For those who cherish the "not yet," the possible, the expectations of life's potential, it is an irresistible force to stir their passion.   Therefore, when we are drawn by the potential of our strengths, we are already paid in currency that makes life bearable, fascinating, challenging, and full of desire.   Nothing in us is more creative of potential and hope than the use of our strengths.

The Satisfaction of Fulfillment

Ah, now we arrive at the real payoff. To be fulfilled is to be satisfied. Fulfillment and satisfaction are not physical; they are mental realities. Even when we feel a physical act fulfills us, it is in inner satisfaction that we really experience fulfillment. The inner response is what makes us content or excited, and that helps us grasp that our inner life is what everything in life is all about. Inner satisfaction, contentment, peace, happiness, and, yes, summing it all up in one word, fulfillment. Fulfillment is having an order filled. Order any of the above and following your blueprint will ensure the order is filled.

What really fulfills us? Money? Rank? Status? No. What really makes us feel we have arrived is that feeling that what we are doing completely satisfies us or, better still, that what we have become is fully satisfying. It fits.

We have a number of words in the English language to describe this feeling of the human heart. Every language creates words for referring to fulfillment and satisfaction, but the nations who are most stirred to achievement have the greater need for words that express more meaningfully the feeling of fulfillment. Therefore, they create them. This is not surprising since we create language out of our experiences and desires.

Fulfillment is so rewarding because it is the carrying out of something we expected, were promised, predicted, or hoped for — a successful life's fruit: the rising of the sun on the human spirit, if you like, to stir yet more desires and make us believe in a happy cause-and-effect and in the fruits of our labors. In reality, being fulfilled urges us to believe in ourselves and that we can function reliably and rewardingly. It is, as well, a promise of more to come.

The greatest fulfillment that we can experience is to know that the use of our strengths is worthwhile and builds our sense of self-worth, which no amount of money can buy. It lifts our self-image and makes us face the world with confidence, conquering its fears and its denials. If we live our lives feeling fulfilled, we have no more to ask for.

Sarah hated her condition. A back injury resulting in the inability to stand or sit for long, a heart condition that further limited her mobility, and seemingly no chance of getting a job that would support her led to despair and then to depression. However, she found fulfillment after she completed her Adult Temperament Key and realized for the first time how she was made.

"You are made for encouraging people. You have strengths that others will recognize. Your temperament will only be fully fulfilled when you lift people and help them to their goals. You could do this," I told her.

It took a while, experimenting with the possibilities of how she could do it, but she recognized from the start that this was what would bring her reward and happiness. Some training and a limited amount of time spent with each person soon led to her being recognized as gifted in a unique way to lift and reinvigorate the lives of others, and her marketability rose with her perceived value.

Now she finds she can support herself and go to bed each night content and with a sense of worth that thrills her. Our strengths fulfill us because they are us. Find the fulfillment you were meant for.

The Nutrition of Happiness

Happiness is nutrition for the human spirit. The body needs nutrition to keep it alive and operative. What makes us think we can starve our spirits and not witness them wither and die.

Spiritual nutrition (the nutrition for the human spirit) is essential. The surprise is that it comes in the form of immaterial values like love, joy, peace and related virtues. Joy (what we call happiness) is one of the three essential foods that our spirits need to survive in the pressures and stresses of a fast-paced, demanding life. There's no doubt you have been introduced to this kind of life.

Use your strengths and follow their direction and you will find happiness that arises out of functioning as you were designed to function. Happiness is found in the healthy use of our natural powers. Nothing approaches the natural high of joy that a skilled use of our strengths can give us.

Our strengths or drives, when used properly, generate this reward so we don't ever need to be without it. Happiness is found in our being what we are and what we are meant to be. Life is more than the pleasure of things and achievements. It's a deep-seated happiness born of this kind of success and not disturbed by the vicissitudes of life. Following our blueprint contains the secret to a deep inner joy.

Emptiness and Dissatisfaction Are Warning Flags

Whenever you feel empty and unfulfilled, suspect that you are not following and using your strengths. It's a self-management tool not to be forgotten.

Jack complained to me of his dissatisfaction with his life and his feelings of failure and emptiness. He was choosing not to follow his inbuilt strengths. Rather, he chose to follow what he had been told by others he should be. He felt he had to. It led to a career in management when, to the contrary, he yearned for the life of a park ranger — outdoors in the solitude and intriguing beauty of nature. The office felt like a prison cell, its walls bare and unchanging. He missed the stimulation of the wind stirring his senses, the warmth of sun or the bite of cold. He was all about his senses, senses that the office failed to awaken.

When the temperament key confirmed his wishes that to be a park ranger would use and develop his deep-seated urges, he felt a rush of excitement and a real relief in his spirit. He hollered with ecstasy. Subsequently, he left the office in his past and started the journey to his wonderland. Life is only rewarding if we are satisfied and fulfilled.

Many have not been diverted by the advice of others but by their own mistaken desires. The value of a temperament key is to crosscheck your desires and tell you if they are based in your strengths or some other foreign soil.

The Reward of Stimulating Relationships

It stands to reason that if different inner powers drive different people they could affect our relationships. They attract or repel others depending on whether others are understood and respected. Our drives can be catalysts in breaking up a relationship or in building one. They always play a part in the dynamics of our associations.

Success in relationships is the ultimate goal for some people. They need loving relationships and find it hard to function when their relationships are disturbed. Disharmony de-motivates this temperament (NF), and they can even get physically sick as a result of damaged relationships. So any discussion of success will, for them, lead ultimately to relationships.

If you are defining success in terms of relationships, understanding your strengths and those of your friends will make it a lot easier to accomplish. For this goal it is imperative. Relating happily to another person is (most of the time) learning to relate to someone whose urges are different, if not opposite, from yours. For the most part we can't be successful in life on our own. We need others and rely on them. It is not too much to say that all success is, in part, a matter of skilled relationships born of understanding and respect.

If people are integral to your success, then become knowledgeable of both your temperament and theirs. Learn to honor someone who has opposite drives to your own and build a healthy respect for their strengths. In doing so, you will increase both of your chances for success.

Define your goal; formulate your possible dream (the best you can be), and the road to it will be lavishly lined with satisfaction, joy, and happiness.

Our motivation to succeed lies in the direction our life is intended to go.
~ Ray W. Lincoln

Finding the Real You

Nature is often hidden, sometimes overcome, seldom extinguished.
~ Sir Francis Bacon

I'll walk where my own nature would be leading.
~ Emily Bronte

The deeper natures never forget themselves and never become anything else than what
they were.
~ Soren Kierkegaard.

The Adult Temperament Key

The Adult Temperament Key used here has been developed using the principles of research into temperament that Myers-Briggs, Keirsey, Harkey-Jourgensen, and others have used for the development of their assessments. These principles, when used in assessments, have proven very reliable and can be depended upon. Any of the above named assessments of temperament are excellent guides to the discovery of how we are made on the inside.

As long as you carefully follow the instructions for the Adult Temperament Key presented here, you should get excellent results.

This is a very positive assessment. We are looking for your strengths, not your weaknesses. There are no wrong answers since it is a self-evaluation. However, be as accurate as possible. Read these instructions carefully since a knowledgeable guide is not looking over your shoulder and you can't ask for help. It is imperative that you answer according to these instructions.

- *Answer these questions according to your preferences (what you prefer), not according to what you think others would have you become.*
- *Answer each question individually. Don't try to be consistent.*
- *Aim to get through the key in about 20 minutes or less.*
- *Think carefully about each answer, but avoid over-thinking, which can lead to confusion. If you are over-thinking, ask yourself "What am I the most?"*
- *Again, let me put it this way: You will see yourself as both (a) and (b) in some of the questions. Your answer should be what you see yourself to be the most, or what you prefer the most or makes you feel most comfortable.*
- *Your preferences are often different at home than at work. This can be because, at work certain things are required of you and, therefore, they have become your work preferences. You prefer to do it that way at work since that's what is good for you. If your work preferences differ from your home preferences, answer according to your home preferences.*
- *We want to know what really beats in your breast, what really satisfies, fulfills, or pleases you the most.*

The results should be accurate but if you attend one of my seminars, ask to be checked again. It's a service we provide. When you read the descriptions of the temperaments in chapters seven, eight, nine, and ten, you will determine whether they match your results in the temperament key. If they do not match the descriptions, then you answered with something else in mind and you will need to confirm the temperament most like you.

This check on your answers is very helpful. The ones who are most likely to be confused about themselves are the NFs. They are the complicated temperament and have the greatest difficulties in understanding themselves for that understandable reason. Now, proceed with careful thought.

Note: You may also go to our website at www.raywlincoln.com/RESOURCES where you will find a free, downloadable Adult Temperament Key.

ADULT TEMPERAMENT KEY

Check (A) or (B) for each question. Please answer ALL questions.

1. At social gatherings do you prefer to
   _____ A. Socialize with everyone
   _____ B. Stick to your friends

2. Are you more in touch with
   _____ A. The real world
   _____ B. The world inside your mind; the world of possibilities

3. Do you rely more on, or take more notice of
   _____ A. Your experiences
   _____ B. Your hunches or gut feelings

4. Are you (most of the time)
   _____ A. Cool, calm, and collected
   _____ B. Friendly and warm

5. When evaluating people do you tend to be
   _____ A. Impersonal and frank
   _____ B. Personal and considerate

6. Do you mostly feel a sense of
   _____ A. Urgency/upset if you are not on time
   _____ B. Relaxed about time.

7. When you see a mess do you
   _____ A. Have an urge to tidy it up
   _____ B. Feel reasonably comfortable living with it

8. Would you describe yourself as
   _____ A. Outgoing/demonstrative/easy to approach
   _____ B. Somewhat reserved/private

9. Which are you best at
   _____ A. Focusing on details
   _____ B. Catching the big picture, the connections, the patterns

39

10. Children should be
_____ A. Made to be more responsible
_____ B. Encouraged to exercise their imagination and make-believe more

11. When making decisions, are you more influenced by
_____ A. The facts or impersonal data
_____ B. Personal feelings

12. Do you feel more yourself when giving
_____ A. Honest criticism
_____ B. Support, approval, and encouragement

13. Do you work best
_____ A. Scheduled; to deadlines
_____ B. Unscheduled; no deadlines

14. For a vacation do you prefer to
_____ A. Plan ahead of time
_____ B. Choose as you go

15. When you are with others do you usually
_____ A. Initiate the conversation
_____ B. Listen and tend to be slow to speak

16. Most of the time, facts
_____ A. Should be taken at face value.
_____ B. Suggest ideas, possibilities, or principles.

17. Do you mostly feel
_____ A. In touch with the real world
_____ B. Somewhat removed, lost in thought

18. When in an argument or discussion do you care more about
_____ A. Defending your position and being right
_____ B. Finding harmony and agreement

19. With others do you tend to be
_____ A. Firm
_____ B. Gentle

20. *Do you see yourself as*
_____ *A. Predictable*
_____ *B. Unpredictable*

21. *Do you mostly prefer to*
_____ *A. Get things done; come to closure*
_____ *B. Explore alternatives; keep options open*

22. *After two hours at a party are you*
_____ *A. More energized than when you arrived*
_____ *B. Losing your energy*

23. *Which best describes you*
_____ *A. Down to earth, practical*
_____ *B. Imaginative, an idea person*

24. *Which do you finally rely on more*
_____ *A. Common sense*
_____ *B. Your intuition/insights or your own analysis*

25. *In other people, which appeals to you most*
_____ *A. A strong will*
_____ *B. Warm emotions*

26. *Are you more controlled by*
_____ *A. Your head/thought*
_____ *B. Your heart/emotions*

27. *Are you typically*
_____ *A. Eager to get decisions made*
_____ *B. Not keen on making decisions*

28. *On the whole do you spend your money*
_____ *A. Cautiously*
_____ *B. Impulsively*

29. *When you have lost energy, do you find yourself mostly*
_____ *A. Seeking out people*
_____ *B. Seeking out solitude/a quiet corner*

30. Do dreamers
_____ A. Annoy you somewhat
_____ B. Fascinate and interest you

31. Do you rely more
_____ A. On your five senses
_____ B. On your sixth sense/intuition

32. Are you more
_____ A. Tough-minded
_____ B. Tenderhearted

33. Would you more likely choose to be
_____ A. Truthful
_____ B. Tactful

34. Do you see yourself as more
_____ A. Serious and determined
_____ B. Relaxed and easygoing

35. Do you feel more comfortable when
_____ A. Things are decided
_____ B. Your options are still open

36. Would you say you mostly
_____ A. Show your feelings readily
_____ B. Are private about your feelings and keep them inside

37. Would you prefer
_____ A. To be in touch with reality
_____ B. To exercise a creative imagination

38. Is your way of thinking more
_____ A. Conventional
_____ B. Original and creative

39. What motivates you more
_____ A. Solid evidence
_____ B. An emotional appeal

40. Would you rather be known for
_____ A. Being a consistent thinker
_____ B. Having harmonious relationships

41. Do you tend to
_____ A. Value routines
_____ B. Dislike routines

42. Do you live more with
_____ A. A little sense of urgency
_____ B. A leisurely pace

43. Do you have
_____ A. Many friends and count them all your close friends
_____ B. Few friends, and only one or two that are deep friends

44. Do you place more emphasis on what you see
_____ A. With your physical eyes
_____ B. With your mind's eye

45. Are you
_____ A. Thick skinned; not hurt easily
_____ B. Thin skinned; hurt easily

46. When you are asked to create a "To Do" list, does it
_____ A. Seem like the right thing to do and do you feel it will be helpful
_____ B. Bug you and seem more like an unnecessary chore

47. Which word attracts you most or describes you best?
_____ A. Talkative
_____ B. Quiet

48. Which words attract you most or describe you best?
_____ A. Present realities
_____ B. Future hopes

49. Which word(s) attracts you most or describe(s) you best?
_____ A. Logic
_____ B. Loving heart

50. Which word attracts you most or describes you best?
_____ A. Plan
_____ B. Impulse

51. Which word attracts you most or describes you best?
_____ A. Party
_____ B. Home

52. Which word(s) attracts you most or describe(s) you best?
_____ A. Common sense
_____ B. Vision

53. Which word attracts you most or describes you best?
_____ A. Justice
_____ B. Mercy

54. Which word attracts you most or describes you best?
_____ A. Concerned
_____ B. Carefree

SCORE SHEET

Instructions for the score sheet (located on page 45):

1. Place a ☒ in the appropriate column (A or B) to indicate the answer you chose for each numbered question. [Please note that the numbers run from left to right across the chart.]
2. Count the number of "As" in column #1 and write that number in box "c," above the "E." Count the number of "Bs" in column #1 and write that number in box "d," above the I.
3. Count the number of "As" in column #2 and write that number in box "e." Count the number of "Bs" in column #2 and write that number in box "f."
4. Count the number of "As" in column #3 and write that number box "g." Count the number of "Bs" in column #3 and write that number in box "h."
5. Add the number of "As" for columns 2 and 3 together and write the total in box "i." Add the number of "Bs" for columns 2 and 3 and write that number in box "j."
6. Repeat the steps in instructions 2-5 above for columns 4/5 and 6/7.
7. Which did you have more of, "Es" or "Is"? _____

Which did you have more of, "Ss" or "Ns"? _____
Which did you have more of, "Ts" or "Fs"? _____
Which did you have more of, "Js" or "Ps"? _____

8. *In the four letters you listed in Instruction #7, which two-letter combination below is present? Circle it!*

S and P   *S and J*   *N and T*   *N and F*

	1			2			3			4			5			6			7	
	A	**B**		**A**	**B**		**A**	**B**		**A**	**B**		**A**	**B**		**A**	**B**		**A**	**B**
1			2			3			4			5			6			7			
8			9			10			11			12			13			14			
15			16			17			18			19			20			21			
22			23			24			25			26			27			28			
29			30			31			32			33			34			35			
36			37			38			39			40			41			42			
43			44						45						46						
47			48						49						50						
51			52						53						54						
						g	h					m	n					s	t	
						e	f					k	l					q	r	
	c	d				i	j					o	p					u	v	
	E	I				S	N					T	F					J	P	

Your Temperament
The Two-Letter Code

I will refer to the four temperaments by a two letter code, the one which you have just identified from your score sheet.   Your temperament will be either SP, SJ, NT or NF.

Letters, Not Words

I use letters instead of word names because trying to put the meaning of a temperament into one word is really not possible. Over a span of 2,500 years, many have tried and they seem always to create new names for the temperaments without a clear consensus.   No one name predominates or will do.

Our temperaments are not narrow streets; they are more like busy, multilane highways. To capture the variety of strengths that travel the highways of our temperament with one word is a failing, reductionist pursuit and one, as I have pointed out, no one seems to agree on.   So let's use letters instead of words and fill the two-letter codes with the multiple meanings of the temperament as we learn them. When you read SP, for example, you will think of the many characteristics of that temperament, not just the one word chosen for its name.

We do not build our strengths if we don't know them. They must be uppermost in our minds.   You will soon be getting to know each temperament for its rich display of strengths and you will fill the two-letter code with a full and complex meaning.

For the meaning of the two letters and all four letters of your code, go to the Appendix.

Section 2

The Real You
Stands Up

Portraits of the Four Temperaments
and Their Variants

Directions to Guide Your Understanding

Please read the descriptions of the four temperaments and verify whether your answers to the Adult Temperament Key have accurately described your preferences.

If the description doesn't fit, you may well have answered the questions of the temperament key with something in mind other than the key intended. Even though care has been taken in the key to prevent this from happening, it is possible.

Caution:
When reading the portraits you may find that a feature of another temperament may sound like it applies to you. It may if you have used and developed that strength, but it may also be because you have not understood it fully in the context of your own temperament or another temperament.

Although this will likely not concern you, let me point out an example for those who may be somewhat confused.

For example:

An NF may be strongly attracted to the SP strength of optimism and feel that he has that strength too. The NF is optimistic. That is true. However, he is optimistic in a different way from the SP and not to the same degree. The SP is optimistic in the sense of always feeling that the next moment will offer something that will excite him or give him an opportunity to find a way out of a negative turn of events. SPs live in the present moment and are focused on it. They always believe in a world of abundance and that means abundant opportunity to find the rush of adrenaline they love and the thrill of change. Therefore, they are optimistic.

For the NF, optimism shows itself when they find a possibility on their future horizons that attracts them and enthuses them. The NFs are focused on the future, not the present. They get all excited about what could, may, might, or should happen. The expectation of some meaningful experience in their future is almost as fulfilling for them as the actual experience itself, and their excitement is not so much the rush of adrenalin or the thrill of change as it is the meaning that this possibility may bring into their lives. This optimism is fed by their constant experiences of turning future possibilities into realities.

The SP is, by nature, optimistic. The NF is optimistic only if meaningful opportunities can be seen and imagined. Otherwise they can be seriously given to depression. A depressed spirit haunts them and stands thinly veiled in the background of their lives.

When confused (this should not be a problem for most people), you will need to pay close attention to the definitions of the strengths in the chapter, "Let Me Introduce You to Your Strengths."

Correct identification of your temperament is important to reaching your potential since struggling to be what you are not is a waste of energy and a dead end street as far as success is concerned. Only our primary strengths will lead us to be the best we can be and fulfill us completely.

As You Read the Descriptions of Each Temperament, Remember:

- They are not exhaustive definitions; they are suggestive and descriptive. To be exhaustive would make for tedious reading and it may not even be possible. We are very complex beings, faced with complex situations, and the options and alternatives for our preferences and actions are almost infinite. The descriptions of the temperaments are enough for accurate identification of your temperament. Of the temperament characteristics that appear as mostly you, not every element has to be you. Within each temperament there is considerable variety of expression.

- The temperament that describes you best is you. It <u>feels to you like it is the real you inside</u>.

- The right temperament will give you the most fulfilling feelings.

- You are the final judge. You must settle on which set of elements or strengths would fulfill you most in life.

- If you have not found satisfaction and real comfort in your life or in what you have been doing for a career, *don't choose* the temperament that best fits what your life has demanded you become and what you don't appreciate.

- If you find the greatest fulfillment in what you are now involved in, then use it as a guide to confirm your real temperament.

The Road Ahead in Chapter 7

A section entitled "On First Meeting" begins the description of each temperament. This is how the temperament might appear to you initially and describes some of its obvious characteristics. This is followed by a "Portrait" which describes the temperament for both identification purposes and to give you a summary of the temperament to help you see it as a whole. Remember, temperament groups similarities.

51

After the portrait you will be introduced to "Keys to Developing an [SP's, SJ's, NT's, NF's] Potential." These cryptic surveys of the temperament's focus, core needs, values, likely talents, how they handle stress, self-image, and what fulfillment feels like are for quick references to keep your success journey on its personal path to your best. They provide you with an outline of the things you must watch for in particular as you develop your temperament's strengths to reach your ultimate potential.

As an additional help to fine-tune your understanding of yourself, brief portraits of the four variations of each temperament are included.

After an essential side trip in Chapter 11 to understand strengths and weaknesses, the next section, "Introduce Yourself to Your Strengths," will delve in detail into the strengths of each temperament and their proper use so that you can develop your temperament's potential.

You should also select within your temperament which strengths beat loudest in your heart, which ones you want to awaken to reach the success you have defined, and which need the most development. You can then focus on your initial selections and develop your strengths to be the best that you can be.

The Real You — SP

The Action/Impact Temperament.

On First Meeting

SPs share most of the following core elements that are important to their identification.

Charming and pleasant It is hard to find an SP that does not strike you as pleasant to meet. They are bold, courageous, impulsive, and daring risk takers. What others would feel is too chancy or alarming, can be positively inviting for the SP.

Their love of action, excitement, and movement that is often expressed in dance and sports, together with their optimistic attitude, makes them stand out as the incorrigible action temperament. They are all about expressing themselves in the present moment, and they live in the external world. To them, it is the only real world, not the ethereal, abstract world of the mind. It's in the real world that they make their impact.

They do not take life too seriously. They are all about image as Plato's Greek name for them, *image makers*, suggests. This means (along with the artisan's skill of making images) having the image that makes an impression.

You may find them busy with their toys (tools, that is) since they are gifted in all the arts — not just the fine arts — and love machinery and tools of all kinds. Rules are not important to them; self-expression trumps rules. Life is lived at full throttle for even the quieter versions (the introverted SPs), and they all drain the last drop of pleasure and excitement from each moment. Today is the world of the SP, not yesterday (which can remind them of depressing memories) and not tomorrow either, for it may never come.

Portrait

SPs are **adventuresome**. They value adventure and are excited about every kind of exploration of their physical world. Adventure stimulates them and presents life to them as a living, moving picture, arresting their senses. They take adventure to its limits and must go where others have never gone.

The physical senses are where they live. **Action, variety, stimulation, excitement,** and **speculation** feed their insatiable senses. They venture to the games, to the ski slopes, following an urge for constant excitement with variety to keep the thrill alive. The same thing over and over is boring and demotivating.

Adventure calls for **bravery** and **bold, daring behavior** is the essence of their feelings of self worth. If they are "chicken," they hate themselves and lose those feelings of self-esteem so essential to their bravery. They are the lion in the fourfold faces of lion, ox, eagle, and man (Ezekiel's vision of living creatures, c580 BC, and the first mention in literature of the distinctions we now call temperament) and it aptly names them.

A **risk** is like a magnet to them. "Where else can you find the ingredients for real, over the top excitement except in risks?" they ask. Risks are custom-made for the brave. It is not a long leap from risk-taking to pressing the limits of the law or the regulations at their job. Is breaking the rules more exciting than testing their limits? That possibility scares an SJ parent.

For the very bold SP, they have not risked until the boundaries have been breached. For the tamer version of the SP, testing the limits is good enough to encourage their self-esteem. If **courage** and bravery is needed, the SP is among the best. They will try anything once, even multiple times, if high adventure is offered.

In the world of things and people, they seem skilled at **tactical moves** that manipulate their environment, which means people as well as things. Tactics is managing situations and events to produce a desired result; usually a beneficial result for the tactician. Tactics must be executed immediately or a change in circumstances can quickly make them ineffective. The SP has this natural skill, given their sensing abilities, to assess and read the situation (including the intentions of others) and project the next move accurately. They are not so astute at predicting a series of moves necessary for developing a strategy. (That is the skill of the NT.)

It seems contrary to the P in their profile to make immediate decisions and to act on them instantly. The P usually indicates a desire to keep options open and not make decisions. However, this is a case where the other letters of the profile condition one or more of the letters and give them an added meaning. The P in the SP seeks sudden interpretations and actions to take advantage of the data that the sensing ability has processed and the present moment has offered.

Tactics is a skill used in sports to quickly see and enact the next advantageous move. **Tactical intelligence** calls for instant decisions and instant application of those decisions. Living so completely in the present moment, SPs are urged to spontaneous action most of the time.

Their focus on the physical world encourages the SP's interest in the forming and creating of things with their hands. **Tools of all sorts**, large or small — anything that is built to achieve a desired purpose — seem to belong comfortably in their hands, and what matters most to them is a strong desire for mastery of these tools and of the physical world they can shape. Tools can mean machine tools, artist's tools, machinery (including heavy machinery), surgical instruments, computers, technology of all sorts, cooking utensils — any instrument or device that can be skillfully wielded or managed. They are, as Keirsey has dubbed them, the **artisans**. Others have called them, **artistic, sensual, aesthetic, artful**.

This leads them also to be **operators** and **executors** and to fit happily into a role where they can direct and manage, also where they can react with skill to sudden changes, keeping their goal firmly in mind and working effectively toward it. In handling people, this means the strengths of a **promoter** and **persuader**, which they display.

As a persuader they excel at presentations of concrete, tangible matters and issues. Seldom will you find an SP successfully making a theoretical or abstract presentation of concepts. It dries out their sensuous minds.

No other temperament promotes themselves and others better than the SP. We should point out that they usually have no difficulty in promoting themselves, because a low self-image or reticence to put themselves forward is not found in the SP unless the SP is depressed or otherwise defeated. They are **confident**.

Along with being promoters and persuaders, they can make great trainers, leaders, communicators, political manipulators, troubleshooters, and business owners (provided they don't have to do the detailed routine work). The SP promoter lives by the motto "You have to make things happen. They just don't happen on their own."

Often you will find the SP in the role of film producer. SPs want to **make an impact on others**, and producing a movie or a skit gives them yet another avenue to make such an impact. **Producers** are **performers** who do their work of making an impact before the show opens. Shocking affects, which seem to be one of the tools of entertainment, is still "impact" to the SP. Most of the time it is seen as very effective impact.

Of secondary appeal to making an impact when making a production is the opportunity to change things, to create different endings or variations on a theme. This **improvisation** uses whatever is available and makes it work, while also using the skill of adaptation. Of all the temperaments they are the **most adaptable**.

Some are talented **composers** — a result, in part, of their improvising abilities. Composing also demonstrates their creative skills in the real world of the arts. A more evident showcase for their improvisation skills is their success as performers.

Spontaneous and **impulsive**, they are ever in the moment, seizing opportunities and reading the physical clues others display (often before others are aware of being read). Frequently, they react so fast that others see them as reactionary rather than thoughtful.

Of interest is the producer who creates a message that skillfully manipulates the viewer or listener to respond to the message when they perhaps did not even want to be involved. SPs are masters of the art of drawing people in. Sometimes the production leaves the viewer with several ways to respond based on their own beliefs and values. Giving options is as much part of the SP skill set as wanting to keep their options open.

"Crisis manager" fits many of these skills perfectly. I know several firefighters who love their jobs for this reason alone. Reacting spontaneously and with purpose to emergency situations turns them on. They are called on to improvise, think tactically, and show bravery while they get the rush of excitement and the rise of adrenaline, all in the process of having a real impact on others. Rescuing people is high on the SP's list of meeting the needs of others.

Place them in the right tasks and they shine. They will get the job done with flare, skill, and fashion and are proud of their artisan achievements.

SPs seek to control the external world by doing whatever it takes while gladly throwing existing rules or cautions to the winds. **Freedom beats in their hearts** and they hate to be confined or ruled over by some arbitrary authority. To them authority invites challenge. Authority is also viewed as a potential threat so they dislike any form of authoritarian control. Try to force them to follow rules and they may find a way to pay you back. It is their sense of justice.

Freedom means the ability to do whatever one wants, and this is the only view of freedom that makes sense to the SP unless they have personally adopted more restrictive (or what the SJ calls "more responsible") values. Try to cabin or confine them and they resist with vehemence.

In a milder form, freedom for the SP is the **carefree attitude** that lives life at high speed while focused on his own immediate needs and always ready to squeeze every last drop of excitement out of the present moment.

Wheels and balls are favorite toys from their earliest years — both symbols of speed. They create **movement and action** for which the SP is named. It's very hard for an SP to sit still. Their inner urges impel them to move. Movement in itself is stimulating. Being stimulated fulfills the physical senses of the SP. Restlessness can often be seen toying with their spirit. If they have to wait, or if delayed gratification is enforced, they have the urge to find something else to do or simply resist the waiting by becoming irritable and unnerved.

A **cynical attitude** is evident but not always expressed. They will examine anyone's conduct with the question, "Are they doing this for their own benefit?" or "What's in it for them?" Seeing the benefit that others are seeking and making fast adjustments in their favor is an innate skill. (The intuition of the NF that also reads the mind and feelings of others can outmaneuver them.)

Altruism and pure motives are also questioned by the SP. "Where is the benefit in altruism?" they ask. This again leads to a cynical attitude. This cynicism is the nearest an SP comes to being judgmental because they pride themselves on being **tolerant**. The SP is cynical; the SJ, critical; the NT, skeptical; and the NF, trusting. All can be overdone.

Keirsey calls the intelligence of an SP "tactical." Berens calls it "contextual thinking." To me, it is both. The tactical mentality produces tactical results in the immediate context. Reading the immediate context produces the tactical result.

Tactical mentality is based on relevance. They see the relevance of every move. Relevance can become a virtue and an ethical standard for the SP.

They are **optimistic, fun loving**, and quite **charming** with people. The spice of life flows in their veins. The pleasure of encounters and their accompanying challenges stimulate and motivate them. Even their charm makes an impact.

Generous with what they have or don't have, they waste no time to bless the lives of others. This generosity can also be another way of making an impact on others. Sometimes it is designed to be.

They work best to the thrill of **competition**. Competitive games at work, play, or in learning situations is like being asked to play on their home field. Competition is their home advantage.

"Spend and enjoy" is their living style, and they care little about the past or the future in their quest for life's pleasures. The present is their stage, so why wait for tomorrow to spend what you have today. For them, saving for the rainy day is all a matter of your point of view. They will argue that the rainy day may never come.

Individualistic to the core, they **crave self-expression**. Being told they act just like someone else is a put down. Expressing oneself in unique ways draws attention and to have attention is to gain the chance of making an impact.

If it seems as though I have described an SP at play more than at work, it is because they are always at play! Life is a quest for play, pleasure, and excitement. Their work ethic is **play first; work when you must**.

The introverted among them are all of these things, although a somewhat muted version and their adventures are less daring. But they still feel in their hearts the beat of excitement that drives them to live freely as fun-seekers and make an impact.

The joy that pulses in the rhythm of their lives is an essential nutrient for the human spirit, and they avoid much stress as a result.

To the rest of the temperaments, they are a reminder that joy cannot be absent without damage to our systems. Optimism, joy, a free spirit, and fearlessness are some of the essential elements for the healthy development of all of our strengths. They also point the direction in which all of our lives must go if we are to function well.

Do you know anyone who is like this? Check! Is this you more than any of the other temperaments? Read all four temperaments before you decide.

Keys to Developing an SP's Potential

The relationship of the individual strengths of this temperament to success will be addressed in the section "Introduce Yourself to Your Strengths — SP." Here we will outline the things an SP should be aware of to be their best. Repeated items only reinforce their importance.

SPs are born to reach for some kind of success. Life is a performance and the applause of the people is, for many, essential to a high self-image. Trouble trails them when they equate a high self-image with personal acclaim. Achievements alone can never hold your self-esteem high. When the applause is over, so is the rush and the self-esteem falls.

Remember, a low self-esteem means a low performance. So when your self-image falls, so does your performance level and your private life becomes a poor act as well. It is hard for an SP to remain optimistic when there is no attentive audience. A steady high is all about who we are, not what we do.

Many of the things SPs excel at are high profile jobs. Those who don't have high profile jobs must discover their audience among their contacts and play to that audience's needs. They generally do this, so most SPs remain positive and optimistic. If an SP has a specific goal in life, they should seek with all their power to attain it. Success is what they need.

The following are areas of importance to becoming successful and to reaching their ultimate potential.

Focus

You must keep the focus of your *innerkinetics*. Any digression from the natural focus of your temperament will lessen your potential success.

Some, not all, of these focus points must be in the center of your aim and your goals. The more the better, of course, since they multiply your power and increase your potential.

The Focus of an SP Is On:

- **The present moment.** SPs <u>must</u> honor this focus. The present moment is all-important to them. If their focus wanders to the past or the future, it will be counterproductive to all of their strengths.

- **Action.** Without action the SP can become bored and restless.

- **Impact.** Making an impact is essential to the SP's self-image and it is a core focal point of the temperament.

- **Variety.** SPs must focus on variety since it keeps them positive and keeps refreshing their inner energy.

- **Technique.** Living with flair, skill, and excellence is also, for the SP, a key focus for creating confidence and a high self-image.

Core Needs

Meeting an SP's needs keeps the essential ingredients for the effective operation of their temperament supplied. The more of these needs that are met, the easier it is to achieve a life of rewarding fulfillment and to reach their goal. Does their dream allow these needs to be met?

- **Freedom.** Freedom for self-expression and creative improvisation (not fenced in by limiting, arbitrary boundaries) is a must-have.

- **Excitement.** Danger lurks for the SP who does not find excitement and refresh from it.

- **Applause.** Applause for the SP is confirmation that they have been successful and effective. It is essential feedback.

- **Learning by doing.** We all must learn, but we all learn effectively in different ways. Hands-on learning is the SP's way to learn fast and with pleasure. It is a core need.

- **Keep things moving.** Anything that drags is a waste of the precious, present moment. Interest then flags and distractions take over. For the SP, this is more important than for others.

Values

SPs are most satisfied when their values are being honored and rightly represented. Their needs and values often overlap.

- **Aesthetics.** Beauty is a value in their creative personality. Beauty in all its forms — the fine arts, performing arts and all artisan skills — speaks to them.

- **Tolerance.** They value tolerance since they don't naturally tend toward being judgmental and they react cynically to those who do.

- **Relevance.** This is a key value. Their minds are always aware of relationships and to their relevance to the present moment and its goals. All they do must be relevant.

- **Movement.** Movement is valued because of the ill effects that the absence of it causes.

Likely Talents

We are best when we can use our strengths and talents. Multiple opportunities to use our strengths is essential to the building of our strengths. The SPs must make sure their goals give them ample opportunity to use their talents and their supporting strengths.

- **Improvisation.** Improvisation of all sorts is their forte. Finding what can be done with what is immediately available is a talent that other temperaments envy.

- **Tactical intelligence.** This is a mental gift. We all use tactics but SPs are particularly skilled at tactical intelligence. They must center on this skill and develop it. It is a certain path to their success.

- **Sensory data.** Picking up information with their five physical senses, quickly and continuously, is what feeds their tactical skills and a number of their strengths. We could call it "the skill of a keen observation."

Skills:

- Alive in the present context and reading it quickly
- Skillfully able to find the best moves in the present moment
- Ability to act without hesitation and capture the opportunity
- Flexible in any situation
- Performing, persuading, producing, promoting, giving lively and moving presentations
- Skilled at avoiding obstacles
- Natural skills at defusing stress

How This Temperament Handles Stress.
(Stress is a key factor to manage if SPs are going to reach their potential)

Stress, which is inevitable for all of us, must be successfully handled — handled, not eliminated — or we derail.

Optimism keeps stress at a lower level for all SPs. SJs, in particular, envy this ability to dispel the pressures of stress that the SP makes look so easy and natural.

Likely Stress Factors
• Limitations
• Boredom

How this Temperament Prefers to Respond to Stress
• Gets even, breaks boundaries

How They Can Effectively Handle Stress — Their Antidotes
• Move on and find excitement

Self-Image
(We can't outperform our self-image.)

A high self-image is important to high performance. It is also essential as an aid to reducing stress. In a subtle way, what we think about ourselves affects the quality and quantity of our performances in all things. As an SP, don't underestimate the importance of this factor in success.

Typically, an SP will have a high self-image. Therefore, they may overlook whether their self-image is healthy or not. Awareness of the level of their self-esteem is a mental skill well worth learning to avoid unexplained breakdowns in performance.

What Builds the Self-Image of an SP?
Among other things, the following stand out in the SP temperament.

• Success at making an impact
• Being adaptable and coming up with successful adjustments (tactical skills)
• Courage and daring in the face of options
• Graceful physical actions

Fulfillment Will Look Like This

An SP is best when multiple strengths in their temperament are being fulfilled, their needs are being met, their talents are being used effectively, and their values are being honored.

As a result, they will then feel deep contentment with themselves and their life. It will feel as though life is serving them rather than that they are serving life. They will be happy and content in their relationships. Their lives will be oriented to the fulfillment they are bringing to others and to themselves.

The SP Variants
(ESTP, ESFP, ISTP, ISFP)

Let's use the four letters of your profile to fine-tune your path to your highest fulfillment. What will really satisfy you? What are the central drives of your *innerkinetics*? How can we best put into words the direction your life is intended to go if it is to follow your inner drives to the top? In this section we will confine ourselves to answering this major issue. The direction for the *real you* is about to stand up.

Much research has gone into discovering the basic drives and directions of the sixteen types: four SPs, four SJs, four NTs, and four NFs. I will summarize the findings and interpret them for you.

The four SP variations are ESTP, ESFP, ISTP, ISFP. If you are an SP one of these four-letter combinations will be yours and you will find your profile listed here.

ESTP

Driving the *innerkinetics* (inner powers) of the ESTP is an urge to direct and control what is happening in the "now." They do this by promoting, persuading, and expediting whatever they see as the best tactic for the moment. The ESTP excels at identifying winning tactics and promoting them.

The best tactic for the moment (if you always choose the best tactic for the moment) will, by extension, to the SP mind be the best tactic for the future. (This is not always the best solution because the SJ, NT, and NF have valuable perspectives too.) However, there seems to be no better way to go to the ESTP. It should be kept in mind that they are the most persuasive of the SPs and can effectively sway opinion.

SPs succeed by engaging others and obtaining their trust because they seem to anticipate people's actions. Confidence is another of their tools to engage others. This is done by being very observant, optimistic, and "in the moment." Hence, they often find their road to success in such things as selling, making irresistible deals and negotiating on the front line of action. Any venture that needs a sharp leader who can respond quickly and appropriately to the current needs fits the mold of the SP's *innerkinetics*. People become like musical instruments in the ESTPs orchestra and the ESTP blends them all to make the music of success.

If an ESTP will choose a path in life that gives the opportunity to exercise these drives, they will find the fulfillment they were made to experience. They will function smoothly and rise to the top.

ESFP

Whereas the ESTP is the skilled promoter, the ESFP is the skilled performer. Inside the ESFP is an overwhelming desire to perform with skill and hear the applause of observers. Sometimes this talent has been squelched when they were young and that is a loss to all of us. They entertain and thrill us. The world needs its performers.

Whether it be on the stage or at a party or simply lifting the spirits of their family, the ESFP is charming and charismatic and appears to be "on stage" wherever they are. This can be a noble urge to help and inspire the rest of us and meet our external social and personal needs. Making an impression drives the ESFP's *innerkinetics*.

They find fulfillment as presenters, actors, artists, motivators, entertainers — any opportunity that life presents that can trigger our senses and fire us with enthusiasm.

As an ESFP, they must find the opportunities to inspire and impress the rest of us with high-spirited joy. Personal warmth, with a lightness of spirit, infectious humor, and talent waiting to be released is the ESFP's inner path to their potential greatness.

ISTP

Hands-on talents express the inner drives of this skilled artisan. Instruments, tools, and the opportunity to design and create motivate the ISTP. Solving a problem in the physical world awakens their brilliance. They simply must craft, analyze, create, and cleverly solve problems using their skills with all kinds of implements.

No piece of machinery lies outside their urge to master and control. They will face risk and danger for the stimulation of using a tool or operating a piece of machinery to its limits and beyond. If it tests their metal, it excites them.

All crafts, trades, and operations (from carpentry to piloting a military jet, to wielding a weapon or using a scalpel) lie in the path to their greatest fulfillment. Don't forget the building of instruments and sports equipment of all sorts, of course. Physical, active, hands-on, creative work is their forte. This broad path to reaching their highest and most satisfying potential gives the ISTP many options.

The ISTPs must follow their *innerkinetics* and, if they do, they will live with "never a dull moment" and thrill to life's greatest fulfillment for them. What thrills an ISTP might scare the socks off a more cautious temperament.

ISFP

There is a high sensitivity to the physical senses and to their environment in the ISFP. These are the composers who become absorbed in the sensations of the moment and in their creative use. Like all the SPs, they are highly adaptable and skilled at improvising. ISFP excels not only in the world of the arts but in all sensory moments.

One comparison is necessary to make the role and skill of the ISFP clearer. The NF is noted for super sensitivity, but theirs is not primarily in the physical environment. It is in the abstract, inner world of the spirit and the sensitivity of emotion, imagination and intuition in that world.   Although the NF and the ISFP overlap a little (both experiencing a high degree of emotion, imagination, and intuition) the distinction is that the ISFP experiences these sensitivities primarily in the physical world and in the present moment, while the NF is more sensitive in the virtual world and to the possibilities of the future. Also, the SP is concrete and the NF is abstract.

So the ISFPs find fulfillment and reach their peak in composing, directing films, designing, decorating, cooking, editing, graphics, etc. All are expressions of sensitive creativity in the physical world.

As we might expect, the ISFP is also sensitive to the plights of people and to relationships of all kinds. They display a real caring spirit.

The ISFPs must follow their inner path to greatness and satisfaction if they would live to their utmost.

The Real You — SJ

The Responsibility Temperament

On First Meeting

SJs share most of the following similarities.

Obvious at first glance is their **cautious attitude toward life**. Caution and seriousness will be noticeable in most conditions and circumstances. SJs are the most cautious of all the temperaments. Caution leads to risk avoidance. They play it safe at work and at play and make preparations for all they do. To offset this businesslike image is their pleasantness and joviality. Even the introverts among them come over as warm and friendly.

SJs are solid citizens, establishing home and social organizations to protect and educate and establishing clubs for the lighter but still structured side of life.

Practical and down-to-earth, they see to all the routine matters and the mundane considerations of life as though they take pleasure in them. They are loyal and keep to the rules and regulations, creating systems to protect systems and, therefore, they are largely predictable in their decisions and behavior. Simply learn their systems and routines.

These observations lead to the deeper elements of their makeup: their responsibility, reliability, and their insistence that not only they but everyone should do their duty and not shirk responsibilities.

Fun, for the SJ, is with family and friends. A picnic, a family outing, and similar adventures define acceptable fun for most of them.

SJs are helpful (good Samaritans). It is a true key to unlocking their nature. However, they can be given to worry and stoicism. When they are feeling insecure, they attempt to control the things they cannot control.

Portrait

SJs fly closer to the ground than SPs and, perhaps, than all temperaments. They keep their feet solidly in **reality**. Ground zero, for SJs, is not the present moment with all of its choices and opportunities but the solid experiences of the past. They look backwards to find stability, something in which they can trust. "If it worked in the past it will work today," they reason, and who wants to change what works.

If we change it, they nervously wonder if it will open the floodgates of chaos and disorder or break down the already proven methods of conducting life and constructing society. Since they cannot know the answer to that all-important question, they prefer (prefer is far too slight an emotion; try insist upon) **the status quo**.

When the past is the most important timeframe for their lives to be oriented to, it leads to a slew of other **conservative values** and behaviors. In brief, the SJ faces the past, trusts the past, and elevates it above the present and the future. The present is chancy, the future uncertain and anything that is uncertain makes them nervous.

Cautious behavior is one of the offshoots of this orientation to the past. Add to their caution a strong desire to **protect** and **preserve** and the SJ temperament begins to take shape. Their protection is first of themselves and their family and then, in widening circles, embraces their immediate society, reaching out to their nation and the world. All are to be protected and preserved, even if their ideas of protection and preservation may have quite varying meanings.

Caution means looking first at the negative possibilities and making sure they are protected against them before the positive possibilities come into focus. From this point of view, it is a natural step to feel that if anything can go wrong, it will go wrong — Murphy's Law.

However, let's see this negative behavior in the context of its positive motivations. Because they have the care of their loved ones and of society firmly in their sights, SJs look to protect and then guard them with meticulous care. Caution, therefore, operates in the SJ as a strength and not a weakness. It becomes a weakness only when caution is overdone.

Cautious attitudes introduce us to the need for **responsible behavior**. Acting and feeling responsible becomes a deep need of this temperament. If responsibility does not follow caution, then the effort to be cautious is useless. They know that if they are responsible but others are not, there are no brakes on society, so they preach with fervor the need for all to be responsible.

Because many do not share this concern for responsibility, SJs feel the need to take on all the roles of responsibility that are not filled and overload themselves in the bargain. Besides, there is a pride in being responsible and society honors those who are creating a desire for recognition, for doing one's duty. If they turn down a responsible post, they feel guilty, and if they take on too many, they experience stress. These makers of a safe and worthy society are caught by their own passions.

Doing their duty almost amounts to a religion. Public shame and punishment, in the minds of many SJs, should be the consequence to all who show no concern for this laudable philosophy. Presidents of the USA who were SJs, from George Washington to George W. Bush, have all spoken emotionally of their need to serve their country and exhibit a fulfillment of duty that they sometimes perceive as a divine calling.

Once you have proved to be responsible, you are seen by SJs as **useful**. Usefulness is a down-to-earth idea. It is **practical** and **pragmatic**. It creates relationships with others of like mind. Many clubs have been, and are, formed by those who feel the same way.

Society cannot hold itself together without honoring the values of **reliability** and **dependability**. Change comes too fast and runs out of control where these factors are not treasured.

SJs are sensible and realistic. Rules make sense to them when a group of people attempt to live together in peace. Therefore, **rules and regulations** create standards for the judgment of responsible, reliable behavior. SJs see rules and regulations as not only making sense but as imperative for happiness and peace. To all SJ minds, that ugly word "chaos" threatens the dissolution of a society that is without rules and the policing of those rules.

Why would you not want rules if you want things to be under control? If everyone did what they wanted, the world would collapse. **Instability** and **insecurity** describes the door to a living hell for all SJs.

An SJ's **appreciation of authority** is coupled with their insistence on the justice of rules. You will often hear an SJ say, "I'll take on that responsibility only if I am given the authority to make the necessary decisions." The value of authority that has teeth fits with their whole sense of societal control and welfare.

Authority figures, for the SJ, must be duly authorized. All temperaments agree that authority figures that prove unworthy or who are corrupt should be removed and not obeyed. It is just the definition of "corrupt" that is in constant argument. The SPs trump with personal freedom and the SJs, with personal responsibility.

Risk is foolish to most SJs unless they have reduced it to a controllable factor. They often talk of taking **calculated risks**. An SJ parent can overreact and try to remove all risk for her child and this develops a child who, in adulthood, has not faced risk and does not know how to handle it or how to instinctively try to handle it. Usually, hard times and hard lessons follow.

Controlling their world and the people in it and not letting it get out of control feeds the SJ desire for security. This means we are dealing with **preparers** and **planners** who construct systems, rules, and routines to protect their own safety and their fortunes as well as those of society. The SJs are monitors, protectors, providers, and inspectors, and they take seriously the task of making sure everything is going according to plan and done correctly.

The role of providing is important to the SJ since controlling the environment but failing to provide for its needs is counterproductive.

"Be prepared and save for the rainy day" is a true SJ principle for living. Another is to establish routines, and even additional routines to protect the sure functioning of the initial routines. This is the spirit of the SJ as well as the intent of their protective actions.

With their sense of responsibility, SJs make the world go round. They can be depended upon in the workplace, unless you have caused them to feel insecure. For example, don't threaten an SJ worker with the loss of their job if your goal is to get the best performance out of them. They **thrive on approval and encouragement** and fall into less dependable behavior if it is absent. They are the backbone of the workplace, structured in their behavior and stedfast. Their energy sources are used sparingly and very efficiently unless they are pressured, in which case they pay no attention to replenishing or preserving energy. They just work. All Js are subject to the disease of **"workaholism."**

Don't rock the boat that is full of SJs (which means most organizations) and if you want change to be accepted, proceed slowly and in steps that maintain a feeling of security. Teamwork means "work with me and don't make me feel unsettled or unappreciated." They are **team players, disciplined,** and **determined** to be **loyal.**

Logistics is their world. Moving, storing, scheduling, saving; and providing, protecting, supervising, and inspecting are native skills. Logistics is the intelligence that makes sure everything is where it is supposed to be at the right time, in the right quantity, and delivered to the right person.

Sequential thinking is also a mark of logistical thinking. They learn step-by-step, and their mind is the epitome of orderly procedures. If confusion rules, an SJ will sort out the mess and create a procedure to ensure it never happens again.

This often leads to their taking care of things others don't believe need attention. Like the SP, they have an S in their profile which means they are sensory and observant. They seldom pass by when something needs straightening or picking up or adjusting. It is easier to keep things **in order** if you standardize and make things and procedures uniform. Therefore, they will tell you where everything should be.

Logistics require the careful measurements of everything including time. SJs are time watchers.

They are helpers and keep an eye on the **traditions** and welfare of the people who make up the organization. They take pride in their **organization**, wanting to protect its name and functions. Keirsey calls them "**helpmates**" and they exhibit the trait of being attentive Good Samaritans.

They are hardworking, believing that work must come before play. They follow procedures well. Helpmates, workers who follow routines, dependable machines of industry describes the SJ at work very well, and when they are not, something is amiss.

It should be obvious that they also have a strong sense of right and wrong and they worry about the loss of moral measures that stabilize society. Supervisors and inspectors must focus on the impact morals and ethics have on logistics. SJs watch with an eagle's eye.

Because of their **social nature,** they are quite **pleasant** and it is a mistake to view their serious attitude toward life as a prediction of their being dull, spoilsports or even prudish.

That word "**worry**" is, of course, their Achilles heel! If they are underperforming, check to see what is worrying them. Worry, for an SJ, is living in their weakness since it is not part of their temperament's strengths. Whenever they sense they cannot control something or are destabilized by insecurity, worry will raise its ugly head. Worry leads to the companion demon called **pessimism** and they can be very pessimistic, too, if they are troubled or financially at risk. They represent the ant in *The Ant and the Grasshopper*. Storing for the rainy day is the natural action for those who must care for the welfare of society. They hate to spend what is not absolutely necessary. Some are misers. You never know what an SJ is worth, since they seldom tell you of the amount they have stashed in the bank or the hole in the back yard.

Montgomery calls them the cornerstone temperament and this well-describes their strong, supportive nature. Others call them **sensible, traditional, guardians of society, melancholic, and dutifully serious**.

Their positive potentials are obvious. They are loyal workers who follow rules and need, as I have noted several times, security to perform at their best. Responsible to the core, it leads them to work with persistence and tenacity and, if constantly approved, they will spend their last drop of energy for a cause they believe in. These are not quitters.

Perseverance develops strengths and they can quickly succeed in business since they are solidly devoted to making things happen by hard work and sheer doggedness. Hard work is their natural road to success, but they need to know that a mix of pleasure and work sharpens the senses and avoids boredom and many a false step. It lessens the friction on the path to success as well.

Perhaps the tendency to pessimism and the all too ready acknowledgement of Murphy's Law is a sad commentary on a loss of direction in their lives. When worry sucks the life out of their motivation and purpose, it clouds their strengths and their progress toward success grinds slower. The proverbial "Rock of Gibraltar" shatters as it surprisingly shakes.

Do you know anyone who is like this? Check! Is this you more than any of the other temperaments? Read all four temperaments before you decide.

Keys to Developing an SJ's Potential

The relationship of the strengths of this temperament to success will be addressed in the section "Introduce Yourself to Your Strengths — SJ." Here we will outline the things for an SJ to watch to be their best. Repeated items only emphasize their importance.

SJs are born to serve others. Life, for them, is being responsible and reliable while making sure that their duty is preformed. If you are an SJ, your self-image is lifted whenever you are approved for your sacrificial, efficient, and beneficent service. Trouble trails you when you begin to worry and become negative. Pessimism can quickly follow. Approval alone won't keep your self-esteem high; you must work on maintaining a more optimistic attitude. Remember, a low self-esteem means a low performance. When your self-image falls, so does your performance level and your private life becomes too serious and lacks excitement and thrill. It is hard for an SJ to remain optimistic in the company of negative people. A steady high is all about who you are, not what you do or how you serve.

Many of the things SJs excel at are in the world of business, teaching, and law. SJs are second-to-none at logistical planning and operations. Wherever detailed work is involved, such as accounting or record-keeping, they have no equal.

In succeeding, they not only have to be in the right job or attempting a goal for which they are gifted, but they must also manage their tendency to pessimism.

The following are areas of importance to becoming successful and reaching their ultimate potential.

Focus

If you are an SJ, you must keep the focus of your *innerkinetics*. Any digression from the natural focus of your temperament will lessen your potential.

Some, not all, of the focus points of the SJ temperament must be in the center of your aim and your goals. The more, the better, of course, since multiples increase the energy of the focus.

The Focus of an SJ Is On:

- **The past**. Let the focus on the past be enriching, but an SJ must not let it hold them back from needed change. The past must be their guide, not their dictator or their only informant.

- **Order, organization, planning, structure.** The urge to control is a strength that can run wild easily in the SJ. Order, organization, planning, and structure are attempts to control their environment and, at times, people as well. SJs must develop this strength so as not to damage themselves or others.

- **Rules, regulations, norms, roles, responsibilities.** These also help control their environment and are a part of organizational structure. Of course, if they did not try to control how a business operates, it would quickly fail. SJs must put these strengths to good use not only in their business lives but also in their private lives. Control helps fight off the demon of insecurity.

- **On getting things done.** SJs like to come to closure, and fast. Hence their drive to get things done.

- **On being respectable.** Being the social temperament, SJs focus on cooperating and being acceptable to a group. Respectability is a mark of success.

Core Needs

An SJ's needs must be met to keep the essential ingredients for the effective operation of their temperament supplied. The more of these needs the SJ meets, the easier it is to achieve a life of rewarding fulfillment and to reach their goal. SJs, don't neglect your needs!

Incorporate the fulfillment of these needs in your life's dream.

The Needs of an SJ Are:

- Security. SJs are very stable, but their sense of stability is based on their having a secure world in which to work. Secure relationships and secure employment brings out the best in them. Keep everything secure, which means stable environments and even set routines.

- To belong. This is a deep need. Belonging gives an SJ a reason to put down roots and establish themselves.

- To be cautious and take no wild risks. Risk must be carefully managed. Risks are inherently unsettling to all SJs.

- Connected with the past. The present is the arena for the past to be reenacted. The future will hopefully be like the past and the past is where an SJ lives and feels comfortable.

- To do their duty. Self-esteem falls fast if the SJ does not prove reliable, responsible, and faithful.

Values

SJs are most satisfied when their values are being honored and rightly represented. Their needs and their values often overlap. Values shape the life of an SJ. They are usually much more conservative than the SPs.

Key Values of an SJ Are:

- Home. They are the guardians of home and hearth. SJs settle down quickly and center their lives around the home. Family is super-important.

- Structure and routine. For SJs, everything must have structure. A place for everything and everything in its place. A time for everything and everything on time. A way of doing things that, once it is established, becomes the rule of the home.

- Authority. Authority is valued and obeyed. Chaos (what the SJ believes will happen without law and authority) is a frightening thought. Therefore, authority must be clearly understood.

- Being useful. Everyone must contribute to society and be useful. To sponge off others is shameful.

- Historical connections and consistency. History, for the SJ, holds value because it informs us of patterns we should honor and keep. What we do today is to be done tomorrow. Don't try to fix society unless it is broken.

- Social Status. Status has value because it recognizes the contributions that have been made to any group. Status is sought after and prized by SJs.

- Conservative ideas. Conservative ideas slow the rush of change. They are built around the lessons of the past and discourage untried experiments. This champions and consolidates a number of SJ values and, therefore, influences the SJ's chosen belief system.

Likely Talents

SJs are best when they can use their strengths and talents. It is true for all, but particularly needed for the SJ temperament, that they use their strengths. Multiple opportunities to use their strengths are essential to the building of strengths.

They will show a helpful spirit when they pursue more opportunities to use their strengths.

- Management. SJs are born managers. Management presupposes a set of rules and regulations, clearly defined goals, and allocated authority over systems and/or others. For logistical tasks, the SJ is a natural choice.

- Supervising. Supervisor is a name that Keirsey gives to the ESTJ. They, and all SJs, are suited for the above reasons.

- Inspecting. Inspector is Keirsey's name for the ISTJ. SJs naturally inspect everything and everyone. They must keep their eyes on proceedings.

- Logistical operations. It takes a mind focused on details and fashioned for creating order with sequential steps and systemized procedures to excel at logistics. This is the SJ mind.

- Teaching. Most SJs are effective teachers, and many seek out the teaching profession. Instructing others seems essential in the pursuit of social wellbeing.

Skills

- All logistical planning and support
- Serving the needs of others
- Caring for others
- Detailing procedures and taking care of details
- Security operations, keeping law and order
- Historical record keeping and preservation of its lessons
- Maintenance of routines and procedures

How This Temperament Handles Stress.
(A key factor to manage if they are going to reach their potential)

Stress, which is inevitable, must be successfully handled or, like all of us, an SJ derails. Stress must be handled, not eliminated.

Determination to succeed drives the SJ through their most stressful situations. The SJ can be very determined, sometimes crossing the line to stubborn persistence and unreasonably persisting just for the sake of finishing. Stress is an enemy and they must show their superiority over it.

Likely Stress Factors
- Insecurity
- Instability
- Being rejected or unappreciated

How this Temperament Responds to Stress
- Doggedly works through it
- Worries and becomes pessimistic
- Generates tiredness and illnesses
- Becomes flustered and complains

How They Can Effectively Handle Stress — Antidotes
- Activate their sources of appreciation. Move in these circles.
- Increase entertainment and down time.
- Retreat into the comfort of spiritual beliefs.

Self-Image
(We can't outperform our self-image.)

A high self-image is important to high performance for all of us. It is also essential as an aid to reducing stress. In a subtle way, what the SJ thinks about themselves affects the quality and quantity of their performances, causing them, at times, to miss details. SJs think they can push their way through anything and gain some of their self-esteem from their determination. The SJ should not underestimate the importance of a healthy self-image to achieve success.

Typically, an SJ will have a solid self-image. However, their Achilles heel is insecurity and worry caused by rejection, a lack of appreciation, or failure that has caused them to lose the belief that they can be who they are and live successfully in their strengths. They place less emphasis and value on self-image than the other temperaments, certainly much less than the NFs, who are at times almost obsessed with it.

Awareness of the level of their self-esteem is a mental skill well worth learning to avoid unexplained breakdowns in performance.

Self-image can also be essential as an aid to reducing stress.

What Builds the Self-Image of the SJs?

- Awards, achievements, and certifications — any recognition of service
- Serving and being beneficial to others
- Constant feedback in the form of encouragement and approval

Fulfillment Will Look Like This:

An SJ is best when multiple strengths in their temperament are being fulfilled, their needs are being met, their talents are being used effectively, and their values are being honored. Insecurity and worry will then be kept at a safe distance.

Fulfillment causes them to feel deep contentment with themselves and their life. It will feel as though life is serving the SJ rather than the SJ serving life. They will feel happy and contented in their relationships. Their life will be oriented to the fulfillment they are bringing to others.

The SJ Variants
(ESTJ, ESFJ, ISTJ, ISFJ)

Let's use the four letters of your profile to fine tune your path to your highest fulfillment. What will really satisfy you? What are the central drives of your *innerkinetics*? How can we best put into words the direction your life is intended to go if it is to follow your inner drives to the top? In this section we will confine ourselves to answering this major issue. The direction for the *real you* is about to stand up.

Much research has gone into discovering the basic drives and directions of the sixteen types: four SPs, four SJs, four NTs, and four NFs. I will summarize the findings and interpret for you.

The four SJ variations are ESTJ, ESFJ, ISTJ, and ISFJ. If you are an SJ, one of these four-letter combinations will be yours and you will find your profile listed here.

ESTJ

There is a deep interest and concern in the ESTJ for the social unit or the organization that is responsible in some way for the welfare or protection of society. These are the supervisors who make sure that the rules and regulations are kept and that adequate protections for these regulations are in place. Also, they keep a sharp eye on resources and ensure that the resources are where they are needed at the right time and in the right condition.

Where order, regularity, reliability, and trustworthy performance are needed, they excel. Follow through is a native skill. Therefore, we can expect that they will enforce consequences, good or bad, and be very serious about it all. They feel responsible for themselves and others and are not in the least bit shy about calling another to account.

They seek administrative, supervisory, managerial, and leadership positions. Law, education, law enforcement, business, politics — oversight positions and tasks call out their best. Where the maintenance of tradition or the preservation of values are of importance the ESTJ finds great fulfillment in serving and none surpasses their responsible and gifted contribution.

If you are an ESTJ, then you must seek out and aspire to these positions and to the status they offer since, in them, you will find your greatest contribution to society and complete satisfaction for yourself. This is the path your *innerkinetics* suggests.

ESFJ

In the ESFJ there is a softness not found in the ESTJ. This softness emphasizes their concern for people and their desire to provide for people's needs in any social or physical way possible. They are the truly friendly, sympathetic ones.

Therefore, they are the providers par excellence. The supply chain and the response chain are where the contented ESFJs are to be found. To be the best they can be, they seek out harmonious relationships as well as opportunities to serve. ESFJs are the supreme helpmates and makers of a caring home.

They can be most satisfied in such roles as nurturers, teachers, support workers, and suppliers of all kinds of services. Schools, churches, nonprofit organizations, social groups, welfare organizations, and hospitals are typical places where they find fulfillment. Their alternatives for reaching their potential are many. The main thrust of their *innerkinetics* is to be of service in a meaningful way and better the world in which they operate.

ESFJs should follow their inner design to be their best. If they are placed in demanding, harsh environments, they cannot thrive with the same success. Their path to a successful life is undoubtedly paved with the opportunity to care.

ISTJ

Called the inspectors, they watch with eagle eye and are the true policers of society. Therefore, they must struggle to project a loving attitude and not be shunned for their stern, all businesslike exterior.

They excel at operating systems, administering policies, regulating procedures, checking results, and teaching and monitoring others in their respective roles. Nothing gets by them. Like the extroverted STJs, they organize, plan, delegate, and conserve resources. ISTJs are loyal, down to earth, sensible, logical, and insist on doing things in the accepted way. "Follow instructions" could be their war cry.

If their role is to see that things are done as they should be done to control outcomes and keep order and preserve quality, there are none better. Their homes reflect their orderliness, everything with a place and in its place.

They are detailed, duty minded, and responsible. Therefore, they find pathways to success in law, teaching, inspections, security, and anywhere in business where such characteristics are treasured and super-dependability is needed. The ISTJs will find their path to their greatest success and fulfillment in making order happen and in keeping that order. Following this design in their *innerkinetics* will propel them to the top.

ISFJ

The security and safety of society and of individuals is of prime importance to the ISFJ. Like the ISTJ, they are detailed-oriented and duty bound. Their introversion makes them quiet and the F in their profile makes them friendly and personable. Therefore, their path to the top is via a devoted service to the needs of society, whatever that social unit happens to be.

They find satisfaction in being of service. That service, however, needs to be in supplying the protection and the necessities of life, particularly to those who are most needy: the downtrodden, the under privileged, the disabled. By comparison, the champion of causes (the ENFP), while not limited to needy causes, joins interests with the ISFJ and needs the ISFJ to take care of the details that all SJs are good at processing, while the ENFP provides the drive and enthusiasm for the cause. The ISFJ can be quite firm and resolute when in the role of caretaker.

Following this path will lead the ISFJ to be the best they can be. At the same time, it will provide that all-essential feeling of fulfillment that all satisfying success must create.

The Real You — NT

The Technology Temperament.

On First Meeting

NTs share most of the following similarities.

On first meeting NTs appear **calm, confident** and **disengaged**. Several characteristics help create this exterior. They are **logical to the core.** If it does not make sense, they refuse to do it. Why should they? It doesn't make sense? With this rational mind comes a skeptical attitude and you may find them questioning you and acting as though they don't believe you. They don't — not until they can verify it. They don't accept the expert's statements either. Even their professors are subject to verification, so belief or praise can be something they hand out very sparingly.

They don't mean to be cold. NTs must investigate everything. Curious to the core, they must find out how things work and solve each problem they encounter — at least theoretically. That coldness is also evidence of their intense independence.

They are, as Montgomery calls them, the "technology temperament" and they must use all available knowledge and devices to expedite their discoveries. If on first meeting you would like to know how to build or structure something, ask.   They will begin to overwhelm you with information, and you had better be ready to keep up with their slew of knowledge.

NT's are pleasant, although somewhat remote; caring, although appearing not to care; and deep down, a little emotional, while on the surface unemotional.   Their theoretical approach to everything only confirms the above feelings.   Often, when approached they will give you the impression that they are being disturbed.

Portrait

NTs have a love of and skill with **technology**.   Is that computer misbehaving and threatening your sanity? Find an NT, but don't stand over them with your suggestions; it will infuriate them.   It actually insults them. (If no NTs are available to help you, try an SP or, maybe, an SJ.)   For NTs, technology is a tool — a tool to be thoroughly understood.   If it can help them in their constant examination of all things material, they will engage its abilities.   After all, technology is the result of their scientific experiments and they know only too well how skillfully crafted inventions, backed with solid theory, can improve the world.

NTs are **theorists** and can follow and **plan complex strategies with delight.** Their **strategic mind** thinks of all the possible contingencies that might develop and they are great users of the phrase "What if?" Successful strategy examines all the roads and dead ends to understand where everything might lead.   Projecting results into the future like this is a superb way to achieve a sense of control over one's future. It requires an imagination able to construct mental pictures of possibilities and follow each possibility's development and effects.

In this way it is different from the step-by-step analysis of the logistical mind that thinks in terms of concrete operations, not abstract possibilities.   The NT excels at this strategic thinking in the realm of things and theories but leaves the strategy of diplomatic relationships and theorizing in that realm to the other inner-world experts, the feeling NFs.

Mundane, repetitive work bores the NT and causes them to malfunction. There is little knowledge required to do routine work and it feels beneath their dignity to waste their giftedness on such simple tasks. Creativity, especially in the form of **ingenuity**, is their world. It is of interest that in the sixteenth century, when science was in its infancy and beginning to promise great things, the word "ingenuity" came into use in our language from the Latin. Ingenuity is an inborn trait, as the Latin word would have it, and truly part of the NT's hardwired temperament.

NTs are all about their heads. **Reason dominates** and the world of **emotion is subjugated and despised**. That world of emotion, however, is not absent in an NT. It is just buried deeply beneath the weight of logic and analytical thinking that dominates them.

Emotion has a habit of disturbing one's thinking because it brings emotional facts to light and calls for attention to these facts. The NTs do not want such interruptions and exclude them, to their loss in certain circumstances and to their gain in the purely rational processes. That's not quite the way an NT sees it.

Evaluation of truth can be a **skeptical** process. Every fact can be viewed from different perspectives. Therefore, one can be skeptical of any point of view. Skepticism is often, in their hands, a negative process or a tool to break down theoretical opposition. They skillfully use it for good and bad purposes. Often, they critique themselves to the point of self-damage. This is a wrong use of the strength. However, **criticism** can be a powerful, positive tool and they use it in this way to fine-tune their strategies and improve their findings and those of others. They will mercilessly use it to create greater competence in themselves.

Rationality and the worshipping of knowledge make them crave **competence**. To imagine that they would not be competent fills them with a real fear. They feel anointed, if you like, with the task of bringing rational competence to the world and discovering how the world operates so they can harness its wonders for all of us. Self-confidence is based on their knowing that they will deliver and that they will not be ashamed in the day of scientific judgment. Therefore, they seek and excel at **scientific research**, application of new knowledge, **theoretical** musings, and solving problems, particularly of an **abstract** nature. The ability to see the relationship between the parts and to discern the connections and patterns is an ongoing operation in the NT mind.

They **live inside themselves,** as do the NFs. Once you have crossed over from the S world (all about the outside world and the physical senses) to the N world, you have entered the ethereal world of the mind. NTs (some of them) are not good with their hands and physical tasks can unnerve them. Think mental — all about reason and planning and theories — and you have them tabbed, as we have noted already.

A narrow focus causes them to be **absent-minded**, and they can forget the simplest tasks related to life's mundane needs. They will not always notice you, even if you are someone they care about. Lost in the world of the mind, they share this characteristic with some of the more intense NFs.

They will not do anything that does not make sense to them. You will notice this at first glance. If what you ask them to do does not make sense to them, you can always reason with them that it can make real sense to them on the basis that a paycheck is at the end of the week or it serves their purpose to cooperate.

Maintaining their **cool** is not just necessary to assure clear, uninterrupted thinking, but it is a part of their self-image. It advances the aura of **intelligence** and the mystique of these, the ingenious ones.

Therefore, with this cool exterior the NT concentrates intensely, working well with data. Data excites them if they are looking for patterns and trends or reasons why. Give an NT the task of graphing the trends of the past year and projecting suggested changes for the year to come, and they are in their element. They often become engineers and planners.

Design is also their field, whether the design of physical objects (as in the inventor) or the design of mental **strategies**. Designing a building or a schedule is appealing, but don't expect much in the more artistic field of, say, interior decoration or the fine arts. *Artistic* is a word less appealing than the word *functional*. Design, to them, is the gathering of details, categorizing, systematizing the relationships of the parts, and ordering the steps to create functionality and practical usefulness. Therefore, fine arts do not usually attract them as much as pragmatic, functional design.

As kids, they hold their forks a different way because they believe finding a new way to do things is what they must do, and they are likely not to have outgrown this tendency as adults. At work, they are constantly finding **new ways of doing things**.

To summarize thus far: They are **ingenious, pragmatic, rational, independent**, and **more about their head than their heart**. The head or brain could well be their mascot.

They are often seen as prideful as they can tend to project a feeling of superiority. They have confessed to feeling more intelligent than others and some have looked down on their inferior counterparts at times.

An NT's relationship to time is unique. If they are engaged in a project, time is of no importance until the task is done. Time will not hurry them or slow them down. They can be late to an event without conscience since they were simply completing the project their minds were engaged in. After all, who would not understand that an ingenious mind has to work this way and complete things? Time is relevant only to the achieving of their goals.

Outside of their projects or concerns, NTs don't think of time. All they do transcends time. Transcendence is a quality often attributed to God and, although most NTs don't think of themselves as God, some have theorized about the possibility. NTs think into the future with a practical intuition, but they do not live in the future. That quality will be left to the NF.

The values of an NT are abstract or they are values that support their abstract lives. **Truth,** to the NT, is a value, but it is often narrowly defined within the scope of scientific principles. They see themselves as the discoverers and protectors of truth, but truth cannot be caged within one temperament's strengths and design. Because truth is abstract and they are logical, they reach it via the development of principles, theories, and ideas, all of which must have a presuppositional base. The processing of data is used to develop their **theories** and is a value in itself to the NT.

Myers' definition of the NT as the thinking type truly sets them in contrast to the feeling types and points to **thinking** and the mental processes as another value of the NT. Since brain is all important, NTs conceive of thinking as a physical brain process in contrast to the NF who sees it as more of an ethereal mind exercise.

Another value of the NT is **progress**. They promote it and insist on it, truly conceiving of it as improvement for society. Of course, **scientific inquiry** and **mathematical order** are deep-seated values. Berens is right in seeing not just logic, which is a tool we use for communication, but **logical consistency** as the true value of the NT. Consistency attached to logic takes the importance of logic to a higher level. Consistency is something that can be projected into the future or the past and is a well-used tool of science. Inconsistency bodes of error to the NT.

Aristotle called them logical. Others use the words reasoning, skeptical, thinking, scholarly, phlegmatic, and even insensitive to describe their core. Keirsey, who is one himself, calls them rationals. Hidden in all these titles is the desire to master their environment. They must succeed at whatever they attempt or they prove their incompetence. Proving yourself incompetent as an NT is a self-image fall of the greatest proportions.

NTs are purveyors of exactness in language. They argue over semantics and can dissect a meaning into a thousand pieces. Their words are carefully chosen, if they have a substantial vocabulary, and rational argument is one of their passionate skills.

Their strengths lead to the positive potentials and occupations of discovery, analytical theorists, strategists of all kinds, mobilizers, and leaders of people (both military and civilian). The NTs with a J in their profile are serious directors of others. Negative potentials develop chiefly in their lack of people skills or insensitivity to the feelings of others.

Do you know anyone who is like this? Check! Is this you or is some other temperament more you? Read all four temperaments before you decide.

Keys to Developing an NT's Potential

The relationship of the strengths of this temperament to success will be addressed under NT strengths in the section "Introduce Yourself to Your Strengths — NT." Here we will outline the things for an NT to watch in order to be their best. Repeated items only emphasize their importance.

NTs are born with a very strong drive to succeed. Life is discovery for the NT and we know that discovery doesn't wait for us. It presents its opportunity and we either take it or loose it. NTs, although they exhibit a calm exterior, are in a panic at times inside. Success to them is a successful ending to a long project, or an ingenious invention, or even the confirmation of a long-held theory. However, time marches on. They do not want to be troubled by time's inevitable march onward, but they can hear the ticking of the "enemy machine," counting down to success or failure. NTs do not suffer often from low self-esteem. They have an innate pride in themselves and in all they do, which boosts their self-image.

Trouble trails them when they equate a high self-image with success. That's the wrong way around. A high self-esteem must contribute to our success, not trail it. Self-image is usually high for the NT, even higher than it should be at times. When it falls, the NT is nonplussed. They can't figure out why they feel empty and tired, as though a hole has sprung a leak in their energy tank.

Remember, a low self-esteem means a low performance. So when their self-image falls, so does their performance level and they feel disconnected from their source of power. They must guard against many things to run on full energy for long periods. A steady high is all about who they are — not what they do.

The following are areas of importance to achieving success and reaching our ultimate potential.

Focus

NTs must keep the focus of their *innerkinetics*. Any digression from the natural focus of their temperament will lessen their potential. Some, not all, of the focal points of their temperament must be in the center of their aim and the NT's goals. An NT who has lost touch with his powers is a miserable misfit wherever he happens to be.

The Focus of an NT Is On:

• The present project: NTs don't live in the past, present, or future. They are wrapped up outside of time in the project they are engaged in. Time is not of the essence. Focus is on the project.

• On "Whys?" The question "why" was made for NTs or by NTs. Not "how," but "why." Once they understand why, then "what ifs" come into play and are the focus of their minds. "Why" leads to discovery with understanding.

• On being problem solvers: A problem is made for an NT. Their success is chiefly in solving problems in a pragmatic way. An NT's life is often spent trying to solve just one problem.

• On reason, logic, and what makes sense: Because they are all about their heads, logic is their prime tool.

• On pragmatic competency and efficiency: If an NT is not competent, they hate themselves or the issue over which they fail to meet their competency standards. Efficiency is second to competency and all must be pragmatic. (Pragmatic, for the NT, is useful, rational, and down to earth.)

• On the abstract and theoretical: The combination of an inward focus on the mind and analytical skills creates an atmosphere in which theory, speculation, and strategy can flourish. Success, for the NT, is in exercising all these points of focus.

• On being independent and autonomous: Their focus is on living autonomously and with a detachment that makes them appear cold at times.

Core Needs

We must keep our resources well stocked. The more needs of an NT that are met, the easier it is for them to achieve a life of rewarding fulfillment.

Mastery of themselves and others by willpower and competence is highly developed. Their self-image is supported by their overpowering willpower. This means they seldom experience a low self-image, which means they seldom run low on the need to feel good about themselves.

Core Needs Are:

• Intellectual competence: Without real pride in their intelligence (sometimes warranted and sometimes not) they would not easily withstand the mistakes or dead ends in the formation of their theories or the struggle in their ingenious pursuits. In comparison to the NF, this is a real advantage to building and sustaining self-confidence. Intellectual competence for the NT is IQ rather than EQ.

• To be pragmatic: Whatever is not useful is worthless. It needs to work and benefit them or others in some way. If they are not pragmatic, they feel useless and that makes pragmatism a real need.

• To be efficient: Although they seldom consciously race against the clock, to be efficient and use time without undue waste is a drive that amounts to a need. Hence they often become workaholics.

• To be ingenious in their creativity: If they do not find a new way to do something, they can feel they are failures. They are the makers of all things new. To them, ingenuity is skill with the use of ideas and imagination in a pragmatic way.

Values

NTs are most satisfied when their values are being honored and rightly represented. Their needs and their values often overlap. Value, for an NT, does not usually center on moral standards as it does for the SJ. NTs simply value all that makes them more efficient and successful.

The Values of an NT Are:

- **To be skeptical**: Skepticism is the need to question everything and take no one's word for granted. It can be both beneficial and hurtful to the speed in which they accomplish things and the quality of their work. Skepticism can be overdone and must be managed.

- **To be praiseworthy**: Personal worth for the NT is more about being worthy of the praise of others than feeling worthy regardless of the opinions of others.

- **Rationality:** The mind is the ultimate guide for an NT and reason is its light. They often see the mind as operating successfully only when all emotion has been removed. This is, of course, not true in all cases.

- **Knowledge:** Knowledge is the gold the NT mines for a lifetime. Without it they feel weak and vulnerable, so they store it and prize it. To the NT, knowledge is power.

- **Ingenuity:** This is the ultimate skill of an NT. Ingenuity is the quality of being inventive, clever, and original in one's thoughts and creations. The NT, as we have said, is the creator of all things new.

- **A calm exterior**: NTs value this virtue of keeping a calm exterior even under stress, but particularly in interpersonal relationships. Cool, calm, and collected is how they like to see themselves.

Likely Talents

We are best when we can use our strengths and talents. Multiple opportunities to use our strengths are essential to the building of our strengths.

NTs have a slew of talents and they use them best wherever they are given the freedom to analyze, theorize, design, and create.

The Likely Talents of an NT Are:

- **Strategic thinking:** NTs make formidable chess opponents. From the Greek *strategikos*, thinking strategically is finding the most effective way to a long term goal.

- **Insightful use of the means to the end:** To the NT, it is not so much the goal as the discovery of the way to the goal that is their skill.

- **Discerning possible contingencies:** "What if" is the NT's mantra, repeated for the obtaining of more knowledge. Unlike the NF, whose focus in on the future and its possibilities, the NT is focused more narrowly on the possible steps to the current goal they are attempting to reach.

- **Creating hypotheses and theoretical patterns:** This talent is a necessary part of their strategic thinking.

Skills:

- Designing buildings and projects
- Discovering unexpected consequences
- Finding new ways to do things and designing new products
- Evaluation and long-range planning
- Leading and mobilizing others to achieve a goal
- Teaching

How This Temperament Handles Stress.
(A key factor to manage if they are going to reach their potential)

Stress, which is inevitable, must be successfully handled or an NT derails. Stress must be handled, not eliminated.

Determination wards off stress until the task is completed. None can be more determined than the NT. At times, their determination even clouds their ability to see the facts and changes the mental game. They have a high tolerance for stress.

Likely Stress Factors
- Failure at being competent
- Lack of knowledge, which is also destructive of self-esteem
- Unrecognized for their work
- Relationship breakdowns
- Not thought of as credible

How this Temperament Prefers to Respond to Stress
- Work harder and become obsessive about their work
- Lapse into inactivity

How They Can Effectively Handle Stress — Antidotes
- Find confirmation for their ideas
- Move to a new project

Self-Image
(We can't outperform our self-image)

A high self-image is important to unlimited performance. It also is essential as an aid to reducing stress.

The self-image of both the SP and the NT are routinely high. The NT has been accused of being proud. Their abundant confidence and their cool, remote image can lie behind this accusation. It can also be generated by genuine pride in their own estimate of their intelligence.

What Builds the Self-Image of the NTs?
- **Recognition of ingenuity:** They depend on recognition of their labors and successes.
- **Offer of more independence:** To be worthy of being trusted with independence in their work is a natural high.
- **Mental force:** Sheer willpower that pushes through the challenges.
- **Success at a project:** If, after theorizing and designing their work, it is finally acknowledged as useful and pragmatic, the NT's self-image reaches its apex.

Fulfillment Will Look Like This:

An NT is best when multiple strengths in their temperament are being fulfilled, their needs are being met, their talents are being used effectively, and their values are being honored.

They will feel deep contentment with themselves and their life. It will feel as though life is serving them, the NT, rather than the NT serving life. They will be happy and contented in their relationships. Their life will be oriented to the fulfillment they are bringing others.

The NT Variants
(ENTP, ENTJ, INTP, INTJ)

Let's use the four letters of your profile to fine-tune your path to your highest fulfillment. What will really satisfy you? What are the central drives of your *innerkinetics*? How can we best put into words the direction your life is intended to go if it is to follow your inner drives to the top? In this section we will confine ourselves to answering this major issue. The *direction* for the *real you* is about to stand up.

Much research has gone into discovering the basic drives and directions of the sixteen types — four SPs, four SJs, four NTs, and four NFs. I will summarize the findings and interpret for you.

The four NT variations are ENTP, ENTJ, INTP, and INTJ. If you are an NT, one of these four-letter combinations will be yours, and you will find your profile listed here.

ENTP

Written into the *innerkinetics* of the ENTP is invention — pragmatic, theoretical invention. All problems need solutions, or so thinks the ENTP. The ENTP is certain that all problems can be solved — by the ENTP, of course. Confidence and a faith that is inspiring fill their hearts and drive their efforts. If it requires ingenuity, is innovative, and never has been done before, they are stimulated. A limitless number of things in this universe require ingenuity, innovation, and the desire to create something new to unlock their usefulness, so the ENTP is constantly stimulated — if they are awake.

Because all NTs are pragmatic, these solutions must have application to something or they are useless. The ENTP starts with an idea and finds ways to make life, in their terms, better. As extroverts, their interest is, of course, in people and in satisfying people's needs. They must believe in the idea or they are not motivated. They work naturally with systems, creating and revising them.

Research, science, and engineering are reliable fields for them to operate in. Any system is likely to get an overhaul — even home routines. A variety of occupations outside of the above three are attractive but, for most NTs, any routine, mundane work destroys their spirit, and they do not last long in such environments.

To follow the path written in their drives they must be inventive with opportunity to make all things new and work in the abstract world of ideas, crossing over into the real world to fashion their inventions for use. ENTPs should follow their *innerkinetics* for the highest fulfillment.

ENTJ

ENTJs mobilize people. They are born leaders and, working efficiently with order and design, they can affect the marshaling of people and materials to meet a need. As abstract thinkers, they work with plans and ideas to bring about pragmatic change.

They are not so skilled with people, often lacking the sensitivity to intuit the feelings of others. Therefore, they work at implementing systems and theoretical concepts and, at times, unknowingly disconnect from others. They work well as executives, CEOs, consultants, teachers, and organization builders.

Their *innerkinetics* make them a force to be reckoned with in leadership. They excel in this area where they implement accepted ideas or ideas that are new to them but usually with their own theoretical twist and application. Control of the issue or project gives them independence to use their talents. They are not shy and they mobilize people with the goal firmly in mind.

A significant drive is their ability to visualize the means to the end. ENTJs, if they accept and believe in a goal, will bend heaven and earth to find the means while keeping a sharp eye open for the priorities.

With these drives, their road to success lies in finding or constructing a well-defined goal and in finding an opportunity to lead where they can apply their strengths with the clear-cut purpose and independence all NTs insist on.

INTP

These are the champions of debate who notice inconsistencies with ease and speed. They give the word "theoretical" its most intense meaning. Principles underlie everything for the INTP. The Universe is made up of consistencies and they search these out and use them to find the relationship of the parts to the whole.

They fashion and compute outcomes to create better designs or better architectural systems. Anything that can be analyzed, explained, and understood — educational systems, engineering, construction, anywhere the structures and patterns of the universe can be examined — is where their attention is focused.

INTPs are logically and mathematically inclined. You will find them in science, all technological fields, design and architecture, also teaching: wherever pragmatic issues require an explanation. However, if they do not have freedom to explore and explain, they will not achieve their best. In a technological world, opportunities abound for them to be fulfilled and reach their goals.

INTJ

The INTJ is the contingency expert. Where planning needs to take into account the unexpected and be broken down into easy steps, this type finds their natural home. "What ifs" and "if thens" are foreseen and dissected with a connection or adjustment for every observed unknown factor.

The fulfillment of the INTJ is found more precisely in defining a goal, setting out the logical sequential steps to that goal, processing and accounting for all the details, creating in-depth plans, providing for the unplanned, and then forming strategies.

However, their fulfillment and their road to success do not end there. They want to make their plans and theories work and they press toward pragmatic application. They will even supervise their plans to make sure they work as they were designed to operate, but once someone has been taught to implement the plan, they leave for greener theoretical pastures.

Many opportunities exist for them to be successful: business plans, all kinds of engineering, politics, science projects, the development of institutions, the coordination of anything. They must avoid the routine and mundane. The road to fulfilling accomplishment is to find where their drives can be implemented with the freedom of independence.

The Real You — NF

The Personal Growth Temperament.

On First Meeting

NFs share most of the following similarities.

What is noticeable is their **high sensitivity**. They are sensitive to everything. Many will feel unhappy after stepping on an ant. Chiefly sensitive to you and your needs, they will also sensitize you to things you previously did not notice. Furthermore, they will make you feel that you are truly at the center of their world.

Their warmth and their emotional intuitiveness will attract you and make you feel they are inside your heart, if not your head (that too, at times). You may have occasion to notice their romantic leanings as well!

They will empathize and project their personality into yours. They want to please and are trusting on first contact unless their intuition has flagged them to back off. Their desire to please is a projection of their deep longing for harmony with all individuals, but especially with those close to them. Discord is hated with a vengeance and disconnectedness is equally disdainful.

Kindness and extreme empathy fills them and you will soon find they are intent on helping you to your potential. Montgomery, whose insightful title calls them the "personal growth temperament," flags their need to grow in knowledge and experience and their need to help you to the same goal, ever lifting your self-image. It lifts theirs as they lift yours. "Who am I?" is the constant question and pursuit of the NF who is not asking "why" and "what if" with the same insistency as the NT.

On meeting them you may not notice their emotional volatility. It can be quite vesuvian at times if they are angered. Extremes mark the NF temperament — from deeply rewarding love at one end of the spectrum of emotion to being capable of poisonous hate at the other.

NFs are social, pleasant to meet, and some can be the most vivacious of all the types. Even the introverts are socially engaging. Their people skills will show and they will make you feel as though you are more important than they are.

Portrait

NFs are **charming and friendly** — all about people. Charming, in this case, means likable, agreeable, winsome, having an attractive appeal, and full of endearing qualities. It might seem they went to the school of "How to Win Friends and Influence People." They did! They **must please**.

They are the **influencers** of society and, if their influence is used for the benefit of others, they excel at positively changing people's lives and beliefs. If this strength is used to manipulate, it can be a sad misuse of what can benefit society. They influence people naturally and, if practiced, are skilled with language. Their **passion** for **integrity**, **ethical wholeness**, genuine **altruism**, and for an **ideal society** drive them to create a just world.

They live on the other side of the S-N divide, as do the NTs, sensing and feeling what is going on inside themselves and others and showing high **intuitive** abilities.   They can be flooded with premonitions and given to visions, prescience, and other "spiritual" tendencies more than others.

It would be fair to say that, because of this inner life, they are excessively **introspective** as well.   Introspection is often overdone to their own harm.   They compare themselves to others constantly and even compare themselves to the conditions of their environment.   This makes them sensitive to atmosphere and moods, not restricted to people's moods.

NFs **live in their minds,** an abstract world, most of the time.   Their mind is constantly active and **focused intensely.**   Sleeping is a problem for them because, when they close their eyes, the distractions of the outside world vanish and the mind in which they live is now in full focus.   How can they shut it down sufficiently to sleep?   Most go a lifetime wondering why they can't sleep as well as, for instance, the SJ sleeps (who typically is asleep moments after their head hits the pillow).   NFs must learn how to shut their minds off by centering and relaxing techniques.

When they focus they are 120% centered, but they can shift focus in a flash.   Their focus can be disturbed by **powerful feelings** that reside in their overactive virtual world.   For example, they cannot function well when there is disharmony and division.   The emotional disconnectedness disturbs their focus to the point, unbelievably, of making them physically sick.   Feelings can steal their focus for periods, days, even weeks at a time.

Therefore, they work constantly at keeping morale high and disagreements at a minimum at work, home, and play — preferably nonexistent, so that they will not be disoriented.   Disharmony de-motivates them so much that they lose all creativity (some are creative writers or artists; all are creative inventors of relationships).

Harmony activates their giftedness and **passion**.   Peace inside is heaven on earth for them and a condition that makes all things beautiful.   I have an NF friend whose pronunciation of the word beautiful is artistic and passionate in itself.   Something like, beeeyuuuuu-teeful with an energetic emphasis on the "yuuuuu." It comes out in her speech constantly as she enjoys her world.

To the NF, the world dances with a happy rhythm when all is harmony and peace — in relationships especially. Perhaps this is why they can make such passionate and successful diplomats and mediators.

Did you guess that they are **supersensitive** and wear their feelings on their sleeves? Some say they are oversensitive. As I will explain in "Introduce Yourself to Your Strengths — NF," their sensitivity is one of the poles around which their temperament revolves.

This results in sharp emotional reactions to any cruel or inconsiderate comments and to any condition that does not **consider people's feelings** or is not **fair and just**. Their sensitivity extends beyond themselves to others and ignites anger in the presence of ethical dishonesty.

When aroused, they can deliver verbal broadsides that are quite frightening and, after their emotions are settled, they apologize meekly, and usually over and over again. (The SP, in contrast, is also known for sudden bursts of anger, but for them, it is over in a flash and all is back to normal — usually with no apology.)

Sometimes, for the NF, their reaction is kept inside themselves — most of the time, for many. This practice of **introjecting** everything (turning everything toward one's self or against one's self) causes them much pain. They are also good at hiding in the secret world of their minds. Of course, introjection builds up pressures that have to go somewhere and when (maybe a week later) a very tiny incident sparks the powder, the NF explodes completely out of proportion to the incident that sparked it. Others are amazed and wonder at the mental stability of these incendiary people. Not only do NFs suffer for their volatile emotions, it is the pursuit of their lives to control this heavy load. They must find the answer.

To add to their confusion they are **perfectionists** and, when they don't live up to their own standards, they punish themselves mercilessly. No temperament is more **self-demanding** and self-condemning. It's the emotions, sensitivity, and passion again. They will take the blame when it is not really their fault because of their desire to avoid disharmony.

They constantly set the bar too high for themselves and, when they fail to clear it, they set it a notch higher and try again. Sounds ridiculous? It feels to them the only thing to do if you demand perfection of yourself. "Try again, and try harder," they tell themselves. They must reach perfection, or at least a hair below it — not just some low standard unworthy of true greatness or true goodness. The two Js are intensely driven in this regard. They damage their own progress at times.

Because they typically have **low self-images** (caused, in part, by their perfectionist drives) they feel they are not very good and don't deserve better. The result can be self-flagellation. It is impossible for other temperaments to empathize with their feelings and, therefore, the NFs receive comments like "What's wrong with you? Can't you pull yourself together?" They can, but they need time for emotions to cool. Of all the temperaments, they are the most difficult to teach healthy self-talk.

To return to the title Montgomery gives them, they will sacrifice considerably for the **personal growth** of all, not just themselves. In all they do they search for the ideal. They are the **true idealists,** as they well know in their dreams.

They dream about removing walls of discontent or reducing conflict and anything that divides people. They are the essence of **kindness** (if not angered) and work extremely well with needy, complicated people.

Their personalities and their temperament are highly **complicated** — the most complicated temperament — and it helps them in dealing with complicated people and situations. Emotion is the most complicated element in our mental and physical makeup and they are the purveyors of emotions in all shades, creations, and sizes. Furthermore, remember, people are the most complicated creations in the universe. Hence, as people-people, we expect their obvious skills with people or wonder what is wrong. If you are reading this and saying they certainly have difficulties to overcome, you are right. You are right, also, if you recognize what gifted people all this sensitivity creates and what blessings they are to the rest of us who need the touch and healing of their emotional richness.

Because NFs are superbly skilled at finding solutions to the most **complicated ethical and personal problems,** they often end up

111

counseling, coaching, and teaching people skills, or working in human resource departments using, in all these realms, intuitive insight.

Their lives are dream-worlds of aspiration and hope. They live in the future, ever probing its possibilities. A dark horizon is devastating to these hope experts.

By now you may also have decided that you don't want them in the work place because of their sensitivity. You would be making a mistake. Not only are they needed, they can be your greatest asset. As supreme diplomats, they are skilled in bringing about harmony and creating a work environment that produces the greatest chance of productivity and pleasure in the process. They can settle differences and get people to work together, all the time obsessed with doing so for their own sense of peace as well.

An NF manager is liked since they are people-people. However, as a manager they find it hard to be "tough" (unless angered) and will focus on making the work atmosphere the best they can for everyone. They act like friends more than managers and, although not tough, they can be demanding at times when slackers get under their skin or hinder the progress or when they feel their kindness is not being honored.

Everyone is trusted until they prove (for the good of others and the NF's welfare as well) that they must not be trusted. They want the best for everyone and are skilled at leading people to perform at and find their full potential.

They are easily bored with mundane tasks (like their cousins the NTs), but they will try their best since they are always trying to please others.

Hidden in all this emotion is a logical mind that is much like the NT's but warm, not cold. Many philosophers are NFs, causing them to search with both logic and intuition into the hidden realities of life. Their logic, however, includes the emotional as well as the rational facts. As I have said, emotions are facts. But we must add a further twist to their logic.

Because they experience the world of the spirit, NFs are other-worldly as well as rooted in living a life of personal growth in this world. They are **futuristic, imaginative,** and they honor the world of **fantasy.** Hence, they often see the need to include the things of the spirit to interpret the logical and illogical in this world. Because of this they have been dubbed the "spiritual temperament."

When they do include "spiritual" facts in their world view, in their logic, and in their beliefs, their logic is inevitably influenced by the ethereal. Logic is a tool of language and is not limited in its use to things material or mathematical. It can aid the discovery of truth beyond the reach of material things and beyond our laws of physics — meaning the world where faith unlocks the secrets.

Logic takes on a new category in this context, reasoning with the consistency of a world that cannot be tested in typical scientific ways. It is logic nonetheless — the consistency of logical reasoning applied to spiritual facts and experiences. In this way the NF has often emerged as the logical champion of things unseen.

NFs are also **visionary** and **imaginative** and, with their **intuition,** face the future, searching for its possibilities and dreaming of its potential. They can almost eerily detect the feelings, motivations, and inner world of another. Their intuition is also in play when interpreting events and explaining the meaning of people's inner urges. When the future is bright, so are they. When the future is dark, so are they.

They live a life in search of **meaning and significance.** Everything must have meaning — even their fun. Meaning is connecting to a purpose within themselves and outside of themselves, such as some cause or lofty significance. They are the closest to the SP in **optimism of spirit,** closest to the SJ in living a **responsible** life, and closest to the NT in the **use of the world of the mind**. One could say they take the NT's use of mental dominance one step further and include all things emotional.

NFs are cooperative, authentic, idealistic **self-actualizers**. We can add to their talents and roles in society such things as mentors, leaders of causes, fighters for justice, spiritual leaders, advocates, and directors. They fill the role of "catalysts" in society (as Berens names them), and they help people be the best that they can be. They are the transformers of society and its subgroups. People who are around them often find a positive energy that lifts them and helps them travel through "this dark world" with less pain and anguish.

Two types of NFs are discerned by the way they handle encouragement. There are those who "inform" and those who "direct." They are both effective in lifting people. They encourage by praising others and pointing out their worth as well as leading them to new insights of themselves.

The intelligence of the NF is in **seeing the big picture** almost instantly. Also, it is in their ability to see **similarities** as opposed to differences and to strategize their effect. The NT sees the differences; the NF sees the similarities and forms patterns based on these. It leads to more optimism and to working toward unity and wholeness. They are all about the whole, not the unit.

Harkey and Jourgensen call them the "intuitive and feeling" temperament; Keirsey, the "idealists." Others call them enthusiastic, spiritual, ethical, inspiring, choleric, oversensitive, and **soulful**.

Their language is **abstract** and **global**. They speak in generalities and in metaphors, often excelling as poets and creative writers who can especially use language effectively for motivation and self-development. Metaphor mixes with symbol. This kind of language sees the similarities between one reality and another and takes you across the divide to view yourself or a truth in the light of another reality. Often, their metaphors bridge the gap between human and other animal species or between life forms and non-life forms. A richness of understanding develops.

The positive potentials of the NFs' strengths lie in their concern for people and their unending passion to make it a better world. They are deeply hurt by what they see as injustices in the world. They live in their virtual world and this makes them talk of love and peace rather than their concrete expressions. They find their ultimate fulfillment in teaching and developing people and helping them reach their potential. They climb to their potential often by encouraging the potential of others.

When any of their strengths are used in mundane (to them), meaningless routines, they lose all motivation and purpose and look for something to do that is significant. NFs are unhealthy mentally and emotionally when **meaning and significance** are not in their lives.

Do you know anyone who is like this? Check! Is this you or are you nearer to one of the other temperaments? Read all four temperaments before you decide.

Keys to Developing an NF's Potential

The relationship of the strengths of this temperament to success will be addressed under "NF Strengths" in the section, "Introduce Yourself to Your Strengths — NF." Here we will outline the things for an NF to watch in order to be their best. Repeated items only emphasize their importance.

NFs are born to **reach for their potential**. Life is a journey to meaning and **significance**, a road to being ever better than they are, to be the best that they can be. Self-image is built by helping other people successfully along this path. Trouble trails them when, realizing their failures, they whip themselves and berate their self-worth. Achievements alone can never hold their self-esteem high and NFs know that all too well. When they do succeed, they feel the emptiness at the top and say to themselves, "Well it wasn't much of a success anyway." Then they fall to the bottom of their self-esteems and try again, only to repeat the critical performance.

Remember, a low self-esteem means a low performance. So when their self-image falls, so does their performance level and their chances of success don't rise any higher. It is hard for an NF to remain optimistic when they keep failing or when their future is dark and hopeless. A steady high is all about who we are — not what we do — and the lifelong quest of the NF is to feel meaning and significance as a person.

Many of the things NFs excel at are people-to-people jobs. Those who don't have people-related careers suffer from a lack of meaning in their lives.

Success for an NF is to first find a rewarding goal and then to build their self-esteem daily. It is a big help to gather around themselves a battery of encouragers who will lift them.

The following are areas of importance for becoming successful and reaching their ultimate potential.

Focus

We must keep the focus of our *innerkinetics*. Any digression from the natural focus of our temperament will lessen our potential. Some, not all, of the focal points of the temperament must be in the center of our aim and our goals. The more the better, of course.

NFs have an intense focus when they apply it. They tend to scatter their focus when emotionally disturbed and weaken its power on any one center.

The Focus of an NF Is On:

- **The Future:** This, for the NF, is essential. When they focus on the past, or even on the present, their momentum slows. The future is where their mind is while they translate its possibilities into the now.

- **Why people do what they do:** People, including themselves, are to be understood. NFs who do not understand people limit their success. Their intuitiveness and sensitivity is not being used to its maximum.

- **Identity and significance:** Who I am and who you are sharpens the NF's focus on one of their strongest strengths: the pursuit of significance in them and in others. Significance is a focus, need, value, and the fuel for their sense of self worth.

- **Intuition:** When NFs pay no attention to their intuitive antenna they usually make big mistakes. Often their intuition supports their reason and then the path is clear. When it doesn't, the NF should follow their intuition, even if they do so cautiously. Learn to trust intuition. It is a gift.

• **Imagination:** From childhood the NFs have been using their imagination and, hopefully, it hasn't been ridiculed too much. It provides a great deal of material on which they can ponder and reason. Imagination is more important than reason. All the people who have said imagination is more important than reason have called attention to a principle that changes our world.

• **Possibilities, maybes, and the ideals:** The next best thing is only a possibility at this point. Finding and interpreting the value and potential of possibilities is the NF's home turf and is neglected to their loss.

• **Learning:** NFs, particularly the INFJ, are lifelong students. Learning in itself, to an NF, is rewarding. Shut this focus down and they tend to act lost and without a passion. Knowledge is power to the NT. However, together with intuition, it forever fills the mind of the NF, feeding new insights.

• **Relationships, harmony, love, and bonding:** The NF can't help not focusing on these. The success comment on this issue is that an NF's relationships must either be healthy, healed, or forsaken. Relationships can catapult an NF to success or shackle them with ball and chain.

• **Personal integrity:** Guilt will haunt an NF who pays no attention to their inner calls for truth and ethical rightness. More NFs have fallen short of their goals over this than we would like to think. They then live in torture.

Core Needs

NFs must keep their resources well stocked. Each reservoir of need should be well supplied with plans and actions. The more of these needs that are met, the easier it is to achieve a life of rewarding fulfillment.

Note that some of these needs will be mentioned again under comments on focus, values, etc. When you come across them repeatedly it means they are all the more important.

Key Needs that Affect Performance and Success:

- **Meaning and significance derived from purpose and personal worth:** Without this need being constantly supplied, an NF may as well stop and restart with new goals. Without meaning and significance, an NF's potential is jeopardized.

- **Personal growth that never ends:** Without this learning curve, stagnation invades such strengths as: potential, intuition, passion, sensitivity, and imagination, to name a few. The growth of a healthy NF is not only in self-actualization, they must grow in knowledge and in insightfulness to feel true fulfillment.

- **The spiritual and ethical:** Not often given its true value, this center of need in the life of an NF often fails to be fed. Spiritual connections are essential to the life of the spirit. The NF, with an intuitive antenna, probes the world of the immaterial and the input wanes if not used and valued.

- **The authentic:** Being real and authentic runs parallel in these perfectionists to being right. Authenticity keeps company with integrity and the two, at times, can't be separated. As I noted under "The Spiritual and the Ethical," neglect this and experience ruin.

- **The feedback of love:** To me, this is a core need as great as any other. NFs wither without love, both the love they receive and the love they give. To be devoid of love's response, saying you are much needed and precious, opens the door wide to depression.

Values

NFs, like the other temperaments, are most satisfied when their values are being honored and rightly represented. They don't need agreement to their values or beliefs, but they do need to be respected and not laughed at for what they believe. If an NF's values are disrespected, the

NF will go elsewhere because they cannot work profitably where their is dislocation.

Needs and Values Often Overlap
Listed here are some of their main values.

- **Integrity:** Valued for the inner peace it brings.

- **The world of the unseen:** Since childhood, this has been a key element in the NF's value system. Fantasy, fiction, dreams, visions, and the imaginative is where they refuel, refresh, and where they gain so much of their inspiration.

- **Intuitive flashes and gut feelings:** Valued because the NF believes in their guidance and validity.

- **Emotional richness:** Valued for the way it feeds their emotional needs and warms their souls.

- **Passion:** Valued for how it increases the intensity of all strengths.

- **Romance:** Valued because it keeps the NF in touch with the beautiful and the aesthetic side of life.

- **Recognition:** Valued because of its ability to lift the spirit and the self-image when crushed by hurts and saddened by failures.

Likely Talents

NFs are best when they can use their strengths and talents. Multiple opportunities to use their strengths are essential to the building of their strengths and the reaching of their goals.

- **Empathy:** Definitely a strength that transposes easily into a talent for encouragement and healing.

- **Creating harmony in relationships:** No temperament is set up for a greater talent in this area of life.

- **Leading people to realize their potential, mentoring:** Mentors and healing advocates make up the NF profile of types. Mentoring feeds both the one mentored and the mentor, and that makes the NF happy. NFs are uniquely fitted for this task also.

- **Visionaries:** A brace of strengths create this talent. Empathy, intuition, spirituality, imagination, sensitivity, passion, and the intelligence that finds patterns of similarity, sees the big picture, and fuels visions.

- **Dealing with complex human issues and situations:** This talent is supported by the emotionally complex nature of the temperament.

- **Mediating:** Similar strengths support this talent as they do the mentoring skills.

- **Creative skills:** Writing, the fine arts, creative personal development of others, any creative art requiring sensitivity and intuition.

- **Philosophic insights:** The interest of the NF in people, mysteries, and the reasons behind our existence and purpose is as much a role as a talent. Many become lifelong students in search of the big questions of our existence.

- **Public speaking as teachers, persuaders, and motivators:** These talents come naturally to influencers.

- **The use of people skills:** At this the NF excels.

Skills

- Counseling
- Coaching
- Teaching
- Symbolic and metaphorical expression
- Abstract analysis and problem solving
- Possibility thinkers
- Envisioning, developing the vision, and communicating it
- Inspiring leadership

How This Temperament Handles Stress.
(A key factor to manage if we are going to reach our potential)

Stress, which is inevitable, must be successfully handled or they derail. Stress must be handled, not eliminated. Most of the stress for an NF comes from internal pressures of their own making. A sensitive person cannot avoid creating inner stress. NFs must learn the art of stress management or suffer the destruction of their potential.

Realized Future Possibilities Lower Present Stress Levels

Likely Stress Factors
- Disturbed relationships
- Being treated unfairly or without consideration
- A dark future with no seeming relief

How this Temperament Prefers to Respond to Stress
- Withdraw and shut the cause of the stress out of their life; disconnect
- Looks with incessant urgency for possible solutions

How they Can Effectively Handle Stress — Antidotes
- Use of imagination and day dreaming to refresh their spirits
- Nurture their needs
- Find significance in other areas of life.

Self-Image
(We can't outperform our self-image.)

A high self-image is important to unlimited performance. It is also essential as an aid to reducing stress. For the NF, this amounts to a critical Achilles heel.

What Builds the Self-Image of the NFs?
- A feeling of being meaningful in someone else's life or in the lives of many

- A sense of nurturing a higher purpose in life
- To give and receive love
- Harmonious relationships

Fulfillment Will Look Like This:

An NF is best when multiple strengths in their temperament are being fulfilled, their needs are being met, their talents are being used effectively, and their values are being honored.

They will feel deep contentment with themselves and with their life. It will feel as though life is serving them, the NF, rather than that they are serving life. They will be happy and content in their relationships. Their life will be oriented to the fulfillment they are bringing others.

Their self-esteem will be high and stable, and they will feel as though they are blessed and are a blessing. The NF fulfillment is a calm and a peace inside that rests their spirit and quietens their anxious thoughts.

The NF Variants
(ENFP, ENFJ, INFP, INFJ)

Let's use the four letters of your profile to fine-tune your path to your highest fulfillment. What will really satisfy you? What are the central drives of your *innerkinetics*? How can we best put into words the direction your life is intended to go if it is to follow your inner drives to the top? In this section we will confine ourselves to answering this major issue. The *direction* for the *real you* is about to stand up.

Much research has gone into discovering the basic drives and directions of the sixteen types: four SPs, four SJs, four NTs, and four NFs. I will summarize the findings and interpret for you.

The four NF variations are ENFP, ENFJ, INFP, and INFJ. If you are an NF, one of these four-letter combinations will be yours and you will find your profile listed here.

ENFP

Like all the NFs, they are influencers of people. Inspiration drives the ENFP. Their intuitive perception of another's motives and genuineness is second to none.

Their complexity, as for all the NFs, is seen in the multiple key words that describe their inner drives: significance, inspiration, perception, enthusiasm, exuberance, empathy, intuition, and spontaneity in their quest for meaning.

Their *innerkinetics* lead them to flourish in people-to-people work with entrepreneurial opportunities. Their options are always kept open. Their untamed individualism draws them to champion causes where they feel they can make a difference in the lives of others and in their own life. They must be in a job or a cause where they have a chance to win. If what they do has no inspirational meaning to them, it is boring.

ENFPs are vivacious idealists with powerful convictions. Therefore, to rise to their dizzy heights of accomplishment, they must work with people, be free to bring inspiration to themselves and others, and motivate people to ever higher goals. They must follow the key words listed above and not walk a path that provides no opportunity for these concepts to flower.

ENFJ

These are the insightful teachers of individuals and groups. They educate with empathy and concern for others and show a drive not found in the ENFP or the INFP. They need structure. Like the INFJ, they are mentors of all the people they influence and passionately desire the best for all in their circle. Their circle of friends is usually large, like the ENFP.

Key words that describe their core drives are: enthusiasm, warmth, empathy, connections, creative in dealing with people, stimulating, expressive, structured, and intuitive. Note the central theme and the divergences from their extroverted cousins the ENFPs.

The ENFJ's path to fulfilling achievement lies in their ability to instruct, teach, and lift others, and it can be found in teaching professions, group mentoring, spiritual development, parenting, and any task where their positive idealism can be communicated personally.

ENFJs must follow their inner path and not let circumstances mold them. Like all NFs, they must believe in their abilities since NFs typically have low self-esteems.

INFP

The desire for wholeness and healing for themselves and others fills the INFP. Shy and reserved, their introversion can imprison them in severe introspection and introjection. None of the types is more empathetic and they exhibit a quiet, effective enthusiasm, which the more you know them, the more it appears as a potent passion.

Their path to fulfillment and accomplishment is in caring with intense empathy, and in this they succeed and make an impressive mark on the world. Loyal like no other, they struggle to heal all conflicts, drawing people into their hearts with intense connections.

Words like caring, empathetic, concerned, holistic, ethical, spiritual, introspective, and quietly passionate mark out their main path.

Life is lived in the awe and contemplation of its unexplained issues and they search the moral, ethical and spiritual meaning of everything. So, the path to a meaningful life is by way of their passionate desire for wholeness. Holistic opportunities and the health and wellness industry, together with spiritual paths, lay at the center of their drive for satisfaction and personal wholeness.

INFJ

Studious and visionary, the INFJ is both mentor and teacher with an emphasis, for many, on written communication skills. They can be fixedly driven by the inner urge to lead people to their highest potential.

Highly intuitive and insightful, they deal with complex people and problems, guided by their inner knowing, foresight, and learning. They often know others before the other person can know themselves. Psychic phenomena or the things and happenings beyond logic and material facts are often understood and intuited. Most NFs do this to some degree.

Inspirations, visions, and insights add to the image of their private complex personas. Like the ENFP, inspiration guides them and the logic of the big picture makes them able to understand the parts by the knowledge of the whole. In this they bring a balance to the NT's quest to understand the whole by the knowledge of the parts.

Key words to describe their complex path to success are: studious, logical, wordsmiths, intense, ethical, super sensitive, creative, passionate, empathetic, and intuitively insightful.

Their supreme path is the path to personal development for themselves and all others.   Mentors, coaches, teachers, writers, counselors, consultants, and philosophers identify some of the INFJs' means to their success. They thrive on helping others.

Section 3

Amazing Strengths
And Pesky
Weaknesses

Understanding Strengths and Getting Rid of Weaknesses

I was always looking outside myself for strength and confidence but it comes from within. It is there all the time.
~ *Anna Freud*

The way of defeat is to focus on your weaknesses.
~ *Ray W. Lincoln*

If you can picture a central core of energy inside you that drives and inspires you, you are close to an understanding of the influence of temperament. Picture it this way: We are all familiar with DNA (deoxyribonucleic acid), so imagine your temperament as a bundle of metaphysical "genes" that you can actually feel as preferences or urges inside you. Essentially, you are driven and shaped by your choices but strongly influenced by your temperament's "DNA." Our innerkinetics (all the natural, positive forces or drives that are inside of us) form this intangible "DNA."

I think it is imperative that we understand how this inner core functions. So, let's get a great grasp on how we live in our innerkinetics and how we step out of our strengths to form our weaknesses. We won't want to stop until we understand the dynamics of getting rid of our weaknesses and developing our strengths.

The real you powers you and wants to be you. It wants to stand up and be recognized. Temperament hates to be suppressed. When we are who we are, we feel fulfilled and maximized. Know yourself and don't stop there; be yourself! It's an exhilarating journey.

Before we look at the strengths of each temperament in the section entitled "Introduce Yourself to Your Strengths," we'll journey through an understanding of our innerkinetics and how they work.

The Real You Is the Source of Lasting Motivation

Temperament is a noun — actionless and blah — so we need to rename it and see it as energies (strengths) inside of us if we are going to appreciate its power and purpose. *It is more than our preferences or our makeup; it is our natural strengths, drives and urges, as we found in Chapter 2.* We can use verbs like drive, urge, power, inspire, force, and impel to feel its functions.

These powers drive you from the inside, urge you forward, and want you to choose their preferred way of doing things. It's the SJ's caution that urges them to be cautious. The NT's urge to find out all they can about their world and its ways drives them to intense curiosity. All of our strengths will motivate us to action if we use them. What would you give to find the source of real lasting motivation? It's inside you in the use of your strengths.

When I use the words *innerkinetics*, temperament, drives, strengths, and urges, I mean all those *positive* (not negative), natural forces inside of us. We'll talk about the negative inner dynamics (the weaknesses) and who makes them later. First, the strengths.

Strengths Are Us

The development and nurture of our strengths is our main task on the road to happiness and a life lived to its utmost.

We need a map with some details to use as a practical guide to:

- Understanding ourselves
- Managing ourselves
- Determining our purpose
- Leading us to the ultimate development of our lives

Let's identify three characteristics of our strengths.

Your Automatic Transmission
We usually don't think about the basic drives of our temperament or the preferences they produce.   This is because they act like the automatic transmission that controls the gears in our car, selecting them as needed without our involvement. They are not usurping our control; they are us. Most of life's choices feel to us as though they just happen, and this is the reason.   These choices operate unconsciously most of the time as preferences that are driven by our temperament.

This is why we don't get consciously in touch with our innerkinetics very often.   Temperament is like your brain: It's there although you don't feel it, and it does its job without drawing attention to itself. Becoming more aware of our strengths and when we are using them is advantageous, though, since it will help us develop them.

No Need to Present Our "ID"
The you that others unconsciously know comes mostly from the automatic operations of your innerkinetics, not from learned behavior. Natural drives that exist inside of us surface constantly as our preferences. They don't change, even when our environment changes. This is what we know of ourselves and what others see.

Example: I choose to celebrate my birthday with just a few friends at most, never with a mob of people. I'm an introvert; it is a natural urge of mine. Besides, I feel embarrassed by a crowd.   My extroverted friends can't understand why I enjoy a quiet celebration or feel happy when I'm alone! My natural urge is surfacing.

Whatever is the *real you,* welcome and celebrate its strengths. These strengths are your ID card for which you are loved, appreciated, and known.

Learned behavior is all the time subject to relearning. As our environment changes and presents us with other choices, what we have learned tends to change too. *Innerkinetics* are stable and these strengths emerge consistent to their design — always, even if we modify our choices due to environment or learned behavior.

Our Strengths are Our Best Asset.

Finding the true you is better than finding gold. You've heard the saying, "You are your own best asset." Actually, your strengths are. Discovering and developing yourself is the road to the best you can ever be. Here's one of many stories that illustrate this characteristic of our *innerkinetics.*

"I hate my job. Life is a downer. The harder I search for a lasting feeling of happiness, the more I believe it is a myth." Janet was obviously upset. We were talking because she had come very near to taking her life. She was very intelligent and about to complete her thesis for her doctorate while at the same time holding down a responsible leadership position in a large company.

Her description of her strengths were nothing like the preferences her temperament key revealed. We wrestled with the disparity, and soon it was apparent to both of us that her learned skills, for which she received constant praise and reward at work, were in no way satisfying her. They were adding to her confusion and pain, and they were not her innerkinetics.

Slowly it dawned on her that her preferences were pointing to a temperament she had never really come to know except for happy memories in her youth, which she described as the "old me." She had disparaged this "old me" and thought, because of her success at her job, that her temperament had changed over the years.

When she reactivated the strengths of her real temperament and began to use them, she felt a real happiness and a promise of success. She beams now. It didn't take her long. Her feelings are now in sink with her goals, and her achievements are enhanced with a new drive and fulfillment. Now she lives! The real Janet has stood up. As I told her at the start, "You will be the judge of who you really are and you will recognize yourself when you find yourself." She's glad she is finding more of herself each day and getting to know her intangible DNA.

Strengths Are Complex

Core and Adopted Strengths

The "energy" at the core of our makeup is what defines and produces our natural strengths that in turn make us prefer certain ways of thinking and acting. We will also call this energy our "core strengths" or our "power package."

We observe and experience these core strengths as our natural strengths. They are what we use to achieve and develop to our highest level. That's what we are most interested in. They develop and continue to develop with use and training. We never know just how much we can perfect them because we never feel we have exhausted their possibilities.

When we use our core strengths we feel fulfilled and happy with a sense of inner peace. This is our reward for operating as we were designed to operate: the smooth peace of functioning according to our design and running seamlessly. These strengths feel as though they "are us." We are experiencing our core powers.

All of us have *core strengths* that are natural to us and most of us have used and practiced other strengths as well, ones that don't come as naturally to us nor belong to our *innerkinetics*. Both can be positive but affect us in different ways. We will call the strengths that don't belong to our temperament *adopted strengths*. Let's define core and adopted strengths this way:

- Our core strengths are given to us and belong to who we are. They are our temperament, our *innerkinetics*.

- Adopted strengths are those that we have picked up along the way and adopted for various reasons. (Usually we have become quite good at them and, therefore, we can be fooled into thinking they are our core strengths.)

Core strengths and adopted strengths create different "feels," however, and we find our core strengths fit more comfortably. To know if a strength we are using is "core" or "adopted," ask: "Which fits and feels most comfortable when I use it and which gives me the greatest feeling of satisfaction?" First, our core strengths.

Core Strengths

These form our *innerkinetics*: the strengths of the SP, SJ, NT or NF — whichever temperament we happen to be.

We use some of our core strengths more than others so they soon become familiar to us and develop more. However, *all* of our temperament's strengths may feel comfortable to us and feel as though they really fit after we have used them and tried them on.

Finding our temperament — SP, SJ, NT, or NF — is like finding the ballpark in which we are supposed to play our game of life. Trying out the strengths of our temperament is like building our team.

Core Strengths Fashion Us

The core strengths that belong to our temperament affect us in many ways. Here are a few examples:

- They are a part of us and will always feel as though they belong.

- They fulfill us when we use them and give us that contented feeling of deep satisfaction. Deep-seated happiness and inner peace comes from their use and increases as they develop and become stronger.

- They make us prefer certain things and certain ways of doing things. For example: We prefer to come to closure or prefer to keep our options open. We prefer to decide quickly or prefer not to make decisions and put them off routinely. Preferences declare their presence and we find these preferences hard to dislodge.

- These preferences also let people "see" our temperament. They truly distinguish us and present our "inner ID."

- We consistently act according to these preferences unless we are forced by circumstances or other people to act differently. For

134

example: We may prefer to be fiercely independent or prefer to be social beings or prefer tradition or prefer constant change. However, circumstances can make us want to reverse any one of these preferences. Our peers may influence us to take a dare when risk is not a part of our nature. We have, in these cases, been influenced or forced to act contrary to our natural drives. Choice finally fashions us.

- This consistency of wanting to do things a preferred way is what also gives us our direction in life and lets us and other people know who we are and what to expect of us. Without them we would be Dr. Jekyll and Mr. Hyde all the time. No one could know us and we would never know who we were either.

- They are the foundation of our nature. Humans, like buildings, need foundations to keep them upright in the storms of life.

- Acting in opposition to our core strengths causes us to feel guilty or lost or, in the extreme, at war with ourselves. We then act in uncustomary ways and people notice that something is wrong.

- We also lose the full sense of satisfaction and fulfillment in our lives when we don't live in these strengths, and this can cause us to go searching for fulfillment outside of ourselves when the true fulfillment is inside of us.

- We live satisfied only when we use our core strengths and use them in a non-damaging way.

This last point is important. I come across its effects all the time. People often tell me they feel comfortable with themselves but, when pressed, they admit they are not, as they put it, "really happy." Everything is okay, but they feel flat and have a niggling yearning inside of themselves to experience something more. They are, most likely, opposing their natural drives and throwing away their chance at happiness. We often damage ourselves without understanding how, and often we experience an inferior condition as though it is normal.

Tama J. Kieves was a Harvard lawyer and had a well-paid, promising position in a law firm but suffered from a lack of inner satisfaction. She quit her job and, in a risky financial move, became a writer. Her first book is the story of her adventurous, but necessary, move to find the true satisfaction of her *innerkinetics*. The title is *This Time I Dance*, and I recommend it to you if you need to remove the fears of change. It's a great read, and if you find the same fulfillment in your life, you will have felt the thrill of discovering your core strengths and their satisfaction.

Adopted Strengths
These we embrace because:
• Others have told us we are good at something.

• Our work demands we act a certain way, so we soon prefer to act that way to be effective and please the boss. Besides, that's the way to a continuing pay check.

• Our circumstances make it advantageous to prefer to use a strength that is not natural to us even though it isn't what we feel comfortable doing.

In a marriage the latter situation comes up often.

Veronica, an INFP, was overwhelmed by her ESTJ husband. He was controlling and made all the decisions fast and firm, never looking back to see how they affected her. He thought everyone was or should be like him and his speed at making decisions made him feel superior to Veronica. He was convinced she needed his tutelage and help.

She simply found it advantageous to mask her feelings and to suppress her anger to avoid his angry denunciations of her "procrastinating habits." So she didn't often stand up to him.

In the long run we find it almost impossible to suppress the natural drives of our innerkinetics, and one of her drives was the strong desire to create harmony in all relationships — hers and other people's. She bottled it up inside as much as she could and tried to act calmly like her NT friend had been exhorting her to do. In doing this she was trying to adopt the strength of another temperament and outwardly had some success. However, it couldn't be suppressed for long. She soon felt like the proverbial doormat and he kept scrubbing his ESTJ boots on her wilting spirit.

Finally, after two decades (it's hard to believe she suffered it this long) she revolted. Suddenly without any warning she divorced him. The relief she felt and the shock he felt created a tidal wave of emotions for both of them.

He was simply using his natural strengths, albeit without fully understanding his serious overuse, and she had adopted a set of strengths not natural to her, only to find in the long run they don't fit too well under pressure. Fortunately both found themselves and made massive adjustments that led to respect and a reuniting of their lives.

Choosing to act contrary to your strengths destroys you eventually and choosing to act like some other temperament cannot profit you either.

A Place for Adopted Strengths.

- As secondary strengths, adopted strengths are not part of us. However, since they can become learned abilities, we often try to make them part of us. We can, at best, make them very handy secondary strengths.

- Adopted strengths can feel natural if we haven't identified our natural strengths and don't know the difference. This can confuse us easily.

- They can pad our list of acceptable abilities and, at times, make us quite versatile. (Nothing wrong with this as long as we understand their place in reaching our potential.)

- All of us have some secondary strengths that we have learned to master. Just remember, master something and it feels a part of you.

- These adopted strengths are not bad for us. Look at them as our second string (not our first string) abilities. First-string strengths lead us to our ultimate potential, while second-string strengths (when they become our life) fall short. I know; it happened to me and to many others I have talked with. It is sad to settle for a second best and not to know it.

- We don't usually know we are living in the shadow of adopted strengths until we discover our temperament's natural strengths and start using them. Then the difference is discovered.

- We usually enjoy using adopted strengths simply because we can become good at them and we are rewarded by them. They also gain the approval of others.

- If they are opposite from our core strengths (as some strengths that belong to other temperaments are) they can cause us to lose direction and then search for meaning outside of ourselves. As a result, we malfunction.

How do we sort all this out? Simple. Go to the strengths of your temperament and start using them. Experience for yourself which ones give you the ultimate feeling of fulfillment and pleasure.

Mixtures of Core and Adopted Strengths Can Confuse

As you read through the strengths of the four temperaments in the next four chapters, you may discover that you have "borrowed" some strengths from other temperaments. Whatever we use and train becomes stronger and more comfortable. We become a mixture of strengths and that can confuse us into thinking we have found full satisfaction when we have not. It is a deception that has unknowingly crept up on us and is now determining our life. More abilities often make us feel stronger and more successful when we are not.

Some students of temperament will tell you that you are a mixture of several temperaments. They do not differentiate between natural strengths and adopted strengths and they simply suggest that it is fine to see yourself as a mixture of temperaments. I disagree and I think you will too when you have experienced the difference. Adopted strengths are fine as long as you do not confuse them with your core strengths or expect them to be the catalyst for being the best you can be.

It is fine only if you are content to settle for an inner happiness that is less than what you were born to experience. I want the best, not the second best. Don't you? As someone said, "The good is the enemy of the best," because it stops you short of your ultimate reward in life. We have a tendency to settle for the good since it is good. Not a good idea! Reach for the best.

Let me urge you, as you reach for your potential, to find and primarily use your core strengths that belong to your temperament. You will know if you are on the right track. As you use them, they will develop and the reward rises or falls with how much you develop your strengths and use them.

We Have Only One Temperament

To talk of primary and secondary *temperaments* is not to understand the difference between core and adopted strengths. We have only one temperament, but we may have adopted strengths from other temperaments. It is misleading to call the other temperament's strengths our "secondary temperament."

When people are told that they have more than one temperament, they see themselves as neither temperament. They lose the direction and the focus of their core strengths that describe them, define them, and motivate them most.

Multiple temperaments mean multiple goals for our lives. We then live our lives scatter-gunning and dispersing our energies in more than one direction. One temperament is the way we are made and it gives us a finely focused destiny that maximizes our efforts and our potential.

Strengths Come in Different Degrees and Numbers

You will also notice that some of your own temperament's strengths are not as strong as others. This, too, is natural. It is exciting to discover our natural strengths, which ones are most dominant, and how they reward us and give us a direction to our lives!

Temperaments Are Not Cloned; Everyone Is Different

Therefore, everyone's expression of a temperament, as well as every individual strength, is unique. The variety of urges and drives within us remind us of snowflakes: each different, but each identifiable as snowflakes. The more we use our natural strengths, the more they will grow and show our individual temperament's distinctive nature and focus.

People who object to being placed in a "box" are not understanding the diversity of each individual within that box and that identifying their temperament does not set boundaries around their personalities or their possibilities. If we have adopted strengths of another temperament, we have simply flexed the boundaries of our temperament, not become another temperament.

Infinite Variety Within a Temperament Comes From:

• The variations in the degree of each strength's potential.

• Not having all the strengths of a given temperament and having different combinations of strengths within that temperament.

• The reaction of one strength on others that can "color" them differently.

• The freedom to chose whether we use the strength, over use it or wrongly use it. If we develop our own weaknesses, of course, these define us too, and negate our strengths.

• The variety of talents that can arise out of one strength in a given temperament. Talents are not the same as strengths.

• How environmental factors or influences have forced us to modify a strength or not.

• The amount of effort we have put into building and developing our strengths.

• Other non-temperament factors that come into play in our lives.

The possibilities for variance and uniqueness are endless. With all these possible variations, the amazing thing is how accurately the similarities of our temperament describe us.

Core Strengths and Adopted Strengths in Real Life

Let's take hypothetical Pierre and see how core strengths and adopted strengths might work out in real life.

Pierre is an SP temperament, preferring to take risks and find excitement in every present moment. His parents are SJs and he is always being told to be careful and look before he leaps. They cautiously parent him away from trouble and danger, but he wants to face danger and prove to himself how brave and effective he is.

Their relationship becomes tenuous as a result, since he feels he is not understood nor his feelings respected. Pierre wants to be who he is. They want him to be more cautious. In the process, however, he picks up the ability to act cautiously, which makes his parents proud of their parenting, of course.

So he grows up not having developed his own strengths and is somewhat miserable and cranky, feeling inside that he is somehow living with a residual unhappiness for some reason.

He goes to work at an accounting firm. His parents are accountants and they provide him with the job in a poor economic climate, all the time exhorting the benefits of the financial security it brings. He learns the details of figures and numbers well but is not as good as his parents who are suited for the serious, detailed work that accounting demands. They feel they have done their son a favor. After all, they feel the reward of this kind of dependable work and, surely, he will too. However, he feels life stinks and hates going to work everyday.

Now he is a misfit at his job and his core strengths are still not satisfied. His adopted strength has increased his marketability and his standing among many of his friends. The more he uses his adopted strength, the more it seems to fit since the stronger it becomes.

Pierre starts to search for fulfillment in his life and thinks that perhaps other people or pursuits his friends suggest will give it to him, but things never really satisfy so he lapses into a mild depression and acts somewhat bizarre. His parents are worried. He feels sick in his spirit.

He stumbles on a temperament key and, when told what his temperament and type is and when it is explained to him, he sees for the first time that this is really who he is, who he wants to be. He is a risk-taker, an adventurer, and although he hasn't developed these strengths much, they have a fulfilling ring to him. He is encouraged to use his newly found strengths and to find a job he likes that will also exercise his strengths. He becomes a hunting guide and a guide for exploring parties. He finds he loves this life and feels really happy and fulfilled. His depression leaves and Pierre has found himself and found his direction. Life is now what he dreamed it would be. Pierre has followed his innerkinetics.

This story is a collective tale of many people I have talked to. What a relief they feel when they find who they really are. The relief, however, is not as great as the sense of fulfillment they experience when they use and develop the natural strengths of their temperament.

Our Strengths Give Us Stability, Direction, and Fulfillment

Stability
Remember there is a package of strengths in you that give direction to your life. If there weren't you would constantly oscillate with whatever force or influence that had an impact on your life, changing direction and never feeling a solidifying purpose. Our core strengths stabilize us when we face life's challenges. Change is good, but not if it robs us of this stability.

Being at peace with yourself enables your strengths even more. The only way we can be at peace with ourselves is to consistently be ourselves. I am not denying a spiritual connection since that means peace in a larger context. Accepting ourselves and our *innerkinetics*, and learning to love who we are, centers us. Another way of putting it: We must function according to how we are made to function. If this makes sense, find, develop, and live in the basic strengths and drives of your *innerkinetics* — as an SP, SJ, NT, or NF.

Imagine what would happen if our digestive system worked at whim in reverse, accepting poisonous foods and rejecting the foods we love without reason. Its unpredictability would make life impossible. We would never know if chocolate was going to make us throw up, or poison us, or cause our tastebuds to smile. We only operate effectively when our systems operate predictably. Stability is reached when we rely on our *InnerKinetics*™ and don't try to function as another temperament, which can be the reverse of how we are designed. Is stability a requirement for your life?

Direction

Having a temperament gives a tilt or leaning to our lives. The tilt gives the sense of direction we have been talking about. Our lives need to move in the direction of our positive preferences to find fulfillment and journey toward our potential. Whatever way we tilt by nature, we must go.

If we had no leaning, if we were perfectly balanced in our preferences, we would not have any motivation either. Suppose you preferred equally to make decisions quickly and come to closure and, on the other hand, to not make decisions and wait for more facts to turn up in the hope that the decision would be made for you. You would be in anguish over your decisions all the time if you did not lean one way or the other. You would never know who you were, decisive or not wanting to be decisive. The lack of motivation and direction would paralyze you. This is why I say we are one temperament and not a mixture of temperaments.

Balance is not a good thing when it comes to temperament. It robs us of motivational energy. Leaning to one side or the other is a good thing. Without a clear leaning, we would not achieve consistently either. Imagine if I were pulled equally in opposite directions all the time. I would be forever frustrated and irritable. No meaning comes to the life that has no leaning or direction.

To know who I am before I leave the starting blocks of life is essential to knowing how to perform. Be thankful for your temperament's bias.

Fulfillment

A person locks into the moment when they are using their natural strengths and you should be able to feel the intensity of focus and pleasure. Repeated use will reinforce the strength, and you will clearly know if you are really happy in the positive use of that strength as you exercise it. Don't confuse the outer rewards you receive for using an adopted strength with the inner satisfaction of a core strength that settles kindly on your spirit.

It's hard to define fulfillment. It comes in the satisfaction we feel with life and with ourselves. An inner peace flags us of its presence. We simply feel great. Teenagers ask, "How will I know when I am in love?" We tell them, "You will know!" It is similar when describing fulfillment: "You will know when you are fulfilled and inwardly happy. You will know!"

You may have to fight the influence of parents, society, and your friends who have their own plans for your satisfaction. They mean well. Live exercising your own strengths and you will hear the bells of an inner coherence ringing with a satisfying melody in your spirit.

Now let's turn to how weaknesses are made and how they affect us.

Weaknesses Are <u>NOT</u> Part of Our Temperament

Surprise! Nearly everyone I have talked with assumes that weaknesses are a part of their temperament.

"I guess that's just me," Jay reluctantly and somewhat fatefully said of his weaknesses.

Eyes open with the comment, "You don't have to live in your weaknesses. You can get rid of them — easily."

Weaknesses are not you or a part of you. They are a distortion of who you are and they don't have to be your destiny or your fate.

Here Are Four Presuppositions to Begin the Understanding and Management of Our Strengths and Weaknesses.

Presupposition One:
- Strengths are given to us and form our temperament or *innerkinetics*.
- Weaknesses are not given to us; they are self-made.

Presupposition Two:
- Strengths are positive in nature.
- Weaknesses are negative in nature.

Presupposition Three:
- Strengths fulfill and bring us pleasure.
- Weaknesses damage and weaken us.

Presupposition Four:
- Strengths are best managed by conscious use and development.
- Weaknesses appear when we mismanage our strengths. They are a negative reflection of our strengths.

When we follow what these realities teach us we are able to effectively release ourselves from our weaknesses.

How We Create Our Weaknesses

Since our temperament is made up of our strengths and we all know we have weaknesses, where did our weaknesses come from? Just like the first presupposition says, "Weaknesses are self-made." We create them when we:

- Don't use our strengths
- Overuse our strengths
- Use our strengths in a way that is destructive to us or others. (Others include *ALL* other personal beings.)

Weaknesses Cannot Be Inherent to Our Nature

If we don't create them ourselves, they must be inherent in us. However, this cannot be the case. Let's see why:

- Weaknesses are a negative force in our lives. We cannot be given a negative! Therefore, we can't be given weaknesses as part of our temperament. I have already argued this.

- We can be given an opportunity to create a weakness, but opportunities are not part of our temperament either. They are what life presents to us and what we react to.

- Weaknesses begin with a mental choice, usually a damaging choice. If weaknesses don't begin with a mental choice we are doomed with our weaknesses for a lifetime and may as well resign ourselves to living with them and their damage.

- A chosen course of behavior can become a habit. When a negative course of action becomes a habit, it is easily identifiable as a weakness. Habit is a learned behavioral pattern, not an inborn element of our temperament.

- We are not created with weak spots in our nature. We have tendencies or strengths that, if wrongly used, can become weaknesses. This is my thesis. Overused, not used, or misused strengths create weaknesses. Consider these 2 points:

  ✓ As I have just pointed out, when we don't use our strengths we create a vacuum in our personality. This vacancy or nonuse of a strength creates its own weak spot, an area where failure waits

146

and weaknesses rush in to fill the vacuum. This makes sense if we think about what happens when we fail.

✓When we overuse our strength we also create a weak spot since an overuse of any strength damages ourselves and others. For example: When an SJ overuses the strength of supervision (an overuse would be trying to control others rather than just supervise their work), we alienate people and we corrupt the power we have, which in turns corrupts us. So weaknesses are self-created, not intrinsic to our nature.

Personally, I'm glad that I create my own weaknesses because if I were born with fundamental weaknesses I could do little about removing them. I'd rather believe that I can do something about my weaknesses rather than swallow the fate of having to live with them.

Experience has taught us that when we focus on our strengths rather than on our weaknesses the weaknesses leave our conscious mind and release their grip on us.

For those who have a belief in God, you can view it this way: God does not give us weaknesses since he is not in the business of handing out weaknesses to anyone.

Whether you rely on such a belief or not, it makes sound sense that we create our own weaknesses by our choices. Weaknesses are not part of our temperament. Now the door is open for self recovery from our self-made weaknesses.

Identifying Weaknesses

Since all weaknesses are negative, we can identify them by asking whether our thought or action is negative or positive. That's simple and quick.

I am so thankful for all the emphasis on positive thinking or thinking with faith. It has directed us to an easy way of assessing the impact that our thoughts or actions have on our lives. We are indebted to people like Robert H. Schuller, Dennis Waitley, Norman Vincent Peale, Napoleon Hill and many others for this emphasis.

Humans are constructed to function positively, not negatively. Therefore, positive thoughts are healthy thoughts and they encourage the production of healthy chemicals in the brain.

- Positive strengths increase our potential, while negative strengths decrease our potential.
- Positive thoughts lift our self-image. Negative thoughts lower our self-image.
- Positive thoughts of someone we love increase the feelings of love toward that person. Negative thoughts decrease feelings of love.

We have all experienced the effects of a positive or negative mindset. Simply put, if an action is negative it is the result of a self-created weakness.

The road map, at this point, is not complicated. To live in our strengths we need to increase our awareness and acceptance of positive thoughts, feelings, and actions.   We will become more attractive and more effective in all our relationships and tasks when we do and we will race with greater speed to our goal. So, let's identify all our thoughts and actions as positive or negative and we will know when we are living in our strengths or our weaknesses.

How Do We Get Rid of Our Weaknesses?

If you are like me, you have been waiting for this one. By focusing on our strengths — that's the answer! Please, **not** by focusing on your weaknesses and struggling to defeat them! That's the worst thing you can do! Let me explain.

Focus Magnifies Its Object
Whatever gets our attention and we focus on grows in importance and size in our minds. Focus on your weaknesses and you will likely **never** get rid of them. You will simply increase the attention your mind is giving them. This means you are increasing the problem you are trying to resolve and turning a molehill into a mountain. This is obviously not the way to increase your chances of overcoming your weakness.

Life is lived best by focusing on positives and magnifying their importance in our lives. Our full potential is only reached by pursuing our strengths, not by trying to remove our weaknesses.

However, even if we pursue the building of our strengths, we still must get rid of our weaknesses or they will dominate us. How do we accomplish building our strengths and getting rid of our weaknesses? With one action! One action on our part achieves both objectives at the same time.

We can get rid of weaknesses by taking the focus away from them. We build strengths by focusing on them. Rob your weaknesses of your attention and they begin to wither. Change the focus to your strengths and they, not your weaknesses, grow and develop. Changing focus is the key. Wherever we focus, that's where the activity and energy is concentrated in our brains and in our spirits. That's what we are self promoting!

When we focus on our strengths, we are not focusing on our weaknesses. We can only focus on one thing at a time. Again, let me emphasize: Whatever is outside of our focus weakens and whatever we focus on is magnified. Better still, remind yourself that if no attention is paid to your weakness, it vanishes from your conscious vision and then where is it? Gone, and whatever you are now focusing on takes over your consciousness. Your weakness only returns when you give it your attention again.

We grow our weaknesses or our strengths by where we place our focus or to which we give our attention. We are all painfully aware that when we obsess over a hurt it grows into gigantic proportions and we ruminate on it with ever-increasing negative results.

Keep your mind firmly focused on what you want to develop and grow. Stay focused on your strengths and you will have little trouble driving with power and purpose to your potential. Weaknesses cannot then derail you.

Want to get rid of your weaknesses? Then stop focusing on them; it's as simple as that.

We will return to focus and its other roles in Chapter 19.

149

Don't Blame Your Temperament

We will never get rid of our weaknesses if we believe that our temperament is the problem. Each strength in each temperament can be overused, misused, or simply not used, and when this happens the temperament's powers are weakened. When they are not functioning as they are intended to function our strengths are open to attack and defeat. The problem does not lie in our temperament or its strengths, but in our misuse of our temperament's strengths and our negative focus.

This can happen in many ways because there are so many possible distortions of each strength. Here are two examples of how we go wrong.

Suppose an NF overuses his trusting attitude and trusts a stranger instead of heeding the warning of his intuition that the person he is about to trust is not genuine, a fake. As a result, he will be taken advantage of by the person he trusted. He will then commonly believe that he must not trust people and that trusting people is bad for him. Therefore, he adopts the strength of the NT, for example, and becomes skeptical of others. He becomes distant and cold in his relationships. For good measure, we'll say he also becomes suspicious and cynical.

He now believes that he needs to defend himself against what he has perceived is a weakness in his temperament: too trusting. However, he has made a mistake. Now he is struggling to become what he is not and failing to see that his problem was caused by an overuse of his strength that, when not used, places him in a position of weakness. He should be the trusting person he is and listen to his intuitive voice.

Our temperaments don't have weaknesses. Our misuse of the strengths of our temperament create weaknesses and we often blame it on our temperament.

Let's take another example. Suppose an SJ overuses her strength of caution. As a result her over cautiousness causes her to miss a very valuable opportunity. She misread the cause of her problem and becomes convinced of her need to be more reactive and spontaneous in her actions. Her temperament is blamed for the weakness — too cautious — so she starts jumping at opportunities in the belief that she is correcting the fault in her temperament. The result is that, without the practiced skill of the SP's fast tactical mind, she lacks the SP's advantage and makes big mistakes. The problem is not solved. She has jumped from the frying pan into the fire — from a false reading of what went wrong into the fire of trying to be what she is not.

The mistake was to overuse a strength. Her temperament did not fail her. Caution is a great strength for the SJ temperament, but not if it is wrongly used. Our temperaments are not made to function smoothly when their strengths are overused. Furthermore, it is never a solution to the problem to try to be what we are not.

This misunderstanding of how we are made is very common. This SJ should return to being cautious, but not overcautious, and she will function smoothly and walk her path to success. If she continues to believe she needs to change and be something else, she will drag failure with her.

When any temperament overuses, misuses, or doesn't use their strengths, they are open to hurt or failure, not success. The desire to correct the fault by being the opposite of their strength is understandable. However, this is simply the worst thing they can do.

The motivation to find success or protect themselves against failure is not at fault. Believing that their temperament has weak spots and that they must counter-react is the problem.

If we all use our strengths and don't misuse them, we are armed to win and we will win. Let's stop creating our weaknesses, return to our strengths, and use them. Our success is in the building of our strengths, not in our changing who we are. I simply can't say that enough!

How to Develop Your Core Strengths

Here Are Simple and Proven Steps:
- Read through the strengths of the your temperament — SP, SJ, NT, or NF — in the next chapters.

- Check those strengths you observe as your current strengths.

- Use these more and train them to be stronger. You will want to focus on them because they are already familiar to you. Your increased focus will cause them to grow even more and give you an immediate sense of stability, direction, and fulfillment.

- Develop an awareness of their use in your life hour by hour. You must know when you are using them if you are going to develop and train them. People are attracted to you because of your strengths, not your weaknesses, and you will become more appealing to those who love you and need you when you use your strengths correctly.

- Learn how to use your strengths when you need them. If you are intuitive, ingenious, reliable, or spontaneous, learn how to put your strength into operation effectively. That's called training your strengths to be at your command. Only when they are at your command are they really useful to you.

- When you have developed these strengths, try using some of the others to see if they, too, are part of the real you, fulfilling you and slaking your thirst for real happiness. Not all the strengths listed under your temperament will fit with the same degree of comfort, but most will.

- As you develop your natural strengths you will become all that you can be.

Now we are going to discover the blueprint of each temperament within the details of their strengths.

Section 4

Introduce Yourself
To Your Strengths

SP Strengths — Featuring Self Expression

All strengths, to some degree, may be found in any temperament. The following strengths are native to the SP and are found with greater intensity in the SP temperament. These are the core strengths at which SPs naturally excel if they take the time and effort to develop them.

The path to success for each of us is written in our strengths. Here, for the SP, you will find that path.

The strengths are not set out in any particular order, nor do they have to be understood or practiced in a set order.

Take any strength of your temperament, one at a time, and develop it until you:

- Are aware of when you use it and when you don't
- Have developed it as best you can
- Feel ready to go on to the next

To help you develop your strengths, a convenient "how to" list is at the end of the discussion of each strength. You might copy it and take it with you as you get used to operating your strengths.

Lives Happily In the Present Moment
(Orientation to Time)

We draw lessons from the past, but we cannot live in it.
~ Lyndon B. Johnson.
(An SP's point of view.)

I don't think of the past. The only thing that matters is the everlasting present.
~ W. Somerset Maugham.
(Another SP's point of view)

The SP's strength that relates to time is to be in the present and live in it with gusto, tactical skill, and free abandonment. "Where do they get all their energy?" is a common puzzle to most who are not SPs. SPs get it largely from the use of this strength. It is tiring to be constantly focused on the past or searching the future. Narrowing their focus to the present keeps their optimism fresh and an optimistic attitude produces positive hormones. Positive energy drives them.

Living for the present moment demands that you catch it. If you watch an SP, you will notice how they seem to drain the last drop of excitement and pleasure out of every present moment. This is especially noticeable in the SP child. This energy, enthusiasm, and focus is the perfect example of how to use any strength.

If asked to sit still and do nothing, the SP fidgets and fusses (even as an adult) and quickly becomes bored or is up and gone, searching elsewhere for some ounce of pleasure. Watch them! Life depends on the nutrition of excitement. They are hummingbirds in constant motion, needing also the hummingbird's high-energy nutrition.

The counseling room is not an SP's best performance, nor is meditation, the doctor's office, prayer, or simply having nothing to do.

Tony was in a tight spot. His girlfriend was pregnant and he wasn't ready to walk the aisle. No sir! He wasn't sure he loved her, and conflicting pressures were on from all his friends at the bar. He had other relationship problems that also forced him to come to me for help (an unusual commitment for an SP).

Sheepishly and reluctantly he sat there. Constantly, he wiggled and stretched and stood and sat, crossed his legs and uncrossed them. He was a moving target, hard for my words to hit.

I thought, at first, that the constant motion showed that he was nervous and worried, but as the session continued it was clear he was an SP in eternal motion and nervous too. After his problems were settled, he was still moving around. He also showed evidence of an SP temperament that is panicked by a counseling room's confinement and bored by a real lack of excitement. He said he wasn't nervous (as I had supposed) at all — just acting like a shackled SP.

SPs will find a way to inject action and fun into the moment because they are compelled by an internal force to rescue the moment from waste. This quest for the moment's pleasure can result in distracting behavior that can lead to destructive behavior if nothing else interesting shows up. Their inner drive to find excitement and stimulating movement seizes life in a hammerlock and squeezes the thrills out of it.

It is painful to see an SP at a boring party. They get up to look at a picture, go to the rest room often, longingly strain to see out the window, and act like a caged animal. "I want room to breath and I have to know what is out there that I am missing," says a burning fire in the SP's bones.

Therefore, seldom are SPs obsessed with the past or excessively concerned about the future. If they live effectively in the present they feel the future will take care of itself and, to them, it is a downer to live in the frustrations of the past. Both the past and the future can blow dark clouds over the sunshine of the present. They will insist, "Why are you so concerned about something that has passed?" or "Why are you worrying about the future? Its not here yet." Try to get an SP to focus on the past or the future and they will not show much potential.

This focus on the pleasure of the present moment is supported by their faith in the abundance of life. They believe the present moment is rich with rewarding opportunities. Life will always give them of its abundance, so there is no need to save for a rainy day. Their optimism about life is a gift from heaven but tantalizingly out of reach to the worried SJ.

"Rejoice, and again I say, rejoice," says Paul, the Apostle; and the SP gets it!

If an SP wants to be his best, he must rejoice and that, for them, means to focus on the present: be full of positive optimism and not let others or difficult circumstances redirect them to be focused on what has happened or what might happen. Therefore, they don't plan or prepare much, as does the SJ. Nor do they treasure traditions and connections with the past. They want to be "all there" in the present, and if they are distracted by past or future events, they feel cheated out of a valuable chance at joy.

The external world is their natural home and this is where they enjoy the present moment. Their physical senses are alive, finely tuned, and tingling with its stimulation.

Living in the present helps them find enjoyment anytime, anywhere. To them, all you need is a present moment and an optimistic searching spirit.

A happy SP adult is a pleasant partner too. Don't despise this focus on the present, as some SJs tend to do. It feeds mental health and avoids unnecessary stress. When this focus is absent in an SP, depression and strange behavior is likely.

What do they do when this focus is absent? Find a present moment (not too hard) and restore joy, optimism and excitement in exploring what it offers. At work, also, an SP must live in their present opportunities. Do this, and they will feel the power of this basic orientation to time to heal them.

If you are an SP, make sure this strength is fed and developed, since without it life will lose its sense of worth and you will lose your effectiveness.

How Do I Develop This Strength?

- Use it. Be who you are. Live in the present. You must!

- Sharpen your awareness of what the present moment offers you. Knowing your strengths and being aware of them helps you use them and see the potential they offer you.

- Catch the moment's joy. Don't let it pass. It is often registered with a contented, satisfying feeling that simply says to you that all is well.

- Turn your faith in life's abundance into a firm conviction and a habitual way of thinking.

- Look at your optimism about life as your most important strength and keep your mind positive. This will help you live in the present effectively.

- Convince yourself and teach others that the reduction of stress caused by living in the moment (free of worry over the past or the future's uncertainties) is helpful to all people.

- Tell yourself that living in the moment is focusing on the here and now, and whatever you focus on grows stronger.

Caution:

All temperaments lapse into weaknesses when they don't use their strengths, overuse them, or use them for destructive purposes such as damaging themselves or others. Here are further cautions for this strength.

- Plan a little. Remember, the present moment can catch you unprepared to be able to snatch its thrills at times. Planning is for everyone and, for your temperament, it is an aid, not a demand. Just don't try to overdo it. That will sadden you for sure.

- Think of the future a little too. You will never be an NF, who is oriented toward the future and gains their optimism from it. However, as you develop your strength of being focused on the moment, you will need to look ahead and guard against your resources failing.

- A combination of living in the moment, learning from the past, and preparing for the future is a healthy balance for all temperaments, but each temperament achieves the balance in a different way and to a different degree. Do all three but, for your enjoyment, put the emphasis on the present.

Brave — Bold — Daring

Life is either a daring adventure or nothing. Security does not exist in nature, nor do the children of men as a whole experience it. Avoiding danger is no safer in the long run than exposure.
~ Helen Keller, US blind and deaf educator.

I believe that one of life's greatest risks is never daring to risk.
~ Oprah Winfrey

Security is mostly a superstition.
~ Helen Keller

Be strong and very courageous.
~ Book of Joshua

The policy of being too cautious is the greatest risk of all.
~ Jawaharlal Nehru. (Indian politician)

This is a strength that can be easily observed and seen from the earliest years in an SP's adventures. Ezekiel talks about the lion. "As daring as a lion" gives the analogy true meaning.

Courage and bravery leads the lion and the SP into their daring, even into dangerous exploits. Have you noticed people who seem to seek danger and court it wherever they go? It is a necessary element of their character if they are to succeed and excel at courage. If the lion is not daring, it does not succeed. It must take risks. So must the human lion!

This is very hard for the cautious SJ to understand or approve. Risk-taking is a fool's game, they believe. To the SP, however, it holds some of life's greatest moments. Courage is where the adrenaline is, where the challenge of sudden bravery excites, and where they discover who they really are.

Danger is real excitement. Randal knew that. He had skied where angels fear to ski and, hurtling over an edge, he crashed at high speed amid snow and rocks.

Watching with field binoculars, it wasn't evident immediately what had happened. All his fiancé saw was a cloud of snow and then...nothing. Slowly it dawned. He must have piled up and the lack of movement was a bad sign. The hours passed before he was brought down and, lying in the hospital, badly battered and with broken bones, the smile told of the pride only an SP knows when they relive the rush of adrenaline again — even through the pain.

"How bad?" he asked. Bad enough to assure him of his badge of bravery. Life is rewarding for an SP when its consequences clearly inform the world of his unusual daring. This is an example of this strength in real life.

Daring and bravery creates a rush of adrenaline and this can bring great excitement. So the boldness of the lion is related to another strength: excitement. This is what inspires most of the SP's courageous action, along with the need to be noticed and to take center stage. Take away the opportunity for the SP to be the bold lion, and the SP loses interest in that particular activity.

The SP will not stay long in a group where there is no potential for thrill. However, they will first try their best to inject fun and excitement into the group as though they are commissioned by God or some mighty force to make all creatures bold. Perhaps they are!

Weakness in an SP is most often a nonuse of this strength. If they don't use it, their self-image drops, their pleasure in life fades, and they appear sad. How can they be proud of themselves if they show cowardice or faintheartedness?

SPs can't be successful if they don't use this strength. It is not for the faint of heart. Bravery pushes discovery into the otherwise feared possibilities that others have left alone. Thinking with courage conquers fear before it can develop. The SP uses courage in this way to win the battle over fear quickly and not have to put up a prolonged struggle. Don't forget that boldness alone can win hearts and make the enemy cower. An SP's courage holds many advantages to finding success.

An SP must use the courage, which is their honor, because not to use it breeds depression, and the SP hates depression more than any other temperament. However, wisdom in the use of taking a dare can mean the difference between life or its sudden closure. To weave their way through the intricacies of success, tempering the courage with thoughtfulness and a little planning won't hurt either. The *innerkinetics* of bravery fashions a boldness humans have always memorialized. Use the strength with wisdom, and use it where daring exploits or raw courage will bless or protect society; but use it.

Reward for the brave SP is the acclaim of others and the inner thrill of a life lived on the edge. We always live to our best when we live in our strengths — even the risky ones.

Credit belongs to the man ... who at the best knows in the end the triumph of high achievement and who at the worst, if he fails, at least he fails while daring greatly. So that his place shall never be with those cold and timid souls who know neither victory or defeat.
~ *Theodore Roosevelt*

How Do I Develop this Strength?
• Be brave, courageous, daring, and bold. To do so consistently drives fears out of your life. Fear is the enemy of bravery and if allowed a home in mind or heart, bravery emerges wounded and weak.

• If you want to be brave, don't fear or avoid calculated risks. They are the easy ones.

• Excitement inspires you. It creates the rush of adrenaline. You need to get excited, so refuse living in the dullness of mediocrity.

• However, remember, rash acts of bravery can terminate you. Be brave, but be here.

Caution:
All temperaments lapse into weaknesses when they don't use their strengths, overuse them, or use them for destructive purposes such as damaging themselves or others. Here are further cautions for this strength.

- There are such things as healthy fears. Healthy fears protect us from danger and from things that damage us. Moral standards also fall into the category of healthy fears. There are things fear warns us of that are beyond our limitations. Learn to know the line between bravery and stupidity.

- Calculate risk and enter it with respect. Risk pays great rewards and extracts the greatest of losses. Win; don't lose.

- Thoughtfulness is a healthy addition to the courage of the brave. Great generals and leaders are both brave and thoughtful.

- All bravery should be for a purpose. The lion is brave but always purposeful in its actions.

- Here is a motto to consider: *Never without fear — never without wisdom.*

Spontaneous — Impulsive

All growth is a leap in the dark, a spontaneous unpremeditated act without the benefit of experience.
~ Henry Miller

Impulse is a risk; it is also freedom and a beginning to creativity. Although some who would rather live in the regularity of routine and habit see no silver lining to the cloud of spontaneity, it is a freedom we can't do without if we would be progressive and creative beings.

To the SP, spontaneity and impulse mean room to move and impress, the chance to feel the rush of freedom under their wings, and the reinvigorating force of change.

This is a strength just like sensitivity in the NF. Both can present us with immediate choices and result in immediate action. Spontaneity enables fast reaction to circumstances and can often bring instant positive or negative results. "I must be free to move when the urge calls," the SP pleads. To be the best an SP can be, they must lean heavily on their spontaneity and guard its freedom.

163

The true SP will act on impulse and if the results do not turn out positive, they will simply rely on their tactical skills to decipher the next move and take the fight to their opponent (be it person or thing), confident in seizing the advantage.

Spontaneity is needed if SPs are going to develop their tactical skills. Tactics are the ability to make the best choice in the fleeting moment. Fast on the draw (many of the gunslingers of the early West were SPs who found in this the most excitement they could imagine) and quick to the next move, eye and hand coordinated, they follow their impulses, trusting in their tactical and physical abilities.

Impulse can be an act of faith that jumps into action without the need for thought and mental processing. It is an act of faith! However, that faith may or may not be well directed. An SP shows a ready faith in themselves and that's what they so often trust. Low self-esteem in an SP is rare compared to the SJ and NF temperaments. Belief is an act of the moment for the SP rather than a carefully thought out policy. It is the use of tactical thinking and a courage rooted in self-belief.

An obvious weakness is developed when this strength is used wrongly, without reason and wisdom. When SPs make a wrong move impulsively and prematurely, they simply counter with another to right the wrong they have created — if, of course, they perceive that their move was indeed wrong. Therefore, the argument to think before you leap does not inspire them to become ready followers of this advice.

The strength of spontaneity is needed and can't be put down by the argument that it can be misused. All strengths can be misused. Furthermore, remember that the impulse of the SP is backed up by the skill of tactical insight and seldom lacks reason, even if the reason is short term.

This kind of impulsive faith defends itself as an act of confidence in themselves or in some other belief or divine power. It is their confidence that inspires them to act impulsively without fear, and sometimes without thought.

Fear is their sworn enemy since it seeks to limit and squash their impulsive, brave, in-the-moment action. Worry (a fear) breaks down the rock solid SJ and fear of any kind destroys the impulsive SP. If you are an SP, give fear no quarter or, if you do, you will soon hate the person you have become.

Spontaneity is "in the moment" creativity and, hence, its relevance to success. In the fast pace of games or unexpected happenings in life it proves its worth. The SP is the master of impulsive action in such things as the sports arena.

How Do I Develop this Strength?

- The same way an athlete improves. Practice! Practice does not make perfect; it only makes you form a well-grooved habit. If you dislike practice, you may never develop it fully.

- Become aware of your use of spontaneity. If you don't know when you are using it, you cannot develop it.

- Develop it first in your mind. See things and react in your mind with a sudden spontaneous action and then, as events unfold, check the results of your spontaneous choice. Was your move effective or ineffective? This way you will not have risked anything, but at the same time you will have practiced just as effectively as being spontaneous in the real world.

- Whenever you act spontaneously to whatever the moment presents you are using the next strength, tactics. Maybe not well-chosen tactics but tactics nonetheless. Practice mentally and evaluate the tactic you choose until your skill at choosing the best tactic is impressive. Spontaneous actions will improve along with the improvement of your tactics.

- You should notice that this strength needs to be developed with care and with the help of other strengths.

- You can't build this strength without building confidence, so you benefit two strengths.

- Fear will kill effective spontaneity. Remain positive, not negative, if you would keep fear at bay.

- Spontaneity is a creative strength. The artist feeds on it; the athlete lives by it. Use it to feed your artisan nature.

Caution:
All temperaments lapse into weaknesses when they don't use their strengths, overuse them, or use them for destructive purposes such as damaging themselves or others. Here are further cautions for this strength.

- Spontaneity is not a substitute for reason. Sharpening your reasoning abilities will benefit your spontaneity.

- Wisdom is knowledge that is understood and guided by goodness. Apply wisdom to your actions.

Effective — Tactical — Aggressive

Tactics mean doing what you can with what you have.
~ Saul Alinsky

SPs need to be effective. Achieving results in the present moment is the game of a lifetime for SPs. They seldom concern themselves with the distant future *unless* it really affects the decision in the present. Long range planning is not within the circle of their excitement. They settle for excelling at being able to figure out the best tactic to become effective or efficient in what they are currently engaged in doing.

Tactics for the SP mean quick thinking, fast application of their thoughts, the skill of surprise attack, and the ever valuable asset of not missing a good opportunity.

The word tactic comes from a Greek word *taktikos*, which itself comes from a family of words to do with arrangement and timing. A tactical mind is one that can quickly see what move or what short term arrangement of moves is needed, at what time, and in what manner. The skill shows itself in sports and physical achievements as participants figure out their best move. It is also skillfully exercised in personal battles.

Meagan found herself losing her freedoms as her SJ supervisors in her department created and enforced more routines and more regulations to protect the already protected routines, squelching her freedom and her fellow workers' freedoms more and more. She felt hemmed in and demeaned.

SPs don't take opposition lying down. She began to undermine the "improvements" and tactically frustrate the offending supervisors. After all, they were frustrating her and her friends, she reasoned. She was subtle, secretive, cunning, and, as usual, effective. The offending systems that had been put in place to restrict workers were cunningly and effectively sabotaged. Some routines were overemphasized, others were neglected.

Some of her supervisors started blaming whomever they could and soon the insecurity it all created caused a morale problem that the supervisors were forced to address. "Improvements" to the system were halted. It was finally admitted that the rules and regulations had failed to control people. Oppressive rules eventually undermine their original purpose, anyhow. Meagan had seen the weakness and tactically fought back, stopping the opposition.

This is an obvious case of getting even by using tactics. The SP will, if forced, try to wear down the opposition with fair, or even unfair, tactics. The restrictive pressures of the supervisors were made, by Meagan's tactics, to play a part in their own destruction.

You decide who used their strengths correctly. Whenever we think of strengths that have the potential of controlling other people, their misuse becomes an issue that must not be overlooked. In the story of Meagan, the strengths of supervision and aggressive tactics collide.

One thing that must concern all temperaments is that strengths used wrongly for purposes that hurt others create weaknesses that may not be apparent immediately. What is just and fair in the limited knowledge of humans is not always clear.

However, it is clear that such battles litter the road to success with unwanted debris. Any use of a strength that divides people moves them in opposite directions and to opposite goals, and it hinders progress. Energy, drive, and purpose are then diversified, and forward motion fades.

The degree of aggressiveness differs with each SP, of course, but the right use of aggression is the real issue over which all temperaments disagree. SPs see aggression not so much as attacking others, but rather as effectively executing their tactic without hesitation or fear for needed purposes.   Others see any manipulation of people as personal aggression.   To add to the confusion in our world today, those who claim to be opposed to all manipulation of others use aggression and manipulate others to get their point over too.

Why this discussion? To make it clear that if you are an SP you will need to use your strength of effectiveness, tactics, and aggressive drive to accomplish your goals but without damaging others or yourself. Thinking that through will show you the fast and most effective road to achieve your goals. Ethics must be the concern of all who would push for their goals to be effected.

Each of the strengths we have covered so far is closely related in the real world. Living in the moment, brave, spontaneous, and tactically aggressive are all tools for success in a physical environment, but they can fail in the world of relationships and theoretical concepts.

The SP must win to feel effective; an urge inside demands it. For an SP to lose is to have to painfully examine the loss of courage or a collapse into fear, and that is a distressful thing for a person who is trying to wring the most pleasure out of the present moment. Life drags for the SP when they lose.

Tactical thinking is the SP's mental strength just as for the SJ it is logistics; for the NT it is strategy, and for the NF it is diplomacy, as David Keirsey has so effectively shown.

Aggressiveness (a part of this trilogy) is making a move quickly and effectively to gain the offensive. Aggressiveness is often needed for success.   Tactical thinking along with an aggressive move offers a chance to be effective. All three of these strengths form the arsenal of the SP.

The main weakness is a wrong use of this strength. Since success is not always the highest value, success should not be achieved at any cost. Aggression should keep company with wisdom and goodness.

There is nothing worse than aggressive stupidity.
~ Johann Wolfgang von Goethe.

If the SP succeeds, it is because of having grasped the moment and changed course with wisdom and an innate ease when needed.

How Do I Develop this Strength?

- Practice the skills of tactics. Use aggressiveness appropriately. You cannot develop a strength you don't use.

- Effective tactics have to do with timing, arrangement, and methods. Study these three factors and make yourself a student of them.

- Study tactics in the real world. Observe the tactics and thinking that produced effective moves in your favorite sport and in life's happenings. Be constantly learning.

- Practice mentally, since a tactical move in your mind is as effective for learning as one in real life.

- Have firm boundaries for the use of aggressiveness. If your aggressiveness does damage to others or yourself, it is a questionable strength and can eat away at your personal integrity.

- Tactical effectiveness is not simply a learned trait but also (in the SP) a given strength. Develop it with the belief it is a part of who you are.

Caution:

All temperaments lapse into weaknesses when they don't use their strengths, overuse them, or use them for destructive purposes such as damaging themselves or others. Here are further cautions for this strength.

- Remember, the wrong use of these strengths can destroy your life and your relationships.

- Also remember that losing (which happens to all of us) is a good teacher, not a demon trying to destroy you. Failure is opportunity. Get its definition correct! Don't let it defeat you.

- Focus on good tactics and moves — the ones that will create a life of health and growth. Whatever you focus on you will become.

Easily Excited

The desire for excitement is very deep seated in human beings.
~ Bertrand Russell

Here we draw a distinction between the excitement of the SP and the passion of the NF. Excitement in the SP is an emotion that is raised and enjoyed in the present moment and, just as quickly, lost in the next. Passion in the NF is excitement that is raised in the present by the future (a dream, a possibility, an opportunity yet to be), and the excitement usually lasts long into the future. Passion is nurtured and fed by the future's expectations and dreams, but excitement is rooted in the moment.

Also, excitement for the SP is born in the physical senses, stirring up the emotions. The physical senses produce immediate feelings for any of us. Of the two S's (SJ and SP), the SP is the most emotionally driven to their actions.

It may have been a commercially minded SJ who saw that a fast buck could be made out of the urges of the SP (or an SP who dug deep inside his drive for excitement) and invented bungee jumping. Regardless, it is the SP who is drawn most to the sport. It represents a dare, calls for courage, extols taking uncalculated risks, and is best done on the impulse to keep fear at bay. It gives an adrenaline rush that is unmatched. Perfect for the strong SP, but torture for most SJs.

I know an SJ who was prodded into bungee jumping in Otago, New Zealand. The sheer cliffs of a narrow gorge on the Shotover River provide a thrilling, "Oh-my-God" location for a near 200-foot fall. Friends had dared Peter, and he felt his honor and respect was at stake, so he consented.

He recounts his exploit in this way. "I stood there, frozen with fear, and when they said jump, not a muscle would move. I became noticeably more rigid as though all my muscles were saying, "No." I tried again with no better result. I wondered why I was fool enough to say I would do it. My mind kept repeating, "This is crazy. I'm a lunatic." Then out of sheer embarrassment, when they urged me to try again, I fell off the platform (jumped would be an overstatement) high above the river and, with the stoic belief that whatever will happen will happen, I plunged to my death, paralyzed by fear. I survived, but with the prayer uppermost on my lips, "May I never do this again!" Excitement was what it was supposed to be all about. I found none until it became a story worth telling and a notch in by belt of courage."

"I heard the screams of excitement as others plunged repeatedly into the canyon. They must be made a different way from me," he reported.

No doubt the screams of pleasure must have come from the ultimate pleasure-seekers — the SPs.

The SP is easily excited with the opportunities of the present. Its excitement stirs them deeply in a flash to either perform for the enjoyment of others or for the stimulation of their own senses, or both.

Joy is closely related and feeds the spirit. Easily excited, the SP finds joy that fades as quickly as it is inspired. They must find more joy constantly. So the SP majors in one of the main nutrients for the human spirit, thus dispersing such damaging mental conditions as sadness, gloom, and depression. The nemesis of the SJ is insecurity, but for the SP it is sadness, gloom, and depression. The SP is on a constant lifelong search for excitement and, as they age, memory helps fill in the gaps when excitement is not as easily found as when they were young.

An unhappy SP is unsuccessful in almost all he attempts. The strength of joy and excitement is essential in this temperament to provide motivation. Perseverance depends on an optimistic spirit, which in turn depends on the SP finding the excitement of the moment. To be their best they must be stirred by exciting opportunities.

Nonuse of this strength is certain to cause gloom and halt them on the path to success. It's like going without your food. Excitement drives them forward to success, fuels all their strengths and makes them agents of the impossible.

How Do I Develop this Strength?
• Not much instruction is needed for an SP!

• Catch the moment; accept the dare; make an impact.

171

- If you are an SP of a quieter model (maybe an introvert), you will want to concentrate on this strength to the extent that you feel comfortable. It is a strength, since it lifts the gloom that can settle on life and relieves the boredom of routines. The muted SP usually finds pleasure in more sedate activities (musical performances for example) and in more lasting goals.

- Excitement feeds the optimism and pleasantness of the SP. Continue the search for pleasure that truly feeds the human spirit.

Caution:
All temperaments lapse into weaknesses when they don't use their strengths, overuse them, or use them for destructive purposes such as damaging themselves or others. Here are further cautions for this strength.

- Excitement is not an end in life; it is a means to an end. This strength is a means of activating the other strengths in your arsenal and motivating them to action. Don't make it the goal of your life or you will have made the means, not the end, the goal.

- Use it to help you reach more lofty goals whose rewards last.

- Reward that fades as quickly as the moment passes has to be repeated constantly to keep rewarding you. Exciting events that have to be repeated too often soon lose their stimulating value. Repetition can then deplete your pleasure. However, each moment offers its treasures to the searching SP.

- Excitement is more of a food to ward off the sickness of sadness than a goal for life.

Wants To Make An Impact

SPs do not seek to be significant, but rather to be noticed. Significance is too abstract a concept. Leave that to the NFs. SPs crave a concrete experience that makes an impact in the world of things and people. This is why they crave the gold medal at the Olympics and the winner's stand at competitions. It makes an impact that can, in the case of the Olympics, be heard around the world!

SPs make their mark on the lives of others with their impressive use of their physical skills and senses. The SP artist is motivated more by the first place ribbon than by quiet praise or the approval of some fellow artist. First place makes an impact that is noticed and acclaimed. That's what matters. The greater the impact, the more it motivates.

The impact is in the present and, since they live in the present, we find them constantly endeavoring to impress. What is past is not satisfying today. They press on, ever alive and always performing.
This drive is the source of much achievement in the SP. Therefore, if you would succeed, the path is in making the biggest impact in whatever area of life you choose.

They seek to impress in performances of all kinds, from sports to drama and from fine arts to simply being the life of the party. In all their relationships, they continually try to make an impression unless they know they are trying in vain, in which case they search for someone else to impress. Beware, if you are married to an SP. The worst thing you can do if you wish to keep your relationship healthy is ignore their attempts to impress you. Acknowledge their skills and their performance, and they will return to you for your approval and praise again and again. It is to your advantage in the relationship.

SPs must have approval. Chris had performed as a good husband and thought he was doing more than most women should expect. He was generous and kind and had impressed their friends. Why wasn't Sharon, his wife, impressed? He tried harder and she gave him no feedback on his kindness, skills, generosity, and efforts at making an impact.

The high point for Chris in their marriage had been reached. To ask for praise wouldn't work. He didn't want it if he had to extract it from a non-participating source. Others, it seemed, were easy to impress and he felt paid back and important when other women showed their interest and approval.

Sharon became disturbed at his apparent interest in other women and tried getting his attention by giving him the cold shoulder. She thought she had become too easy and not a challenge any longer. They started talking about their disappointment in each other — their "incompatibility." Sharon was pessimistic about the future, and

173

Chris felt drawn to other opportunities in typical SP manner. Afraid of what she saw, Sharon came for help.

She learned that her temperament was that of an SJ who was focusing on doing her duty as a wife and not on giving feedback to her husband. Realizing that Chris needed her to notice and approve of his impact-making attempts at getting her attention and that he needed to feel she was indeed impressed was an eye-opener.

She admitted she was not responding but she didn't find it necessary to express her approval and admiration all the time. He, on the other hand, needed to impress her and hear that he was who he longed to be: a person who makes an impact in his relationships.

A sudden change occurred when Sharon went home and expressed her admiration for Chris and reacted gratefully to his next effort at impressing her. SPs bond to those they can impress and to those who express their admiration. Respond in a way that lifts the SP's self-image and they will find you essential to their day.

As children, and even as adults, SPs love to perform. Their lives are lived on a stage and are great performances for the world. The world loves its performers. It is just as well that it does or performers would be the saddest of people and turn to destructive exploits for excitement.

Overuse of wanting to impress can lead to a pride that predicts a fall. Watch for the subtle negative power of pride if you are an SP. The balance you need is a high self-esteem that stops short of thinking too much of yourself and that can be difficult to achieve for some.

It is far more impressive when others discover your good qualities without your help.
~ Judith Martin.

SPs must make an impact to be the best they can be. It is their path to greatness. We tend to discourage the SP who is struggling to make an impact when we should help them direct this strength in a positive direction.

SPs must not let this strength be despised. The world is always looking for the best performer — the best performance in anything. To be successful one has to make an impact. To be naturally gifted that way is to be fashioned for the winner's stand.

How Do I Develop this Strength?

- Perform! Make an impact! The use of a strength is the first thing you should pursue to develop a strength.

- Developing this strength is often a matter of training its skills.

- Those who make a career out of performing practice long hours. Persistence is the road to development.

- Perform to earn acclaim. Set your goal for the top.

- Learn that the deepest reward is in the quality of the performance, not in the acclaim, and you will become a better performer.

- Life is one great performance and the opportunities are endless, with many of them improving relationships and strengthening society as well.

Caution:

All temperaments lapse into weaknesses when they don't use their strengths, overuse them, or use them for destructive purposes such as damaging themselves or others. Here are further cautions for this strength.

- Those who perform in their relationships to impress and reward their partner or friends can best add the use of other strengths to their skills since people want more than entertainment to feed their relationships. Use other strengths of the SP temperament as well as the urge to make an impact.

- Perform for the good of others. Performances that degrade others ultimately degrade our own sense of worth as well.

- Remember, all strengths that are not used, over used, or used for destructive purposes become weaknesses. Weaknesses weaken.

Lighthearted — Playful — Tolerant

The human race has one really effective weapon, and that is laughter.
~ Mark Twain

It is the child in the man that is the source of his uniqueness and creativeness.
~ Eric Hoffer

Lighten up to light up. Happy people lighten their hearts with optimism and faith.
The flame of our positive beliefs ignite the fire of happiness in others.
~ Ray W. Lincoln

This makes the SP very attractive and pleasant to know. Life is not taken too seriously by the SP. Parties and adventures may top their list of appealing activities in teenage, and some go to college and suffer the discipline of study because of all they have heard about the parties. The academic activity is often secondary to this innate drive. "Where in academic studies is there pleasure comparable to the fun of parties," they ask?

SPs are always all there, in the present moment, enjoying the excitement and the stimulation. This feeds the lighthearted nature of the SP.

We may have glimpsed this lightheartedness lying behind other strengths of the SP and it serves them well. They should not be taught to be more serious. That is the opposite of the strength and is not likely to take root. Seriousness, the hallmark of the SJ, is a poison to the SP.

Along with this lighthearted attitude goes a tolerance of others and a readiness to welcome all things new. New ideologies and new ways of doing things are tolerated without being judgmental or using a critical voice. Their wide range of tolerance for differences makes them less likely to tolerate dogmatism.

The SP uses this strength best when they include wisdom and thoughtfulness, not seriousness. All strengths can be overused and then they become weaknesses. An SP who has lost his playfulness is open to all kinds of depressive pressures.

This is not a strength that leads the SP directly to be the best that they can be. It is supportive of other strengths and keeps the SP fresh and vital. Develop it for these reasons.

How Do I Develop this Strength?

• Use it with ever present optimism.

• Use it with positive beliefs devoid of worry and concern. The more positive the belief, the lighter our hearts.

• Play is not wasted time. It is renewal and refreshment. Create a balance between refreshment and work.

• Don't try to be more serious. Create a balance between showing concern and encouraging the depressed to find happier activities.

• Lightheartedness lives most comfortably in a mind that is full of faith and hope, both of which should breed optimism.

Caution

All temperaments lapse into weaknesses when they don't use their strengths, overuse them, or use them for destructive purposes such as damaging themselves or others. Here are further cautions for this strength.

• Make sure to learn the rewards of living in some of your other strengths, and their rewards will keep you lighthearted in your work and in the use of your skills.

• Don't fail to realize that true happiness is born in our positive beliefs. The positive beliefs of spiritual faith are an example.

• Always hope and your heart will be light.

Ultimate Optimist

Perpetual optimism is a force multiplier.
~ Colin Powell

177

Few things in the world are more powerful than a positive push. A smile, a word of
optimism and hope, a "you can do it" when things are tough.
~ Richard M. DeVos

The optimistic SPs stand in contrast to the SJs who fall into pessimism. Optimism characterizes their spirit, life, and talk. The present moment is their world, and the passion they generate in the moment can return to feed this buoyant spirit even more.

Optimism for the SP is a belief that produces an attitude. It's a way of seeing their world. It is not a hope built on future possibilities but a conviction of a plentiful beneficent world.

They move with ease from worrisome concerns to enjoyment and fun in a flash! However, if confined and regulated, they can lose their lightheartedness — also in a flash. Freedom and activity are some of their native urges, and they don't want to give these up and lose their lightheartedness in the bargain. Confinement is hard for anyone to endure and maintain optimism. Solitary confinement as a punishment brings out the worst in SPs, not the best. It is hell to them.

Depression is unlikely in their atmosphere of positivism. This strength is clearly beneficial and healthy since we operate best when we are positive.

Many of life's disappointments and troubles are viewed by the SP with a detachment that makes it hard for worry to depress them. Optimism also encourages faith. The SP often confuses optimism with faith. Optimism is an attitude while faith is a belief. Both can appear and be seen to be the same, but faith is really matured optimism. Faith is rooted in a deep conviction, a precise goal, and a firm commitment to that goal. Optimism is its seed.

Marie complained that her daughter was not concerned enough about the possible downside of the economy. "She seems to have no idea of what could happen. She doesn't save enough (to Marie, that meant she doesn't save like me), and she doesn't worry about it." Did Marie mean that worrying was a sign of concern and that it was helpful?

Her daughter was healthily detached from the concerns that she could not control and was making good strides in preparing for troubling times, but Marie found her optimism disturbing. All pessimists are troubled by the attitudes of optimists. Marie was wearing her daughter down, and her daughter texted her more and called her less. Marie was also finding (in her words) "a need to disconnect from her irresponsible daughter."

This kind of attempt to change an SP backfires since the climate of another temperament is being forced on them.

Pessimism also wants to disconnect from optimism since optimism threatens the sad comfort of the pessimist. Optimism calls for a detachment from people who are fed by negative attitudes that threaten the very existence of happiness. Pessimists and optimists live at the opposite ends of the street, produce opposite chemicals in their brains, and decide differently about almost all of life's issues. When a mother and daughter live these opposite lifestyles it is hard on both.

Faith in themselves is almost a given for the SP and endows them with loads of confidence. Confidence disturbs the pessimist too.

Confidence born of optimism shows that the strength of optimism has been developed. Self-esteem swings up with optimism and down with pessimism. SPs can be wonderful encouragers of others, leading others to believe in themselves, if the SP chooses to get involved and pay the price of close contact. Their leadership is often assured because of their ability to encourage and maintain an upbeat spirit. It is an unenlightened leader that appoints a pessimist as a leader.

SPs are not usually financial wizards but, if they venture on Wall Street, they tend to be strongly bullish. The excitement presented by a risky gamble is more than some of them can resist. A positive view on life is a necessity for all of us, so we can all do well to make this a strong secondary strength if we are of another temperament. It will protect the integrity of all native strengths too.

The weaknesses of this strength — over confidence, rash judgment, and failing to see what could be damaging — are all an overuse of the strength.

Optimism is a supportive strength like the previous strength of lightheartedness, playfulness, and tolerance. On its own it will seldom lead to success.   Develop it for its valuable support of all other strengths in the SP.

How Do I Develop this Strength?

• Find and maintain positive beliefs. If you are down on yourself, others, and the world, you will likely lose your optimism.

• Don't dwell on the negative. Dwelling on something magnifies it.

• Protect your freedoms. Optimism is healthy in wisely-used freedoms.

• Be positive at least 51 percent of the time — ppreferably 90 percent of the time.

• Detach from all negative influences and negative talk.

• Indulge in positive self talk.

• Don't spend too much time with pessimists.

• Believe in yourself because you do have reason to do so. Find the reasons.

• Belief in a divine helper has been researched and found to increase the likelihood of a healthy optimism.

• Be confident. Look everyone in the eye and say to yourself, "I am at least as good as they are."

• Keep your self-esteem high. Thank people for their positive comments about you and your actions.

• Encourage others. When we do so we feel an immediate reward internally, and our self-esteem is built as we build the self-esteem of others.

Caution:

All temperaments lapse into weaknesses when they don't use their strengths, overuse them, or use them for destructive purposes such as damaging themselves or others.   Here are further cautions for this strength.

- Overconfidence results in rash decisions.

- Even when confident, live within the limits of good reason and submit your decisions to rational judgment.

Action!

An ounce of action is worth a ton of theory.
~ Friedrich Engels (German socialist and economist)

We often think of the SP as occupied with fast physical action, such as in sports. However, all action — from the surgeon's skillful use of computer technologies or a fine scalpel and the child's speed of the minute movements needed to control a video game to driving large machinery — all are actions that can rivet an SP. The use of weaponry, dramatic performances, dancing, art in all its forms, the skills of a hands-on trade, security careers — are all examples of what might give an SP opportunity to use this strength.

If an ounce of action is worth a ton of theory, an SP is very valuable to society indeed. Anything that keeps them moving can fulfill and excite them. They find it hard to sit still and concentrate on mental activities since physical action is missing. (Reread the story of Tony in the first strength, "Living in the Present Moment.") Not that SPs can't be skilled with their minds; they are as intellectually bright as any other, but they find activity more to their liking and use the mind to decipher the nuances of their movements. Activity stimulates pleasurable feelings in the body and is a form of excitement that the SP takes notice of.

Reading, studying, conceptualizing, or the fulfillment of mental insights are less rewarding to the SP and can go unnoticed. A mental flow of energy that is contained within the mind and is not destined for physical action (such as day dreaming) is not on their want list.

Little Max was an SP who couldn't sit still — one of many. When he did sit motionless, any slight movement got his attention and initiated an immediate response. The teacher punished, warned, cajoled, coaxed, plead, threatened, and gave poor grades — all in the hopeful belief that she would one day hit on the magic solution and Max would become a responsible student.

Max didn't. She did not understand that Max couldn't. He was constantly wriggling and making faces, and the punishments brought him comments from his classmates that encouraged him. Even when his friends applauded the teacher for catching him in some mischievous plot, he was stimulated by the attention it got him and the impact he had made.

The teacher decided that nothing was working and that perhaps she should learn from him. She saw Max as her teacher, offering her valuable lessons. By studying his actions and taking them at face value, she saw that he was not being obnoxious but was driven by urges to be in constant motion. Becoming the student, she learned what was causing Max to be disruptive and assigned him to active tasks and to active hands-on learning. He responded. This is what he was on the inside, and action calmed his mind as it stimulated his body.

Adults need to become the student too. SP friends will be valued and not castigated for their need to move. Action will be seen as a strength that gives context to their meaning in life.

Movement keeps boredom at bay. When SPs must live focused on the fleeting moment, a lack of activity in that moment causes their optimism to fade. If there is no activity offered by the present moment, then to keep them positive they need to find or create some kind of activity. SPs are constantly on the lookout for what feeds their positive spirits because boredom demotivates them and causes them to become nonproductive. Success, for an SP, requires that boredom be kept under lock and key.

Action is also tied to the constant hunger for happiness and stimulation. Keep stimulated, and the flow of sensations will increase the production of endorphins and create more positive attitudes.

Note: Many physical activities produce changes to our attitudes and clean the muddied state of our minds. For the SP, activity is an important means to an end. Have you noticed how SPs take to the gym and the ski slope and thrive when they are given active physical tasks to do? Activity helps keep them mentally bright.

Action contains a major secret of success for the SP. Whatever they set as their goals should, in some way, involve action.

Nonuse of this strength leads to depression. An SP who can't be active is robbed of one of their main sources of refreshment. Overuse can lead to trouble with others at times, and the wrong use can cause them to be introduced to the authorities. Keep them away from these destroyers of true pleasure! Keep them positive, happy, and moving.

How Do I Develop this Strength?
- Not much needs to be said about how to develop action. Choose activities that satisfy.

- If the SP is depressed (an unlikely event for the SP), get them active and keep them active. They will soon find what they love.

- If you are developing this strength in an SP child, join them and model for them the fun and thrill of action.

Caution:
All temperaments lapse into weaknesses when they don't use their strengths, overuse them, or use them for destructive purposes such as damaging themselves or others. Here are further cautions for this strength.

- Learn the sedative effect of quiet times.

- Learn a mental game for calming purposes.

- Curb the constant use of activity. Teach the SP to appreciate the creative arts, like painting and music which SPs can also enjoy.

A Focus On the Physical Senses — Graceful

Although we have mentioned their physical abilities many times, their gracefulness is worth special focus. The SPs physical movements are usually graceful and well coordinated. They even walk gracefully. Their bodily senses are keenly alive. The rhythm of movement and the synchronism of coordinating movements creates subtle enjoyment for them.

Rhythm is an element in gracefulness and dance. It plays important roles in music, cycling, sports, games, and the arts. All are a training ground for the healthy development of an SP's physical skills. For the SP, physical sensations capture most of life's thrills, and there is a special payback for being graceful.

We can calm or excite our spirits by physical movement. Both the body and the spirit are inseparable in this life, influencing each other. The SP emphasizes the body, while the NF emphasizes the spirit. Each sees motivation deriving from a different source. When the body becomes an obsession, emphasizing the mind and the inner life can bring life back to balance and vice versa.

SPs seldom move without a purpose. The purpose is often to offset boredom or attract attention.

The word "grace" comes from the Latin *gratia*, something that is charming, favorable. People have always had words that represent charm and favor in their languages, and that is natural since charm is a quality that gives to life some of its needed pleasure.

A goal for the SP can be all about obtaining grace and teaching others to develop the same. Dance instructors make a livelihood out of teaching gracefulness. If your goal or dream is to be achieved by the use and development of this strength, make sure you become the best and achieve your highest potential.

The nonuse of this strength seems to create more weakness than overuse. Of course, as for most strengths, the wrong use will create a weakness and possible damage too. Use the strength as it was designed to be used to lift your spirit without damage to yourself or others.

How Do I Develop this Strength?
• See the suggestions under "Action."

• Develop grace in all actions.

184

- Coordination is a developed art, and SPs can practice it with benefit to enhance their physical dexterity.

Caution:
All temperaments lapse into weaknesses when they don't use their strengths, overuse them, or use them for destructive purposes such as damaging themselves or others. Here are further cautions for this strength.

- Develop this strength with a distinct purpose for its use. Without purpose, the strength can become an obsession that lives without direction. No strength satisfies for long without a purpose.

Generous Nature

In dwelling, live close to the ground.
In thinking, keep to the simple.
In conflict, be fair and generous.
In governing, don't try to control.
In work, do what you enjoy.
In family life, be completely present.
~ To Te Ching

An easy-come-easy-go attitude contributes to the generosity and kindness of the SP. Since in the confirmed SP not a moment's thought is wasted on saving things for the rainy day, they can give generously of what they have and of what they promise they will have. Saving for a rainy day only robs the present of its possible and pleasurable resources.

Giving things away to someone in need makes real sense to the optimist who sees more coming anyway. "We should all share" is the SP's point of view, and the feeling has developed into a philosophy that suggests that what anyone has should be shared with others.

SPs can give more generously of their money and possessions than their time. If the gift of time inhibits the excitement of the moment, they may not be generous. This is not to say they are self-centered. They can be seriously focused on the needs of others and refuse the gift of the present moment. Their protection of their own pleasure is more like the inflight instruction "Put the oxygen mask on yourself first, then on your child."

Tom was very generous toward his wife.   He would bring home little gifts and occasionally splurge on some excessive luxury, receiving great pleasure when she thanked him dramatically.

His wife became expectant of his generous nature and one day asked for him to forego his golf game and go with her because she was going to receive an award at her writing class. He refused without comment and did so in what seemed to her like record time. She expressed her disappointment and he promptly picked up his clubs and headed for the course. She was now mad at him, her expectations being dashed.

Tom's golf round was his time. He would give her almost anything but not his time for active excitement. Who was right? Both needed understanding of the other. Both needed respect for each other's inner demands. Tom's wife learned that his generous nature was still in tact and ready, but his time and his activity were his need and it conflicted with hers. Tom learned that his wife was an NF whose feelings were hurt and whose expectations he had aroused and now denied. Both came to a respect for each other, and the relationship went on to new and better things.

The motive for generosity differs with the temperaments. In the SP there is a strong desire to bring pleasure and attract attention at the same time and, since they hold their possessions lightly, they use them for making the all-important impression. So free are they with what they have that they earn the name of the "generous temperament."

Motives must be kept pure or generosity can sour.

He loved the applause and the attention, and when it came to giving his friend some generous gift he would wait until he had an audience to play to. When the moment was right and the dramatic stage was set, Lance would call the attention of those gathered and, with flare and pomp, present his lavish gift to his friend. The crowd would gasp and he would bow acceptingly to the crowd for their applause. The moment had fulfilled his craving for attention.

Can you imagine the surprise when one day his friend threw the expensive gift at him and stormed out in tears. His gift rejected, his audience in shock, and his mind reeling, he dashed after her to no avail. She had been deeply wounded by his self-glorifying displays, and the relationship was over for good.

Overuse of this strength is encountered in SPs, and nonuse of this strength is seldom found.

An SP who uses the strength of generosity with little thought or care has been known to give away someone else's time or treasure and feel fulfilled and happy and without guilt.

Generosity is also a supportive strength on the road to the SP's best.

How Do I Develop this Strength?
- Generosity is best encouraged by feeling love or concern for the person. Positive warming beliefs or thoughts can also help.

- Focusing on others saves us from self-centeredness. Wherever our focus is, our interest and love are also located.

- Kindness is love in action and kindness encourages generosity.

- You may notice generosity is a dependent strength. It must have love or concern or some other interest to spark it.

Caution:
All temperaments lapse into weaknesses when they don't use their strengths, overuse them, or use them for destructive purposes such as damaging themselves or others. Here are further cautions for this strength.

- Generosity can be used for selfish purposes: either to boost our ego or gain some selfish result, in which case it loses its purity of motive. It then becomes something else.

- Keep your generosity pure in motive and it will not bring condemnation with it.

- Some people are generous and make a display of their generosity to receive the praise and admiration of others. This, too, distorts the purity of motive.

Dramatic, Concrete Language

Being easily excitable, they probe language for its exciting phrases. Since they are firmly rooted in the real world with the use of their five physical senses, they use its concrete expressions and generally avoid abstract language or discussions of a theoretical nature.

These two characteristics can add up to colorful, vivid language and, at times, inappropriate language in the quest for attention or for making an impact.

A Joy to Live With

All temperaments are wonderful but can have their challenges because their strengths can be used for wrong and damaging purposes. For the most part, the SP is a pleasure to live with and a joy to parent if you don't try to make them into SJs.

The ISFP and the ISTP are muted versions of the above descriptions and appear less dramatic.

If you are an SP, I hope you have chosen a strength already and determined to develop it. Even if you are not an SP you will have sharpened your understanding of your own temperament by the contrast to the SP.

A Convenient List of the SP Temperament's Strengths

Here is a convenient list of the SP temperament's main strengths that we dealt with.

Keep a list with you and develop them one at a time:

- First, focus on being aware of when you are using your strengths.
- Then, with practice and persistence, develop them.
- Training develops them even more and will help you understand them as you discover ways to further their use.

SP Strengths Featuring Self Expression

Lives happily in the present moment

Brave, bold, daring

Spontaneous, impulsive

Effective, tactical, aggressive

Easily excited

Wants to make an impact

Lighthearted, playful, tolerant

Ultimate optimist

Action!

A focus on the physical senses — graceful

Generous nature

Dramatic, concrete language

189

SJ Strengths — Featuring Rules and Regulations

All strengths, to some degree, may be found in any temperament. The following strengths are native to the SJ and are found with greater intensity in the SJ temperament. These are the core strengths at which an SJ naturally excels if they take the time and effort to develop them.

The path to success for each of us is written in our strengths. Here, for the SJ, you will find that path.

The strengths are not set out in any particular order, nor do they have to be understood or practiced in a set order.

Take any of the strengths of your temperament one at a time and develop it until you:
• Are aware of when you use it and when you don't
• Have developed it as best you can
• Feel ready to go on to the next

To help you develop your strengths, a convenient "how to" list is at the end of the discussion of each strength. You might copy it and take it with you as you get used to operating your strengths.

Lives Tied to the Past
(Orientation To Time)

I spent most of my life in the past, so I lean toward living there.
~ An unknown SJ.

Those who cannot remember the past are condemned to repeat it.
~ George Santayana. (Spanish-born philosopher)

Even God cannot change the past.
~ Agathon (400 BC)

The past is certain, the future obscure.
~ Thales (635-543 BC)

The past is what guides and fashions an SJ's life. They live backing into the future with their eyes firmly glued on their experiences and those of others they trust. Phrases such as "You learn from the past," "Doesn't your experience tell you something?" and "You can trust your experiences" are supportive and defensive of this strength, which in the SJ can be very strong.

The correct definition of this time orientation as a strength is "living in the guidance of the past." (Not living "in the past" as though that is a good place to live.) All SJs must live in the present. Living in the guidance of the past is living in the present with a focus on the lessons and experiences of the past and without having them freeze, control or be the dominant influences that molds us.

Moving from the SP's world of the present to the SJ's world of the past sets both in stark contrast. These are lifestyles and drives that are opposite to each other. The SP's preference for living in the present and the SJ's preference for living in the past make a comfortable fusion of each other's lives very difficult. They are constantly at war over whether it is best to live in the present or the past, both thinking the other is crazy to live the way they do.

All that SJs do is guided by the past, even their planning for the future, and they feel confident only when they are repeating the past or maybe modifying it a little. Trusting in change when it hasn't established itself yet is risky and, for many SJs, simply plain foolish. They want someone else to make the change and document its safety and success before they feel comfortable in accepting it. SJs are uneasy about words that describe risk, like chance, gamble, venture, dare, and speculate. They shake at words like chaos, anarchy, mob rule, and disorder. The SP approaches these words with tactical skill and a solid belief in themselves.

How could it be easy to change when you are guided by the past? As we will see, many of the SJ's strengths are fueled by this relationship to time: strengths such as caution, reliability, being prepared, stability, and living in reality.

The J and P preferences in the SP and SJ need to be modified if relationships are going to be successful. Marriages can fall apart on this count alone. If the preferences are strong, the dichotomy can disrupt even the simple matters of timeliness, desire to complete tasks, decision making, and many other issues.

The conflict between SP and SJ is seen in all occupations. Politicians, philosophers, scientists, psychologists, psychiatrists, and teachers are affected by it as much as the average working person, and yet they often claim not to be affected while at the same time giving evidence that they don't understand each other.

No educator or politician or philosopher or anyone can claim to be entirely fair and nonpartisan when it comes to temperament, especially these two temperaments. Perhaps all educators should be required to take a course in appreciating all four temperaments and valuing their point of view.

Wisdom in understanding the "real you" is to accept that all four temperaments are wonderful and make sense within their own preferred way of doing things and to learn to respect each other. Become a student of yourself and see yourself with the eyes of the other temperaments too, not just your own.

Some homes contain all temperaments. Imagine this home. The oldest child, age 11, is an SJ who has been easy to manage but is guided by the way things have always been done and feels it is her responsibility to control the others. She tries.

Because she lives in the past and values the established way of doing things, she cannot stand the attitudes of two other siblings in particular.

Her brother, age 9, is an SP and he is not at all impressed with the established way of doing things. Freedom is his cry and he lives in the present. "I want to do it my way. Why can't I?" he argues. He tactically undermines her in an attempt to get even because he feels he is being restricted and controlled. You can't control an SP and have peace.

At seven-and-a-half, a younger sister is an NT and is calm, cool, and thinks all her siblings are not as bright as she is. To her way of seeing the world, they show evidence of it. She is wrapped up with her projects and pays attention to past present and future only if her project calls for it. She spends time collecting insects and reading and refuses to follow the traditions or accepted way of doing things since she has to feel independent. Mostly, the old ways don't make sense to her. There has to be a better way of doing things and she is born to show them that better way. Her chores are done her way, which she explains is a better way of doing things. Don't try to force her to do it your way. She hates to be cuddled. Mom says she should have been a boy.

The youngest brother is an NF and lives in the future. He is very emotional, trying to keep harmony and, most of the time, losing his temper in anger, withdrawing and refusing to cooperate when hurt. He can be very loving and cooperative or very angry and stubborn and, as a result, he is very unpredictable. He is five years old and, perhaps, the hardest to handle. The future is what interests his imaginative mind that is filled with fantasy.

With four different orientations to time, this home is leaning in all directions, and each is determined they must do it his or her way since there beats inside of each of them an urge to follow their own inner drives.

When they understand that each temperament has a valid way of responding to time — valid in their eyes — each can begin to learn the needs of the other.

Understanding gives validity to all people and sets our own choices in the fuller context of society. We then can better see ourselves as others see us. We can also stop claiming that we practice the only wise way of living.

Plato, as I have mentioned before, was smart enough in his book, *The Republic*, to see this and to envision a society with all temperaments making their own valued contributions. The first volume of *Please Understand Me* (by Keirsey and Bates) also sets out to make us aware of this crying need. Everyone should read it.

The SJ's inner urges, directed by their dependence on the past, hold many valid lessons to be learned, which can be carried with us into the future to make the future less problematical. The SJ understands and believes this with a passion. They fear the future when troubled and hold even more tenaciously to their doctrine of reliance on past experiences.

The past is a great repository of knowledge. Because of the convoluted way we humans make our decisions, it often flags us of the unexpected ways people react. It helps us prepare, but the word "help" is the operative word and should not be used to mean we must act as it suggests.

The danger of this orientation to past time is that the SJ can easily become enmeshed in the past and display reticence to change. They will even tell you they feel imprisoned by it at times. When this happens, they make little progress as they solidify the rules for their behavior and make even more rules to secure those.

For the SJ to be the best they can be they must walk the fine line between valuing and learning from the past and walking free of its constraints. They must condition themselves to welcome change and face it with confidence in their ability to manage what needs to be managed and accept what can't.

To develop this strength and not have it control them, they need to be aware of how it holds them back and slows them down. This leaning toward caution makes them feel more secure, of course, but not without costing the loss of progress at times.

How Do I Develop this Strength?

By first appreciating and believing in its values. Here is a reminder of its values:

- It is intelligent to learn from our past. Not to do so is to invite failure to keep reoccurring.

- Doing things the way they have always been done brings a feeling of security and SJs can't live happily without security.

- Doing things the way they are supposed to be done helps us live cooperatively with others in society.

- Society needs structure to keep it functioning smoothly and surely the past is a solid structure on which we can build our routines.

- Routines are the expeditors of systems and systems have proved invaluable in keeping chaos at bay.

- Hasn't society functioned well with commandments or laws to guide it? Don't we all need guidance?

- Who would not want to live without the boundaries of the past leading us safely into the future?

These values, to the SJ, will help them remember why we need our past and will solidify their belief in the strength we call "living in the guidance of the past." Here's how to develop this strength:

- By listening to your past and the past of those you trust.

- By examining its lessons and learning from them.

- By incorporating into your definition of wisdom what the past can teach you.

- By questioning change but not resisting it per se.

- By developing a set way of doing things but always remaining open to changing those ways for the better.

- By incorporating change in small steps and inspecting the results.

Caution:

All temperaments lapse into weaknesses when they don't use their strengths, overuse them, or use them for destructive purposes such as damaging themselves or others. Here are further cautions for this strength.

- To follow the past slavishly is to discount all innovation. How can that be good for society? Slavishly following the past is not progressive. Educate your drive at this point.

- Change becomes very difficult since it challenges the feelings of security. Who can believe a new way of doing things is going to be safe and even better if you worship security?

- The future is the future, unknown and scary for that reason. Change is inevitable as the future invades, and SJs must believe in their ability to supervise, inspect, and control change to allow its progress, but at a pace they can accept.

- Control of others is never absolute, nor should it be. Control of others can and does destroy liberties and where it has been practiced it has usually had this result. Educate and modify your drive to always do things the way they have been done, but don't give in to complete freedom because if you do your world will shake.

- Life is risk. Trying to eliminate risk is impossible and unrealistic. Accept the necessity to live with risk and make sure you develop a strong faith to enable you to do this.

- Be careful not to adopt an impossible goal. Failure waits if you do. Time may make it an appropriate goal.

It seems to be best for the SJ to reap the benefits of the past while keeping themselves open to the opportunities and innovations of the future, evaluating them and moving ahead with calculated risk.

This strength is not an unmixed blessing. Use it wisely and in an educated manner.

Careful — Cautious — Concerned

The cautious seldom err.
~ Confucius

Some of these quotations should make you smile. All of them contain a degree of error.

The definition of caution as a strength is: The positive evaluation of the next move to assure its safety and wisdom. It is not refusing to move forward where there is danger and risk. It is not evaluating the situation with negative concern either.

Caution is a strength that you will observe in the mood of the SJ as well as in their actions. Because they are cautious, they are focused more on details.

Because SJs want to always be in touch with reality and reality *is* in the details, they will tell you that you need to be very cautious since they have found "the devil in the details." (Why not "angels" in the details? Why does it always have to be the devil — the negative?). Caution in this case has bred a pessimistic attitude. Whenever the SJ sees only the dark possibilities, they have defined themselves as pessimistic. By the way, God claims to be in the details too! There is nothing wrong with paying close attention to the details. The problem emerges when the details are approached with a negative attitude.

Caution is cousin to carefulness and both can give birth to concern. What concern turns out to be is a matter of our own choices displayed in our attitudes. Concern is not necessarily a negative emotion. It can be, and in the SJ it is a negative emotion more often than they are willing to admit. We can be concerned while hope is filling our vision, or concerned while not allowing hope a chance to surface.

Life was miserable. In Amber's words, "It felt like I had been sick forever. Two years ago my husband sent me to a fellow psychiatrist for help with depression. The medications helped marginally but didn't cure anything. It's a long story, but I left my family and moved into a house of my own. My children wondered why I didn't care for myself any longer — or for them — and my previous interests held no pleasure for me."

She came for help as a result of a friend's persistence, and her temperament was assessed as an SJ. Amber had been obsessing over the details of her relationship, as SJs can, and became over-sensitized to her husband's many lapses in attention and his changed attitude toward her. He, in turn, was obsessed with his patients and their health needs and she had become depressed over the obvious loss of love his inattention had developed between them.

Sadly, she interpreted everything as a burgeoning negative in their relationship caused by her own lack of worth to him. Always cautious and concerned, she slid into deep depression fast as she lost self-esteem and everything seemed colored in the darkest tones of pessimism. She was convinced she had to be unattractive and uninteresting and her negative evaluation of her husband's behavior confirmed it to her. She had lost all feelings of self-worth and was quite unable to reverse her extreme negativism. In a desperate grab for relief from all the inner pain, she moved out.

Slowly, with intensive help, she was reintroduced to who she was and the clouds thinned as she understood where all this was coming from. She realized for the first time what her strengths were. As she timidly used them and focused on them instead of focusing on her pessimistic conclusions, the sun peeked through the clouds and, before she knew it, a touch of joy returned. Her cautious attitude returned to a healthy concern. Her interests were encouraged and revived.

First, her children joined her excitement. Then her husband, realizing his part in her decline, reentered her life, and the word "normal" felt like the word "heaven" because she could again look at the details and see both the good and bad possibilities in them, emphasizing the good ones. She packed up and returned home.

When SJs focus on the details and interpret them pessimistically, they can fall quickly, losing all faith and hope in themselves. This has to be understood and they must climb into the healthy use of their strengths, not just try to eliminate the negativity. The wrong focus blocks the return to their strengths. The return journey is just the opposite experience of the fall.

Care has always had a wide range of meaning. From ancient Greek times it could mean taking care of or providing for someone or all the way to an anxious state of fear, just like the English word can and often does mean. Care can be negative or positive, a weakness or a strength. It is either according to a state of mind.

When showing care, the SJ must be cautioned to remain positive or they will fall quickly into the weakness of negativity. Some have mastered it; some have not. This drive of our *innerkinetics* must remain positive!

The Greeks put two words together and came up with *promerimnao*, which means to be anxious beforehand — the feeling you have in the dentist's waiting room. To be negative beforehand shuts out hope and, although the dentist's office may be the last place that you use to master a positive concern, we should practice it always.

Have you noticed the meaning of the word obsession when waiting in the dentist's office? Thoughts can overwhelm your feelings and even panic can threaten at times like these. When the mind turns abruptly from being positive to becoming negative, the ride can be fast and turbulent, as it was with Amber.

The SJs are social beings, protecting social traditions and seeking to increase their value to people. We need their care and concern. Life would degrade into each one for himself if we devalued it.

The SJ is not out for fun simply for fun's sake, though. There is always a serious note in their concern since it leads them to help take care of others, and when their duties are done, then they try to relax and have some downtime pleasure.

Because they are focused on the past, they are more afraid of the future and cautious of how they enter it by the moment. Cautiousness also causes them to establish rules and regulations to protect the downside. What is, is known. What is not is unknown, so the fear of the unknown stimulates their cautiousness and dominates their lives.

Cautiousness leads to a hypersensitive conservatism, which often strongly resists change — not because the new idea is not worthy but because it means doing things differently. That, to the SJ, is a challenge and a road paved with possible traps. "Please don't take risks. Life is trouble enough!" they urge in their attempt to control things.

Care, caution, and concern lead also to a somber attitude, often interpreted as a super seriousness toward life that makes for a clear distinction from the SP's pleasure-loving, in-the-moment mood.

Overuse of this strength is the main cause of weakness in an SJ. Fear (which is a critical attitude), together with social rejection, can result from the overuse of caution.

Caution is a strength that teeters on the edge of pessimism and climbs the hill of success only when it does not destroy itself. Therefore, it is most difficult to control as you try to develop it.

Development of this strength is a matter of remaining positive while cautious. For the SJ, "positive" does not mean "optimistic at all times" (like the SP). To ask that would be to ask the SJ to turn into an SP, which is counterproductive and a false goal. Positive, for the SJ, should be defined as being fully realistic. Realistic is looking with at least equal time and effort at the positive alternatives and possibilities as they do at the negative ones and then choosing the positive over the negative.

To develop caution as a valuable strength, the SJ needs to lean toward being positive with faith and hope, which assures the SJ of a realistic faith. They need to proceed with this positive caution.

How Do I Develop this Strength?

If you are an SP or an NT, you may be saying why would I want to? However, if you are an SJ you will likely side with caution as a necessary value. An SJ must proceed cautiously or they can become jittery. So, as an SJ, how do I develop this strength?

- Positively! Don't miss the silver lining in the clouds.

- Cautiously! Caution almost demands a pause.

- Caution is not to be overdone. The overuse of a strength develops a weakness and with this strength we can arrive at the point of overuse quickly.

- Caution comes naturally to the SJ. It is the way their inner spirit breathes. Even an SJ child can be quickly coaxed to be cautious.

Caution:

All temperaments lapse into weaknesses when they don't use their strengths, overuse them, or use them for destructive purposes such as damaging themselves or others.   Here are further cautions for this strength.

- Great care should be directed to the proper use of caution. Caution is a flag and a low gear for the rough terrain of life. It should not become the fixed wheel gear of one of those bicycles from a long past era of transportation. Release its brake on life whenever caution turns to negative attitudes.

- Too much caution often leads to the tipping point of depression.

- Concern needs hope to keep it healthy. SJs need an extra daily dose of hope. Hope is the formula for SJ vitamins.

Thoughtful and Prepared

Think like a man of action, act like a man of thought.
~ Henri Bergson (French author and philosopher)

In the field of observation, chance favors the prepared mind.
~ Louis Pasteur

The definition of thoughtful as a strength or drive in the SJ's *innerkinetics* is: thinking carefully through the logistics of a matter in preparation for planning or as part of planning. It is not thinking theoretically about the abstract ideas that surround the facts.

The SJ is a planner. Planning brings them a sense of control and security. If you plan, you have at least walked through the possibility with your eye fixed on the details and details bring any idea down to earth. SJs have their feet solidly on the ground. Planning is advocated by SJs with confidence since it makes sense of life and breaks each issue down into orderly steps. If you are concerned about possible problems raising their heads and causing havoc to your goals, planning is a safe and prudent measure.

"Do I prepare? Of course I do. What do you mean?" This was the outburst of a typical SJ to the question "Do you prefer to plan ahead for a vacation or decide as you go?"

As I was being introduced to a man, the conversation turned quickly to his vacation.

Me: *Oh, so you are leaving tomorrow?*
Wayne: *Yes.*
Me: *How long will you be away?*
Wayne: *Oh, about two weeks.*
Me: *Where are you going?*
Wayne: *Don't know.*
Me: *Which direction will you head out?*
Wayne: *I really don't know.*
Me: *I guess you are packed already*
Wayne: *Nope.*

Now that's an SP, not an SJ! An SJ simply can't fathom what is going on in a mind like that. No good thing can come of such irresponsible use of time, they think (if they don't blurt it out).

If the SJ does not plan on paper or in their time management system, they plan in their heads. Most can't go to bed without knowing what is happening the next day and when.

To be prepared the SJ needs to plan. They seldom go to college just to get educated or prepare for something. They go to train for a specific goal. Preparation, for the SJ, is preparing with a goal in mind. For the SP, preparing or planning does not make the same sense since they know the excitement of the day is usually found in the unexpected things that happen. "Why plan them out of your life?" they ask. When you plan you often limit the opportunity for unexpected things to happen. At least the spontaneity and creativity of the moment and impulse is restricted as a result. So the SJ says, "That's what I want to do. I will be creative by my planning and I don't want the disturbance that spontaneity and impulse can create. I will plan the troubles out of my life."

So the SJ and the SP see life differently and, therefore, preparation and pre-thought for the SP is seen as hindering the meaning of life, while for the SJ it enhances the possibility that all will go well, problems will be averted, and happiness will be found.

The SJ continues on course, determined to control his world as much as possible. This is a protective strength.

Their mind operates logistically and step-by-step plans are the favored method. When you think step-by-step, details are seldom missed. Scientific method makes use of the SJ's concern. Reductionist thinking that guides the modern scientific method digs ever deeper to find more detail, believing that in the minute details they discover more "truth." For the SJ, this method of not letting a detail go unnoticed has the effect of making life seem more secure and certain and that is their driving interest.

They often want to know what is happening next in order to be prepared. They feel more comfortable when they are prepared. Again, note that the feeling of comfort comes from the effort to control one's circumstances. For the SJ, it is almost the same feeling as control. They feel comfortable when they have a measure of control and they feel as though things are in control if they feel comfortable.

Returning to planning, it is what offsets their fear of the future in their normal mode of living. Planning is not theorizing or strategizing; it is the formation of a logical step-by-step plan discovered by the question "What do I do next?" Their plan is implemented by the belief that one must follow the directions and do so in the right order.

At times, even the extroverted SJs will look like introverts in their somber planning moments. Being prepared is serious business. They know life is risky and risk is not to be faced without a plan and careful (there's that word again) forethought. Notice that, as in the SP, all the initial strengths are interwoven and support or help each other. *Innerkinetics* is a harmonious package of drives that move us forward with clear purpose and direction.

The SP cannot understand why you would want to plan so much. "Let it happen and release the thrill of the unexpected," is their cry. The difference of these two temperaments can hardly be overstated. Each is right according to his own goals for life.

Over-preparation breeds a stilted existence and joy can be lost in over planning. This is the downside of their strength of thoughtful planning. Immediate response to unfolding events makes planning impossible, in which case the SJ reacts or more likely freezes and waits till they are ready to act, even if in the process they miss an opportunity.

SJs must keep their native strength (thoughtful planning) dominant and build just enough courage to face fear without the emotional panic it can cause those who are not prepared and lack courage. The SJ needs to know how to plan. They also need to know how to react immediately when needed and face the results with confidence in their ability to regain control where they might have lost it.

We all feel fulfilled when we exercise our strengths, so the SJ feels fulfilled when they prepare and plan with careful thought and it results in a successful event. Remember, happiness lives in fulfillment.

Little help outside of training is needed to build this strength. The skills of logistical planning, goal management, time management, logic, system management, and creation, to name a few, should be added to make the strength the best it can be.

How Do I Develop this Strength?

- Thoughtfully! I'm not being facetious. Being thoughtful about how thoughtful I should be is how SJs should approach this strength. Remember, if we plan all the impulse and spontaneity out of life it becomes "grits" every morning. Ah, I hate grits!

- Establish a goal and plan to achieve it. Working toward your goals is a wonderful way to keep your thoughtfulness purposeful and directed.

- Use a time management system. There are many paper and electronic models. However, please remember that they are *self* management systems that are falsely named *time* management systems. Time is not manageable by us. It is simply a condition around which we manage our lives.

- Include, in your preparation, reminders to show care for other people's feelings and needs. Some SJs can become very centered around their activities. Because of the seriousness of the SJ's approach to life, it is a needed caution for them. Anyone can become self-centered, of course.

• In your preparations, pencil in spontaneous time just to feel the variations of life's ride and the freedom of impulse.

Caution:

All temperaments lapse into weaknesses when they don't use their strengths, overuse them, or use them for destructive purposes such as damaging themselves or others. Here are further cautions for this strength.

• Beware of over planning.

• Beware of turning your planning into negative worry sessions.

• Concern and preparation can narrow your life down until you feel you are walking a tightrope. Loosen up a little.

• Beliefs play an important part in our lives. Believe that all will be well and plan to help that happen.

• Don't try to control your world. You can't.

• Control yourself and that will exert all the control you can safely attempt on your circumstances and the lives of others.

Responsible — Dependable
Solid Work Ethic — Disciplined

My country owes me nothing. It gave me, as it gives every boy and girl, a chance.
~ Herbert Hoover

Why such a long list? Because "dependable" is really part of being "responsible." A solid work ethic is a display of responsibility and discipline is essential to making a responsible person. "Well," you say, "why not just call the strength being responsible if everything you have listed either issues from or is a part of responsibility?" Because I wanted to highlight each element and draw attention to all of them.

Let's define each as they appear in the SJ.

Responsible. It means being someone who has proved himself to act or respond in an acceptable and reliable manner, to be trustworthy. Responsibility is a very important value to SJs.

Dependable. It is to be proved reliable and to be someone who can be depended upon. Again, to be trustworthy.

Solid Work Ethic. One who puts work before play and chooses to perform responsibly and reliably at their work whether under supervision or not.

Discipline. The regular use of routines and systems to create consistency and reliability in a person.

SJs exhibit a strong sense of responsibility. It is stimulated by carefulness, concern, thoughtfulness, and preparedness. They long to be known as someone who can be depended upon. Society needs structure (SJs know this better than anyone) and things that repeat themselves in reliable fashion form the firm skeleton of society. When we have rules to determine how each of us should behave on the highway we can depend on a reasonably safe commute. So the SJ proves their reliability by paying attention to the rules and regulations and entrenching them in society.

These rules start in the home and SJ parents teach them diligently to their children in the hopes that they will grow up to be pillars of security in the world, little Rocks of Gibraltar.

You will often hear SJ parents say...

"Now pay attention, this is the proper way to do it."
"We have to obey the rules, remember."
"Rules are for a purpose."
"We have to be responsible."
"Let's all be respectable."

This strength gives the SP cause for concern or rebellion since, in its atmosphere, they don't feel free and open to express themselves. "Why can't I do as I please?" says the extreme SP, and the SJ replies with threatening tone, "You can't, and that's all there is to it!" "Why?"

"Because I said so!" Our laws are built on the acceptance of the SJ's premise for secure societies and people who discipline themselves. When a society makes the shift from being responsible for their actions to using the idea of personal freedom to disregard their responsibilities in the name of self expression, a major shift has taken place.

Testing the limits all the time does not deliver a reputation of reliability. The SJ is therefore less likely than the SP to test the limits or, if they do, they do it cautiously or only to attract the needed attention of peers. Then they suffer from feeling as though they have betrayed something inside themselves.

In the SJ you have a temperament that stays within bounds most of the time. Responsibility is a way of behaving prudently in society and (to their mind) keeping within needed and accepted limits. This is true of both the home society and the larger society.

The solid work ethic of the SJ shows this responsible trait. Work comes before play. "If you wish to eat, you should (if possible) work," is their general philosophy.

It is for the sake of society that they want to be responsible, also for the recognition of being respectable members of that society. In return they expect society to recognize and reward them for their faithfulness in traditional ways.

When they show no concern for society (home or larger groups) something is wrong with the SJ. Either they don't feel that they belong or they have been hurt by society and are rebelling against undesirable authority. Whatever the reason, the SJ becomes less than themselves when they fail to use and appreciate this strength. If they try to live like SPs they soon find themselves square pegs living in round holes.

Jake, an SJ, was having a tough time of it at work. His boss had warned him and placed him on probation. He had requested another job outdoors where he loved to be, but they placed him in a room with few windows and a cubicle that felt like a prison. He believed he had been singled out and unfairly treated when a small indiscretion had been pointed out and resulted in his being placed on probation.

Noticeably, his attitude declined. His workmates loved him, but a sourness crept over his spirit and he became rebellious. Why he was doing it he didn't know, but he defied regulations and became sloppy in his duties. His job now held no security for him. In the midst of other family upheavals his actions clawed at his spirit and guilt made its presence felt.

A friend asked him to go for a walk and they talked. "This is not the dependable, responsible person I know," said his friend. "Something must be wrong, please share." The SJ is tough and their armor is hard to penetrate, but the dam burst and out came the worries, the whole negative cache of pains and, finally, he was ashamed of himself, but he didn't know what to do.

"Be who you are!" his friend suggested. Although he didn't use the words, he told him to live in his strengths and all would be righted. "Focus on your impeccable, responsible behavior, and the old you will return." It did. At times it is all the SJ needs to do: return to the use of their strengths if they know them.

The advice was right on. Whenever SJs fall into their weaknesses the way back is not to pay attention to the weakness and try to right it. The SJs must simply focus on their strengths and the weaknesses disappear.

SJs love routine, and they use routine as a discipline to aid their development of responsible behavior. It is the form of discipline that is natural to their temperament. This is how: Routine creates dependability and, by its regularity, helps a person continue to be dependable. Routine makes it easier to be responsible and not forget what society expects. So they dress in the mornings with a set routine and prepare themselves for the acclaim of being respectable, knowing they have not missed an important detail. Watch how they whip themselves when they unwittingly miss some detail of respectability.

It is not easy to imagine weaknesses that could develop with the overuse of this strength. Stiff, soulless behavior is perhaps one. Nonuse is full of weak, uncharacteristic, damaging behavior and, for the SJ, will certainly produce guilt.

The reward for its use is great. They feel as though they are solid citizens of earth and their self-esteem rises strongly when their trustworthiness is noted.

Developing this strength is a matter of doing their duty faithfully and well. It is further developed by training to be more reliable and effective in which they then take pride. The result? The strength grows, of course. Building all kinds of routines into their daily life further feeds their sense of being responsible and dependable and aids its successful performance. Attitude, belief, and focus are also important elements to being consistent.

Success is certainly down the road of "being responsible" for an SJ. Reliable, dependable, consistent, and responsible describes a strength in which the SJ can take real pride.

How Do I Develop this Strength?

- Responsibility starts with the inner drive to be responsible. It is developed by strengthening our belief in its importance. So, reinforce your belief in the need for being responsible or your belief system will fall victim to the challenges of our age to "look after number one" (a very subtle virus that weakens dependability).

- Along with developing our belief in responsibility, we should recognize that it focuses us on the needs and rights of others as well as ourselves.

- Once your belief system is strong, continue to act accordingly at all opportunities.

- Live out your belief. The world needs you.

- Search your plans to succeed at whatever is your goal and see that at all stages you are being as trustworthy as you can be. This lays a foundation of integrity to your plans that will pay you back and keep you from self sabotage.

- Without joy, being responsible can become a bore. Make sure you have sufficient pleasure in your life to keep feeling rewarded and balanced.

- Teach responsibility to your children, but don't try to control them and produce it by force. No one likes to be controlled. They will likely do the opposite. Let them learn from consequences and example and your modeling.

Caution:

All temperaments lapse into weaknesses when they don't use their strengths, overuse them, or use them for destructive purposes such as damaging themselves or others. Here are further cautions for this strength.

- Limit your demand for responsibility to yourself and to those whom you must teach or train.

- Appreciate the free-wheeling attitude of the SP and the futuristic optimism of the NF, but be who you are.

- See all other temperaments through the belief that all people are wonderfully made and should be respected regardless of their beliefs.

Do What Is Right — Law Abiding

Right is its own defense.
~ Bertolt Brecht

Akin to their desire to be responsible and reliable is their drive to do the right thing. Rules and regulations make absolute sense to all SJs, and established rules are the right thing to follow; of this they have little doubt. They believe corruption is around the corner if people are not compelled to obey the rules at least within reason. "Laws are for a purpose," they declare. If everyone would follow the rules, all would be well. It is part of their responsible belief system. Their actions sometimes fall short of their beliefs, but the beliefs drive them.

If an SJ teenager goes off to college and comes under the influence that says rules and regulations limit the freedom of individuals and individual freedom is promoted as a higher value to protect than laws and authority, they are confused and struggle with the concepts that are foreign to their *innerkinetics*. Their temperament and place in the balance of society is not being understood, and they are likely to rebel against their own inner drives to achieve the all important goal of respectability among their peers.

If the teaching is contrary to the innate drive to do the right thing, they will try to act so they will be thought to be a responsible unit of society while still being acceptable to their peers. In other words, they will be torn between two strong drives: the need to do the right thing and the need to belong.

We must all be respected for the drives within us and for the health they promote when they are correctly used. We must be allowed to be who we are and we must not be molded by any dominant outlook. That goes for all temperaments.

Perhaps this is the place to address the question "What is the correct use of our strengths?" Answer: Any use that does not damage ourselves or others, meaning all others: friends, workmates, partners, our spiritual authority, and even those who would harm our reputation.

There is no doubting the importance of control factors in social life, but this strength is only one side of the coin for society to run smoothly. The other is the need for free expression in a society — the strength of the SP. Both are strengths, and both must honor the rights and needs of the other. Each must profit from their own.

There is no need to point out the positive potentials of a law-abiding attitude. Nonuse of this strength damages the SJ and can cause guilt and can develop further into a self-denunciation and a lowered self-image. Reward and fulfillment come from the safety and security such strengths produce.

Success is negatively affected for all of us if we don't follow how we are made. Doing the right thing is just as honorable and more so than dong something that hurts ourselves or others. Develop this strength, not as a self righteous badge but as a noble benefit for all.

How Do I Develop this Strength?
- Doing what is right is another strength whose power relies on a belief in the value of goodness. Build the belief or this strength makes no sense.

- Examine your values for consistency and integrity.

- This strength is developed by the actions and attitudes that support it.

Caution:

All temperaments lapse into weaknesses when they don't use their strengths, overuse them, or use them for destructive purposes such as damaging themselves or others. Here are further cautions for this strength.

- This strength can be a test for your ethical honesty. Examine yourself.

- People are somewhat uncomfortable when their value system is held up for examination. You are responsible for you. Examine yourself.

Strong Need to Belong — Social — Respectable

The greatest thing in the world is to know how to belong to oneself.
~ Michel de Montaigne (French essayist)

Montaigne's comment uncovers an important truth. Society is made up of individual units. The basis of a secure society is a secure individual. We must first be secure in our belief in ourselves and feel the comfort of being able to belong to ourselves with integrity and without punishing guilt and self condemnation before we can add to the security of others. Therefore, the SJ dresses and lives to feel respectful in their own eyes before they can feel respected in the eyes of others. Once that is achieved they can be a positive force for good and for the stability in society. Furthermore, they feel good doing it. This strength builds a foundation for the other strengths.

The definition of this strength for the SJ is: Belonging creates a sense of acceptance, connectedness, and security. Both rank high in their stabilizing effect on the SJ.

To have to belong is not a sign of weakness — a kind of crutch for the needy. Belonging is a glue, cementing the cords of society as well as being a stabilizing force for the SJ. As social beings, SJs feed the needs of society, keeping it from self destruction while they exhibit the qualities of solid rocks. Society feeds them recognition to create a mutual bond.

The word *society* has come up several times already in the discussion of the SJ. They are the social temperament. Belonging and being respectable and needed in small groups, and also in a larger society, is a paramount drive that gives basic direction to their lives. SJs can hardly pass up the opportunity to belong to clubs and communities and their wallets often burst with membership cards. Whatever group they belong to they monitor with pride and concern as time permits.

There is a sense of security in belonging; there is strength and protection in numbers. The SJ appears rocklike and stable, but it is this strength that supplies some of that solidity.

A society is a group of people of no particular size where the actions of all affect the common welfare of the group. The group makes rules for behavior to protect common interests, enforces those rules, seeks to provide for agreed upon needs, and expects each member to act responsibly as assigned or perform according to expected rules. Mentally, the SJs accept this as their role and it forms a strong belief.

I saw Sarah glued to her TV, watching with furrowed eyebrows to the news. She told me it was a daily routine. Then she confessed she spent all her free time watching the news. What was happening to the nation deeply disturbed her. She waited nervously for news that would confirm her worst thoughts (a mark of a mind that has turned pessimistic). The nation was going to the dogs and she was at a loss why these politicians were not responsible and responding to what she saw as obvious needs and values. "Why can't they live within their budget like we all have to do?" was one of her favorite gripes. But it was her belonging to a crumbling society (in her estimation) that was the real cause of her concerns. SJs watch intently the societies they belong to.

Her small social unit would ultimately be affected negatively by all that was going on, let alone the threat to personal freedom. It wasn't her conservative attitude (most SJs are conservative in values) but her fear of social breakdown (a form of insecurity) that threatened her.

She was finally persuaded to see that her waiting for the bad news was forecasting her own despair. She was ruining her life by letting the painful future fashion her present moment. All optimism had naturally left to provide room for her pessimism.

This is often the action of those whose need to belong has combined with negative thoughts. The need to belong and to feel helpless when the society was crumbling had trapped her spirit in the prison of despair. Whenever pessimism destroys the positives of belonging, belonging becomes a negative energy.

The SJ strives instinctively and purposefully for all this *belonging*. This is because they accept the social model as the norm for human conduct. Therefore, we expect they will feel weaker for not belonging, and they do. It fills the need for connections and feeling wanted and useful. It is about the sense of worth a group gives to an individual.

The SJ blesses society with their careful attention to its needs: safety, security, peace, order, laws, and spiritual togetherness. We have the SJs to thank for most of the positive benefits of society.

The societal units themselves give the SJ a sense of unity and contribution to the whole. When their social being is disconnected they lose the feeling of being useful and needed. They become nervous, lonely, fearful, and then they fall into gloom and despair. As a result, an SJ's home must be a place where all feel connected for the SJ parent to be comfortable. For some member of the family to say they don't feel at home is an S.O.S. and it is taken seriously by the SJ parent as though the family member is complaining of having no food. To make an SJ feel rejected at home, work, or play is punishment indeed.

The sense of fulfillment that comes from belonging arises from the peace and security it brings. We can all operate better when we are at peace in our inner selves. This is peace for the SJ.

The need to belong is a supportive strength. Because we see it as a need as well as a strength in our *innerkinetics*, SJs should aim at satisfying the need, not building a greater sense of belonging.

How Do I Develop this Strength?
- Again, it is a natural urge in the SJ.

- Join a group, club, church or organization. Choose the group carefully and participate. Your sense of belonging will be satisfied if you are an SJ.

- Contribute to society and its needs as the opportunity arises.

- For the SJ, social duty cannot be avoided without a sense of loss and an underlying disturbance.

- Belong and protect the value of your contributions by being an optimist, positive and always hopeful.

Caution:
All temperaments lapse into weaknesses when they don't use their strengths, overuse them, or use them for destructive purposes such as damaging themselves or others. Here are further cautions for this strength.

- Don't worry over the bad news about your nation or community. It does not help to worry.

- Certainly, don't become worried over things you have no power to control or change.

- If there is something you can do to bring about change, do it.

- Above all trust, hope, and make a positive contribution.

Steady — Not Easily Shaken

Slow and steady wins the race.
~ Aesop

The definition of this strength for the SJ is: moving with measured step, unfazed by the ups and downs, while stoically absorbing the blows life sends their way. SJs are not constantly changing and trying to adapt to the many opportunities. Rather, they set a course and follow it with determination, plugging away toward their goal. It is determination on a steady course that makes things happen for the SJ.

When a person feels well-grounded in reality and sure that they are right, they show they cannot be easily shaken. The SJs have their feet solidly planted in reality and their desires and goals are straightforward, making them (when they feel they are right) the proverbial rock of Gibraltar — unmovable.

Society, for its good, needs stability, and SJs know this even if the other members of society don't. They believe that they are the reason social groups succeed. This firm belief only makes them more entrenched in their convictions and they will argue their position with tenacity. "A double-minded man is unstable in all he does." This they seldom display. Double-mindedness is the start of breakdown in their performance, so keep a single mind on all issues.

Steadiness is a trait they show in the face of threat. It is their counterpart to the SPs daring, and it makes them seem equally strong and brave. "Try to move me," is the spirit they exhibit.

To make this steadiness happen they are known for their disciplined attitude, which when they live in their weaknesses is nowhere to be seen. An undisciplined SJ is an SJ living outside of her strengths, if even for the moment.

They will face pain and loss with fortitude if they feel it is in a just or required cause. Sometimes they display steadiness to the extent of stubbornness. That stubbornness is the trait that infuriates the other temperaments since, even more than daring or bravery, it is not easily discouraged or changed. It is an entrenched defense of their position that says, "You must destroy me or I will always be in your face."

SJs play defense more than offense. This, at times, is necessary when their values in particular are under attack, so it is a strength they must use. The SJ's stubbornness will also match any passionate surge of the NF, or even the cold rejection of the NT. They care not what others might think or feel when they dig their toes in and resist. As you may see, no temperament can control the other, and harmony and peace among the temperaments is achieved by persuasion, negotiation and love, not force.

Because they are the J and not the P among the Ss, they want to come to closure and move on. This closing of issues and the setting of firm plans for action immediately is another element in their temperament that makes them look so steady and unmovable. In contrast, closure seems to bring the possibilities of life to an end for the SP. Keeping their options open in case more evidence turns up seems like procrastination to the SJ.

The Js accuse the Ps of procrastination readily, because they believe it is not productive of immediate results, and they want results — now, not yesterday! Loose ends don't contribute to steadiness. They contribute only to the risk of some unknown happening.

SJs see procrastination as laziness and wishy-washy indecision — even irresponsibility. The SPs and the SJs seem opposites, don't they? This is because they live opposing lifestyles.

Weakness enters when SJs are immovable but their cause is not fair and just or loving and caring. It seems to do their relationships harm first. However, it only affects them personally if it ends up breaking down the society that they care about, which usually means their family. They are born to create and protect whatever group they have committed to.

Steadiness has been exemplified in many famous leaders, and history has rewarded some of them for it.

As we might expect there is an inner warmth (fulfillment) from sticking to your guns and fighting it out with staunch resistance. It is your own vote of confidence in your own courage and power. In the SJ, it definitely lifts their self-image and is, therefore, not something that others can root out of them easily.

Again, this is a supportive strength. The rocklike steadiness of the SJ is going to prop up their perseverance, strengthen their responsibility, and help them concentrate intensely on details. It is also a means of controlling their environment. They don't let the circumstances or other people get to them easily and disturb them.

If the SJ has adopted a plan of action, steadiness enhances their ability to execute that plan with concentration on all its steps. Success comes smoothly when the SJs use all of their strengths in harmony to maximize their surge to their goal.

How Do I Develop this Strength?

- Demonstrate to yourself your ability to remain calm and determined in the face of problems and surprises.

- Envision yourself as always remaining steady and unshakeable.

- Exercise the courage to stand for what you are convinced is right.

- Develop your convictions. This doesn't mean to become intolerant. There are many things we should be intolerant of, such as bullies and deceivers, but we can be firm in our convictions while we respect others and yet disagree.

- Plant your feet firmly in reality.

- Learn to take insults and insinuations with dignity and poise. If all they have to throw at you are insults, they have a very weak case against you.

Caution:

All temperaments lapse into weaknesses when they don't use their strengths, overuse them, or use them for destructive purposes such as damaging themselves or others. Here are further cautions for this strength.

- Respect the person, even if you are convinced he is wrong.

- Use wisdom about what really matters and what doesn't.

- Temper justice with love.

- Don't become stubborn when you are wrong or doubtful.

Trust Authority

Trust is the lubrication that makes it possible for organizations to work.
~ Warren Bennis

For the SJ, trusting authority is defined this way: Authority is necessary, useful for the maintenance of order, and should be trusted unless it proves not to be trustworthy.

SJs will defend an authority unless it is showing itself to be unfair in its decisions, lacking in societal responsibility, wasteful of resources, etc. They defend it because they have a great need and a firm belief in the keeping of law and order. In contrast, the SP questions an authority's right to exist. Authority has an uphill battle to prove their worth to the SP, unless the SP is the authority or belongs to the authority in power. Contrasting premises create contrasting viewpoints.

SJs know that authority is needed for law and order to be enforced and they will create layers of authority to protect something as minor as a routine. Enforcement is as important as the law itself. Therefore, they respect people in positions of authority and expectations for authority consequently run high. That in turn means status is created in an SJ society, and since it is their creation and part of their system of authority, it too is honored.

SJs aspire to be in positions of authority and when they arrive, they swell with the pride of newly-gained status, since this is, at times, more valuable to them than the amount of money the position offers. It is a measure of their respectability in society and the more respect, the greater their importance. Other SJs, who are more materially motivated measure their success based on money alone. Both possessions and status are equal drives in a typical SJ. Position in society is measured by both position and monetary status since money has its own way of creating status.

Their overuse of this strength leads to the acceptance of abuses of power and the nonuse can lead to personal lawlessness.

Talking to Joe, a police officer, I was told, "I feel I serve my community. How could they exist without us? It makes me feel good when I enforce the law and bring criminals to justice. All I am doing is enforcing the law and God knows we need laws and authorities that look after our security."

"Tell me, Joe, do you feel that authority is essential to our society?" I asked.

"Absolutely! Why do you ask? Don't you know that the people don't know how important we are until they get robbed or mugged and then they call for us and criticize us if we are not there before they can drop their hat."

There is a pride in Joe, a pride in being a part of the power and usefulness of authority. He is an SJ who, in his eyes, can't fathom why authority should be questioned unless it is corrupt. That's the typical SJ attitude.

As I have pointed out, their trust of authority depends on their view of that authority, and this varies according to personal values and goals. What is present in all is their belief that we need and must honor authority for the benefits that leadership brings.

The level of fulfillment this strength brings is, in my observation, minimal. It's the belief behind the trust of authority that is not to be messed with and is most important for an SJ to protect. The main personal benefit of trusting authority (to the SJ) is the reduction of fear and insecurity.

When it comes to successfully reaching a goal, trusting authority can be helpful or harmful. It just depends on the authority and its effectiveness and on the goal. So the measure in which the SJ might want to develop this strength depends on all the issues at stake.

How Do I Develop this Strength?
• Use this strength appropriately.

• The rationale for this strength is the belief in authority and the need for its protection, services, and security. Build the belief and you build the strength.

• No society has existed that does not admit the need of authority in some form.

- The development of trust in authority is authority's responsibility. Therefore, much of the need to develop a trust in authority rests with authority itself.

Caution:
All temperaments lapse into weaknesses when they don't use their strengths, overuse them, or use them for destructive purposes such as damaging themselves or others. Here are further cautions for this strength.

- Power is often corrupt and support is, ultimately, as Joe thinks, dependent on its honesty and effectiveness.

- The people must ultimately determine the nature of the authority that governs them in a democratic society.

Supervisors — Managers
Systems — Routines

Any supervisor worth his salt would rather deal with people who attempt too much than with those who try too little.
~ Lee Iacocca

This strength is an outcome of several others. The SJ's desire to help, their logistical minds, their sense of being responsible, and their cautiousness and attention to detail, together with their innate honor of authority figures and their urge to control, make them born supervisors and tenders of the affairs of society.

By SJ definition, supervision and management is the control of people and procedures to achieve a certain goal.

SJs recognize rank and desire it. To be appointed to supervise others or things is an honor. They believe that honor should carry monetary rewards, so most often an increase in pay accompanies the honor (but usually not enough for all the responsibility it brings).

ESTJ means "supervisor and manager!" ISTJ means "inspector" and ISFJ means protector. None of the three will shirk their sense of duty to be what they are. We should not ask them to do that either. To do so is to deny the integrity of their own inner drives. With supervision goes the need for standards, routines, and reliable systems. At all of these SJs excel.

What we may be concerned about is the overuse of these strengths, since it can cause damage to others. Too much corrupt or unwise, uncaring, and unconcerned use of management will destroy the group it protects. Overuse of these strengths hardens the hearts of managers and decreases their sensitivity to people's needs. The ugly result is well documented in the history of industry, for example.

This strength (supervision, inspection, protection) is the cause of many SP plans to get even. The ensuing struggle is not always subtle. Revolutions have resulted, so the use of this strength should be most carefully monitored by the SJs themselves.

Along with this strength and its recognition comes power over others, and power itself is thwart with many dangers and, on the other hand, opportunities to be a blessing. Leadership by authority can be much improved if it is replaced with leadership by influence and servitude. The servant leader is a welcome model in any society and a pattern for the SJ to follow.

The ISTJ is the inspector and watches with eagle eye to see that the procedures are followed. Sometimes it can cause aggravation and a serious reaction to get rid of the "inspector."

Jay was a supervisor ESTJ and determined to see that the rules were efficient and followed just as he had carefully planned them. All went well at work among the people who honored the position and where workers expected his supervision.

All did not go well at home. He supervised his wife to the point where she hated his return from work. Not only did he supervise but, in order to supervise, he inspected her every task and corrected her constantly.

"Why isn't the meal ready?"

"Can you stand the mess this house is in?"

223

"I will need my shirt ironed and ready for tomorrow because I am meeting an executive from out of town."

"We are using up electricity. I've told you before, keep the house at 69 degrees in winter."

His wife didn't think she married a supervisor and left him cold one day. His next wife did the same. He was a disaster as a husband and a success at work.

When he was told that he might be the problem he responded with, "Well that can't be right; the people at work love me." Not ready to try to understand, he has settled for a single life. Lesson? Supervision is for work places and even there it must be carefully monitored. Its place is not in relationships or the home unless dramatically modified.

Overuse or misuse of this strength can also lead to SJs thinking they are superior and, therefore, creating friction. The ESFJ also holds to supervision, but not so rigidly and with more feeling.

Society needs supervision and that belief is not questioned by SJs. Only the SP might disagree. It is no surprise that with the natural drive to supervise and the natural strength in place, they would excel at business enterprises where supervision and the regulation of systems are much needed.

When this strength is not over or wrongly used, it brings much satisfaction to the SJ and lifts their self-image strongly. Again, watch for the danger of it over inflating the self-image.

In all fields except relationships supervision is an essential strength to succeed at reaching goals. So the supervisor often succeeds. Blending it with people skills maximizes its importance and its success.

How Do I Develop this Strength?
• By being a supervisor and using the strength.

• By developing supportive strengths like logistical thinking, planning skills, discipline, responsibility, attention to detail, etc.

- By training and practicing organizational skills. There is a definite need for the SJ to receive training in personnel management.

- Watch for the use of power which, if misused, can lead to a feeling of superiority and destroy one's leadership.

- Develop people skills.

Caution:
All temperaments lapse into weaknesses when they don't use their strengths, overuse them, or use them for destructive purposes such as damaging themselves or others. Here are further cautions for this strength.

- Don't overuse the strength or weaknesses will destroy your effectiveness.

- Control the feeling of power and replace it with a mental vision of service and helpfulness. SJs who fall into their weaknesses can be very controlling.

- The care of people and the ability to read people's feelings will be the greatest challenge.

Stoical

The stoical scheme of supplying our wants by lopping off our desires is like cutting off our feet when we want shoes.
~ Jonathan Swift (Irish essayist)

"If bad things can happen, they will." SJs believe we must always be prepared for the worst; then we will never be disappointed. The desire to protect against disappointment is greater than the thrill of enjoying the best while it lasts.

Stoical means (to the SJ) what the British call "a stiff upper lip:" facing misfortune (and even suffering) with gritted teeth and a positive attitude, determined to see it through. Stoical attitudes can breed super seriousness, overcautiousness, and determined resignation — all good if in their proper context and degree.

Perhaps, you wonder if there is any good in this so-called "strength." There is. Seriousness is not all bad and it is essential at certain times in life.   Resignation is an effective way to fight your way through disappointment. As long as this strength is not overused it is a blessing to SJs, but this strength carries with it the ever present danger of being overused.

A stoic attitude develops a belief that is reminiscent of the ancient Greek philosophy of Stoicism. It asks us to steel ourselves against trouble and bear it with an iron acceptance and without complaint since we cannot avoid it. It admits the existence of trouble and adopts a pessimistic attitude toward it. The SJ will often simply say, "Its God's will," and slump into resignation with no attempt to change things. This is not the SJ at his best.

The mental preparation that this attitude requires — namely its carte blanche acceptance of trouble, together with a treasured realism — blended with a very conservative interpretation of life, adds up to pessimism or something so very close to it that it's hard to tell them apart. It is easy to see how this can be overused and become a weakness. A negative, pessimistic attitude is waiting just over the fence, so to speak. Great care needs to be taken to offset the stoic's fateful acceptance of things and a somber, resigned attitude so prevalent in a depressed state.

You will also notice the SJ's seriousness about life emerging whenever the storm clouds of trouble gather. The SP will show hope and optimism at the onset of trouble, while the SJ will display their strength of stoicism and immediately leap into preparations to handle the worst or they will fall into worry. "Better to be serious than sorry," they say.

Christie was about to lose her job. She had been told she had to make improvements in her performance or they may have to let her go. "This was her opportunity, and had she shown a determination to improve and a more optimistic attitude around her compatriots, they would have kept her," so her supervisor later told her.

Instead she resigned herself to face her fate. A fate she believed was coming anyhow and avoidance would do no good. Her sullen response had been a giveaway to her supervisor that soon it would be necessary to terminate her employment.

So her supervisor gave her another heads up and encouraged her to make the changes and lighten up. It was not to be. Christie told me forlornly, "It was going to happen anyway, so better not to try." She stoically resigned herself to her fate. "Less disappointment when it happened that way," she said.

Stoicism is a strong drive in the makeup of SJs. It protects against a flippant attitude to life and, when seen as pure serious determination, is an invaluable blessing. It is to be reckoned with, and the SJ can protect against its dangers by keeping an upbeat attitude.

All the negativities found in SJs are weaknesses, not true productions of their strengths. It is not part of the temperament itself. Many of their strengths need to be carefully used or they precipitate a fall into negative gloom. When I have found a positive SJ, they appear and live like the solid-rock-temperament they are designed to be, and they are the backbone of a healthy society. In their hands stoic attitudes, defined as seriousness in the service of positive hope, can be a driving force to success.

How Do I Develop this Strength?

• Stay positive and don't let pessimism invade your stoic strength.

• Face loss with a belief that every loss is an opportunity, and search for its wonders.

Caution:

All temperaments lapse into weaknesses when they don't use their strengths, overuse them, or use them for destructive purposes such as damaging themselves or others. Here are further cautions for this strength.

• For the SJ, the dangers of worry, pessimism, and loss of hope are to be avoided at all cost.

• Any strength that sails close to the winds of despair must be used with caution.

Logistical in Work and Play

A logistical mind dominates the mental activity of the SJ and is the brilliance seen in their intelligence. Webster's Dictionary defines logistics as "the art of calculation," also as "a complex operation involving many people, supplies, and facilities."

Mathematics appeals to this logistical mind. Calculating and measuring how to get goods or people from one place to another with the attendant issues of placement and timing is a logician's skill. Logistics requires a logical mind devoted to the importance of details and the creation of routines, systems, and procedures.

The difference between the detail-orientated SP and SJ is that SPs attend to detail for tactical purposes and SJs do so for logistical reasons. Therefore, keeping records and lists and making timelines falls naturally into the SJs skill set. Logistics is that branch of military science that deals with procuring, maintaining, and transporting people, materials, and facilities.
The NT is also detailed because their intuition and theoretical bent is directed more to the discovery of things in the real physical world, but they are not as detailed as the SJ, and scientists happily involved in routine research are often SJs.

All business models must deal with logistics. It permeates life, providing efficiency to planning and execution. The world would be inefficient and ineffective without logistical minds. This strength needs developing to its potential in all SJs since it increases their ability to be who they are, carefully taking care of the details and bringing order into their lives and the lives of others. SJs, if operating logistically, typically know where things are and, if not, they know where to look.

Games are the prime world of the SP, but it is this logistical skill that has provided the rules and regulations that govern and control the games that the SP enjoys — a twist of irony to ponder.

Step-by-step planning for the home, doing chores in a logical sequence, figuring out how much and how many, and determining when and where are the logician's brilliance and the natural way they do things. Routines are their love and they depend on them to help them follow sequences. They are the masters of this sequential, systems-oriented approach to life at home and everywhere. Business is just this.

The following story will illustrate one of the limitations of logistics.

Along with this logical approach to life for the SJ is a sense of urgency. Dale runs his business very effectively. "It's my world and it gives me great satisfaction," he'll tell you. "When I make a decision, I check the facts, the records, run the numbers, and then it is clear to me what to do. (He is an ESTJ.) Then I do it. No reason to wait. I want to get on with things." When things are moving on systematically and logically, he is well pleased.

So Dale goes home and his spouse is busy taking care of kids who are not predictable. Just one accident can cause a whole day to be disrupted and plummeted into chaos. Dale instantly sees the mess and explodes ("with just concern," he says). Why can't his mate get a grip on things. Things are supposed to be in control and running with order and the preciseness of carefully planned logistics. He does it. Why can't she? A home is just a small business, he maintains. All she has to do is run around caring for two kids. What could be simpler and a more obvious subject for logistical procedures?

His spouse is a tender NF. She swallows hard as his harsh words discipline her, and she endures the hurt inside until she finally explodes in retaliation for the hurt. This relationship could have been heaven on earth, but now it smelled of sulphur.

For some time this went on — for years. Dale hardly noticed the withdrawal, the quietness, and the collapse of his INFP wife as she suffered.

One day he was shocked when she left. Why? What was the problem? "She must be ill or mentally off balance," he said. The kids must have got to her. She demanded a fair settlement, and that struck him where it hurts a successful male SJ businessperson the most: in his pocket.

In reality, he had lost her years ago. Play was hardly ever in their lives. Work was divine and relationships were supposed to be a given. What an ending this story had. She now demanded that any future consideration of a reconciliation would be on her terms. He was now in a weak bargaining position and had no hand to play. He wanted her.

He agreed to get help, and a slow but fascinating process of learning who he was and who she was began. He would come to a decision quickly and was at a total loss to implement it while he had to wait for his spouse to make up her mind. For her it meant the slow process of: Consult your emotions; adjust and become comfortable with the challengers of these emotions; then decide. That takes time. Relationships, he discovered, were not anything like a business. SJs are not anything like NFs, either!

To both of their credit, it came together. I'm sure they are still learning, and she is becoming herself too.

Satisfaction is found not only in being logistical but in the results it produces: order, efficiency and timeliness. Its development strengthens the self-image of the SJ. When SJs are frustrated it is often because they lack the control over the world that they wish they had, and logistical behavior can and often does restore their sense of having things "under control," as you will hear them say. Having things under control gives peace to an SJ.

Logistics is an intelligence, a way of mental functioning that allows them to see through problems and penetrate life's enigmas to an extent that satisfies their feet-on-the-ground mentality. So, much fulfillment is experienced and, in the process, their self-mage definitely rises.

Logistical intelligence is thinking sequentially and coming to closure, making decisions and plans. Remember, the SP thinks sequentially too but keeps the options open, coming to tentative, in-the-moment decisions that can be easily changed. Logistical thinking leads an SJ to success because it closes options, forms plans and systems, and then they follow those plans with determination and conviction. It may be the most important element in their success.

How Do I Develop this Strength?

- Study logistics and add knowledge to your strength.

- Study business and its systems.

- Study logic.

- Focus on details.

- Practice this strength where it is needed and appreciated.

- Practice in your mind by evaluating what you would have done in a situation you are observing.

- Let the positive results of your successes motivate you.

Caution:
All temperaments lapse into weaknesses when they don't use their strengths, overuse them, or use them for destructive purposes such as damaging themselves or others. Here are further cautions for this strength.

- Remember, not everything in life wants or needs to be regimented.

- Learn the other side of life as well: the soft, unplanned love that needs to be nurtured and tendered, and which refreshes your logistical mind.

- Study relationships in the real experiences of your life and develop people skills to keep you from being all business.

Communicates with the Details

Beware of the man who won't be bothered with details.
~ William Feather

SJs are factual and they focus on details. This strength enables their logistical mind to operate successfully. The details also keep the SJ grounded in the real world and contribute to their stability and stabilizing influence over others.

As expected, their emphasis on the details shows in their communication patterns. SJs communicate with all the details. "What other way is there," they ponder. They insist on the details. You will often hear them say, "But what about ..." and they will name a detail that you haven't addressed. They will do this before you have been able to get the whole story out because the detail is bothering them and they can't proceed calmly until the problem of this detail is solved.

If they skip a fact in reporting what they have done, they squirm at the possibility that someone may have noticed the omission. As children they want to show their skill at remembering all the details of their story and should be praised for it. Of all the temperaments, they handle the concrete facts of life the best. Details keep their feet squarely on the ground.

SJs are convinced, as I have said, that the devil is in the details, and that means in the details of communications too. Their experience says: where the details are left out, communication often fails. They are painstaking in noticing and taking the details into account.

The problem with this strength is that you can get lost in the details, and not see the big picture or discern the overall patterns and relationships of the details. While focusing on the trees, you can miss appreciating the message of the forest. The impressions that the details of the trees leave is not the same impression made by the mass of a forest.

The NT and the NF have problems in communication with the SP and the SJ since they often race ahead of themselves in informal conversation, leaving the detail-oriented listener behind. You may have noticed the escalation of relationship problems caused by this lack of communication.

An SJ and an NF are driving down the road and the NF wants to lay out an idea that she wants the SJ to think about.

"I have an idea..." (First problem: An idea is too vague, and if you want to communicate effectively with an SJ you need to begin like this. "Here are the details about an idea I have," and then launch into the details.)

The NF has seen the big picture, sped through the patterns, and seen the connections but has not sorted all the details yet. It's the big picture they want to convey. Then they will come down to the details and examine them later.

"Let me tell you the whole story first before you say anything. Okay? [Silence.] She starts. Two sentences later he says, "Yes, but what about (he names a detail that is troubling him)? [Pause. Long pause.]

She attempts to answer the detail and then pleads again for the stage to tell the whole story.

Two sentences later, guess what. Another question about a detail.

That is the way communication often goes between an NF and an SJ. One is stuck in the process of having to solve the concrete details, and the other is inspired by the idea that their imagination has just created and can't wait to tell the story. Both the detailed mind and the big-picture mind are necessary in our world, but the communication can be painful.

The SP and SJ speak concretely about the real world that they focus on, and the NT and NF speak abstractly as they theorize and dream up new ideas, possibilities, or theories.

This strength also bores the NF who looks at the forest first and then pays attention to the trees as needed. "Communication should be accurate," says the SJ, and by that they mean "pay attention to all the details; don't skip any." "You should see the big picture first," say the NF and NT, "otherwise you will not know where the details are leading." The conflict is classic.

Overuse of this concentration on the details creates a weakness and leads to getting bogged down in the details. When not overused, the self-image of the SJ rises as they take care of the details. Fulfillment follows for them. Let the SJ increase this strength, since it will make them all the more needed when details are paramount.

Success in all factual matters is in the details, but in the world of imagination and relationships, facts are not life's heartbeat. The SJ who lives in the real world and fashions goals for success in that world must develop this focus on details and become proficient in noticing them and in processing them.

How Do I Develop this Strength?
- Sharpen your observational skills by practice. Try to notice all the details.

- Focus on one detail at a time to develop focus. Multitasking spreads your focus. One detail at a time concentrates your focus.

- It should not be difficult to become a sharp observer and to develop a focus on the details. It comes naturally to SPs and SJs.

- Report all the details and see if you can improve your retention.

- Try to report details in a relevant sequential order to exercise your logistical mind.

Caution:

All temperaments lapse into weaknesses when they don't use their strengths, overuse them, or use them for destructive purposes such as damaging themselves or others. Here are further cautions for this strength.

- Good communication requires that we make sure the other person understands what we intended. It is incumbent on both parties to understand each other.

- Start with an understanding of the communication difficulties temperaments encounter and patiently work your way through until both understand each other.

- When you have the details correct, the task is then to establish the meaning of the details. Both the NT and NF can help you since this is what they have been made to do.

Good Samaritans — Helpmates

No one would remember the Good Samaritan if he only had good intentions.
~ Margaret Thatcher

This helping spirit is a combination of many strengths, chiefly their concern for others and the urge to do their duty and be reliable. In helping they prove their usefulness.

SJs take to occupations such as nursing and childcare (helpful workmates of all kinds) like ducks take to water. Since they want to be recognized as significant contributors to society. Whether in the home, club, church, community, or nation, they logically see themselves as the helpers of their fellow citizens. "Anything that needs to be done should be done" is the way they see it. Everyone has a duty to pay back for the privilege of living in a free society or even for the privilege of living. This is their healthy responsible contribution to our welfare.

When helped by an SJ Good Samaritan, you will feel their care and love in a powerful way. They will attend to details — even sacrificially — and often follow up to see if there is more to do.

You can almost count on an SJ to help. A weakness is developed in their character when they don't use this strength. The practical love their helping generates creates a powerful feeling of fulfillment and satisfaction in them. The use of this strength ranks as one of the best ways to restore a fading self-image or a slide in the direction of depression when neglected or misused.

Developing their helping attitude is sure to propel SJs on the way to reaching their potential and feeling the payback of gratification it unfailingly provides.

The Good Samaritan

I was driving on a back road in the Colorado Mountains with an SJ passenger. As we rounded a corner, we spotted a pickup in the other lane with one wheel off and the drum resting on the road, damaged. The SJ called for me to stop. He got out and ran back to the truck. Finding no owner near and no wheel, he decided that the wheel must be somewhere in the stream beside the road.

Leaping the fence, he started his search, only to meet the owner who also thought the wheel was there somewhere in the stream. Willows made it hard to find anything. After getting wet and spending fifteen minutes searching, my SJ passenger found the wheel about 200 yards downstream. Although it required getting quite dirty, he lugged it back, not to its owner but all the way to the stranded vehicle.

I had joined the search and concluded he had done his good deed and we could continue on our way. Not so. We then took the owner to the nearest phone, which was hard to find, and waited until he contacted help. Then we returned him to his vehicle to await roadside assistance.

Saying goodbye, we set off again. My SJ passenger appeared to have deeply enjoyed helping the man and felt rewarded for doing what he said "anyone would do."

How Do I Develop this Strength?
• Nurture your care for others. It is fed with small caring deeds for family, friends, and strangers.

• Stay positive because a negative SJ is not as likely to help others.

• Work on the strengths of responsibility and trust. They will help build this strength too.

• View your world through the eyes of those who really care.

Caution:
All temperaments lapse into weaknesses when they don't use their strengths, overuse them, or use them for destructive purposes such as damaging themselves or others. Here are further cautions for this strength.

• Don't help others to the neglect of your own family or those dependent on you.

Non-Dramatic — Concrete Speech

As we have just noted under the SJs strength, "Communicates with the Details," they are concrete in thought and expression. Unlike the SP whose language is vivid, SJs tend to a more prosaic way of talking.

Exactness in the reporting of details is expected of all people, not just fellow SJs. Often they will interupt you and correct you if you have made an error in detail. "It was 6:35, not 6:30, when we left!" They can't let it stand as 6:30 since that was not accurate.

If they are caught in saying 6:35 when it was 6:30, they will (at times) argue that it was 6:35, since their honor as accurate reporters is at stake.

Flowery language is not their norm; nor is it to their likeing. "Say it like it is: simple and plain!" they insist. Therefore, some can lack in an appreciation of the arts and prefer science, plain and powerful with its search for accurate facts.

Remember:
If you are an SJ, I hope you have chosen a strength and are determined to develop it. Even if you are not an SJ you will have sharpened your understanding of your own temperament by the study of the SJ.

A Convenient List of the SJ Temperament's Strengths

Here is a convenient list of the SJ temperament's main strengths that we dealt with.

Keep a list with you and develop one at a time.
- First, focus on being aware of when you are using your strengths.
- With practice and persistence, you will develop them.
- Training develops them even more and will help you understand them as you discover ways to further their use.

SJ Strengths Featuring Rules and Regulations

Lives tied to the past

Careful — cautious — concerned

Thoughtful and prepared

Responsible — dependable — solid work ethic

Do what is right — law abiding

Strong need to belong — social — respectable

Steady — not easily shaken

Trusts authority

Supervisors — managers — systems — routines

Stoical

Logistical in work and play

Communicates with the details

Good Samaritans - helpmates

Non-dramatic concrete speech

NT Strengths — Featuring Independence

All strengths, to some degree, may be found in any temperament. The following strengths are native to the NT and are found with greater intensity in the NT temperament. These are the core strengths at which an NT naturally excels if they take the time and effort to develop them.

The path to success for each of us is written in our strengths. Here, for the NT, you will find that path.

The strengths are not set out in any particular order nor do they have to be understood or practiced in a set order.

Take any of the strengths of your temperament one at a time and develop it until you are:
• Aware of when you use it and when you don't
• Have developed it as best you can
• Feel ready to go on to the next

To help you develop your strengths, a convenient "how to" list is at the end of the discussion of each strength. You might copy it and take it with you as you get used to operating your strengths.

Time Is Relative to the Task
(Orientation to Time)

Unlike the SP who lives in the present moment, or the SJ who lives in the past, or even the NF who lives in the future, the NTs seem to be unrelated to time. The uses of their strengths are related to the task at hand more than to time. NTs absorb themselves in a task and time is not a focus until the task is over, and then they wake up and ask what time it is. Even when no task is in process, they still don't seem to be focused on time. Of course, they live in the present; everyone does. But the identifying focus on time that is seen in the other temperaments is lacking.

This takes away the distractions that watching the clock can impose and allows them more inner calm and concentration as they attack their project — definitely a positive for the purpose of focus.

Like the NF, they are abstract and time is a concrete (not an abstract) reality. How can abstract temperaments be related to time? The NT and the NF solve this issue in two different ways: The NT only relates to time (the concrete reality) if their project is dependent in any way on time. As scientists (which many of them are) they can indulge themselves in projects that may take decades. Time is of no relative importance unless a deadline looms and creates a pressure. Therefore, they are unconcerned with time until the end of the project. When the deadline does approach it disturbs them since they must share their focus on their project with a focus on a clock. Split focus lessens creative energy.

The NF will solve their relation to the concrete nature of time by relating to the one aspect of time that is not concrete and, therefore, still abstract: the future.

So the NT seems unaffected by time and grows up at the pace of their interests, showing little stress over time constraints unless, as I said, time is important to their project.

At work, an NT may become so engrossed with a project that he falls behind a company's deadlines. At home, an NT who is immersed in a game of chess may firmly resist quitting for any appointment. Family and friends must understand or be ignored.

Most of their strengths are related to this view of time and, as a result, they appear calm and unhurried. If they are involved in a project, it may be hard to extract them for life's other interests — even those they love. Time is of the essence; time is a reality; time controls us and our achievements; and the NT calmly ignores all these truisms. NTs would agree with Thomas Huxley who said,

"Time, whose tooth gnaws away everything else, is powerless against truth."

The NT would add, "It is truth we are in pursuit of, and we have no pleasure in placating time."

Time is, for most people, simply the passage of events: moments ticking by. NTs are not resigned to time, either. One doesn't resign oneself to something one ignores.

Time can represent stress, bringing with it crisis and opportunity. There is nothing wrong with either as far as the NT is concerned, but if stress means distractions to deal with, they would rather clear their circumstances of all inconveniences if they can. If they can, they shut them out of their minds.

Kent, an NT in his mid-teens, was often lost in creating complicated machines with his large Lego set. If he was working on his design and his mother got angry at his chores not being done (which was often), he would stand, facing his mother as she railed at him (her voice rising for more emotional effect) and just stare at her. She would turn red and almost burst a blood vessel trying, in her words, to get through to him.

He wouldn't even twitch. His mother said, "If only he would have winced so that at least I would know I was getting through. He makes me so mad!" I asked what made her mad. She lowered her voice and tears ran down as she said, "I can't get him to react at all. I don't know what to do, and I know I am losing him"

If only she had understood. He was effectively dealing with his interruption. If you can't control your intrusions, you can shut them out.

At the same time that his mother was "blowing a valve," he was developing his strength. He was doing what an NT can do so well: responding in the way NTs know infuriates an emotional temperament and, at the same time, keeps the NT calm. They enjoy standing there, still and silent, watching an adult fly to pieces in front of their eyes. A few have told me it is amusing to them. Now you should know what __not__ to do in handling the adult NT when they don't meet your fury with their own but simply wait to watch you self-destruct.

Time itself doesn't matter much. It is what is *in* time that matters — its content. What does it represent? To the NT, time represents an opportunity to discover new and important things.

Hopefully, you have been convinced that time is viewed abstractly by both the NT and the NF. Begin to understand them by their relationship to time, and they will make more sense to you if you are the SP or the SJ.

This calm approach to time's pressures rewards the NT and they feel in control. Not only is their attitude to time a control measure, it brings a feeling of superiority to all those who demonstrate frustration over time.

If the NTs are going to succeed, they must adopt this attitude to time or they will lose their path in the many lengthy projects they set for themselves.

How Do I Develop this Strength?
• Ignore the clock!

• The NT starts with an optimistic mental attitude. They believe they can control almost anything and time itself cannot frustrate them.

• Learn how to focus without interruption, closing distractions out.

• Learn how to effectively deal with distractions without disconnecting relationships.

Caution:
All temperaments lapse into weaknesses when they don't use their strengths, overuse them, or use them for destructive purposes such as damaging themselves or others. Here are further cautions for this strength:

• Using this strength to ignore people will destroy your relationships.

- View all emotional displays as signs of ineffectiveness, but do not disrespect the person.

- Non-response can be a form of disrespect.

- Pride may develop and close your mind to the contributions of others.

- Time is an inevitable reality. We can't step outside of it and are wise to learn to live within it.

Strong Will — Determined

Victory belongs to the most persevering.
~ Napoleon Bonaparte

With a detachment toward reality and time, NTs set their jaws and face life with a determination to find answers and to succeed in their search for knowledge. Their road to success leads through the heart of "Determined City." Play is subservient to their goals or projects. Instinctively, they know the power of this single-eyed approach. They will sometimes go for amazingly long periods without indication of the need for a break or a refreshing diversion or even food.

The definition of "strong-willed and determined" for an NT is: Turn neither to the left hand nor the right. Set your course and go where it leads. Nothing must be allowed to divert you. They are not stubborn for stubborn's sake nor determined without a goal or a purpose.

Determination makes them appear rather serious. For an NT, there's not much excitement in life outside of their goals. Excitement itself is viewed as suspect.

Such focus needs a strong will and an unbending determination. They feed each other. Focus builds determination and determination sharpens the focus that creates it. NTs can stay focused on a project for a lifetime.

Their cool calm spirit helps, since determination is most successfully thwarted by emotions. Curiosity also aids a strong will in the NT because they must find out how things work or why things are the way they are and whether they can be changed for the better. What better way to achieve a goal than to be determined, with a mind controlled by a calm, rigid focus?

They seek change because they see it as the panacea for all improvement, and mental force (will power) is the psychological means of bringing it about. Therefore, they seem to many to be masters of the use of quiet, inner strength.

Strength is not in physical might but in mental determination. "The mind rules the body." Tricia believed this and lived by it. She was an unusually strong NT for a woman. Two-thirds of the men are Ts, and she was a strong T. Most NT women are very effective, but more inclined to allow feelings a place in their minds. Tricia had learned to control any emotional surge, and this gave her a power most NT men don't develop as acutely as she had.

She played basketball and, at just over six feet, would often defeat the males in her neighborhood. She wasn't more muscular, but she was mentally tougher and proud of it. Strategy was her secret weapon, and she wielded it with skill and crushing power. She could see possibilities on the court and would set up a move so fast the men would wonder "where did that come from?"

Add to this mental toughness a fierce determination and she could compete with the best of them. The mind rules the body. However, basketball was not her major interest. Debate and theorizing attracted her and, as an INTP, this is no surprise. She took great pride in confusing an opponent in an argument or winning outright. Intense focus seemed to be a force field that surrounded her and others could feel it. She seemed to have no feelings, although she did. They were suppressed and kept under lock and key.

Tricia's outstanding ability to hold her emotions in check and display a calm determination was used to propel her into leadership in the field of engineering.

Determination and focus is available to all temperaments. If you are an SP, it is essential to your success in physical skills and artisan pursuits. The SJ displays strong determination when, stoically, they hold firm in the tremors of life, and the NF will display great determination in making a dream come true.

So why is the NT singled out for this strength? They display it in combination with a calm control of their emotions. Determination is never more threatened than when it is weakened by emotional traumas. In this, the NT can be emulated.

This determination is an emotional commitment, albeit unseen and undisplayed in the NT. Determination needs more than focus to energize it. It needs the support of strong emotions. The emotions that support the NT's determination are like a deep river, running fast and strong, its surface unbroken by waves and its power unnoticed and deceptive.

Determination is threefold:
- A mental decision
- A fierce focus
- An emotional commitment

The NT has all three, with the latter calm, unseen and, therefore, a surprise and an unexpected force. They hate for their emotions to be seen.

Their main weakness is a stubborn will that won't change even when another approach is clearly needed. When they overuse this strength they can lose all objectivity and come to false conclusions. They can destroy the closeness of relationships. Overuse destroys the strength's integrity. The NT can be too determined.

As they journey on the path of discovery they feel great rewards from participating and from the quiet excitement of what might be uncovered in their search for something better.

How Do I Develop this Strength?
- Focus intensely on your idea or task. Focus builds determination and then feeds more focus.

- Keep your emotions in check and under control.

247

- Keep mentally calm.

- Lend emotional power to your decision to be determined.

- Let your curiosity lead you.

Caution:

All temperaments lapse into weaknesses when they don't use their strengths, overuse them, or use them for destructive purposes such as damaging themselves or others. Here are further cautions for this strength.

- You can have too much of a good thing.

- Take care that your determination does not destroy your relationships. Become determined to feed your relationships, as well.

- Don't become so determined that you lose the ability to see what is outside your self-imposed blinders.

Strategic — Theoretical Systems

Emotional control, strategic planning, tactical maneuvers, all of this stuff is so relevant to the way we lead our lives.
~ Lou Krieger (truly an NT point of view)

Let's understand strategy.

Strategy is a way of attempting to leave little to chance. To eliminate unwanted possibilities, the NT needs to devise a plan that understands the possible moves of an opponent or the contingencies of the proposed theory. This requires the forming of strategic theoretical systems — theoretical because they haven't happened yet.

Theory is the NT's homeland, and the mental functioning of the NT is to search for unwanted surprises and produce a theory that marginalizes them.

Strategy also involves the science of planning, theorizing about the options, setting goals, and directing operations. Strategy is not all logic; it can be seen as the artful and scientific means of accomplishing some purpose.

The NT has a reductionist way of thinking, reducing the focus to ever smaller details. The NT is also intuitive but controls the intuition within the bounds of reason. As a result the NT's mind sees the details and the possible contingencies and theorizes with artful and logistical consistency.

Their strategies are all devised with their goal in mind. Then, once the NT has the strategy, they don't hesitate to execute it. They are all about the use of strategies. Strategy requires, at times, considerable research, and research lies in the NT's comfortable territory too.

However, strategy works with least disturbance in the world of things and ideas, research and discovery, and is often disrupted by the world of people. The NT is not naturally skilled at working with people to accomplish a predetermined goal. Often their relationships are only marginally successful, since they lack the intense sensitivity to intuit people's feelings and thoughts and the emotional sensitivity to bond on that level. It can affect their strategies profoundly. (This added human dimension is brought to the intuitive thinking process by the NF.)

The designing of concepts and ideas to form patterns of thought and complex theories excites the NT. They will also spend countless hours designing objects. Seldom are their strategies devoid of some kind of complex design. NTs love to create complex, effective systems and they sometimes lose sight of the superiority of simplicity.

Since the time of the Greeks, the word *strategy* was used for military operations and even for the army itself. Strategy, today, is any plan to defeat opposition or achieve a goal. Chess is a game of strategy where a war is waged to capture the opponent's king. For some NTs, life itself is a game of strategy to defeat all opponents.

A blind spot.
"I have a plan," Ben said.
"Tell me." I asked?

He then launched into a detailed strategy for training people with a plan that laid heavy demands on them.

"Do you think they will really commit to this," I asked?
"Why not? It makes sense."
"But isn't it too complex and demanding?" I replied.
"Not really. You simply ..." (and he outlined the program step-by-step).
"Some people already think you are trying to force them to do what they don't want to do," I advised.
"Why wouldn't they do this?" he questioned with astonishment.
"They won't. They have told me."

At this point there was an uncomprehending stare from this strong NT, followed by a look of disgust. He had not taken into account that the people he was trying to lead had already become resistant to his high expectations and wanted to take things much more slowly. They were complaining that he didn't take their concerns (read "feelings") into account. He didn't listen to them. He didn't understand their other commitments. He wasn't warm and loving. The list has no end when people have already disconnected. His only hope was to listen to them and fashion a path they were willing to tread. A leader is not a leader when the people he leads aren't following.

It's this insensitivity to people's feelings that can foil the NT's leadership.

If a weakness develops, it usually is in their failure to understand people, relationships, and the power of emotions. For many NTs, they do not understand this relevant set of facts. It is an overuse of their analytical strategizing, plus their tendency not to adequately observe the human factors involved in their decisions, that often leads to this weakness.

They must learn that rational strategies are not the only tool needed to solve problems in a world dominated by humans and their interests. NTs need the complex skills of diplomacy and emotional logic to be fully equipped.

To be successful, an NT cannot treat this strength as unimportant. It lies at the center of all they do. Developing sound and effective strategies will lead them to success.

How Do I Develop this Strength?

- Strategize everything. The more you use this strength the more it will develop.

- Think of all the contingencies and try to leave nothing to chance.

- Develop your intuitive abilities because intuition sees things that logic does not see.

- Study theory and strategic skills.

- Always take into account the emotions of people and plan for their unexpected challenges. These are contingencies too.

Caution:

All temperaments lapse into weaknesses when they don't use their strengths, overuse them, or use them for destructive purposes such as damaging themselves or others. Here are further cautions for this strength.

- Life is more than a game of strategy.

- Take care that you do not disconnect from people as you become lost in a world of one-upmanship.

- Consider that winning may be less important than loving and giving.

Intense Curiosity

Only the curious will learn ... the quest quotient has always excited me more than the intelligence quotient.
~ Eugene S. Wilson

The cure for boredom is curiosity.
~ Dorothy Parker (US author and humorist)

The important thing is not to stop questioning. Curiosity has its own reason for existing. One cannot help but be in awe when he contemplates the mysteries of eternity, of life, of the marvelous structure of reality. It is enough if one tries

251

*merely to comprehend a little of this mystery every day. Never lose a hold on
curiosity.*
~ *Albert Einstein*

Curiosity compels the NT to ask why, how, what, and what for
incessantly. If they don't ask it audibly, they are asking it mentally.
"When" is of far less importance to someone who is concerned with
theoretical abstractions, so they live in their theoretical world, engaged
with these four main questions and, as we have noticed already,
disinterested in time.

What is happening is the NT is being intensely driven to discover
secrets to the world in which they live. They believe that analysis and
reason will unfailingly lead to discovery and truth. So they bend their
mental powers to the task. Everything else must take second place to
this inner passion.

Curiosity fuels their ingenuity too. First they must understand how
things work before they can apply their ingenuity to find new ways of
doing things. NTs will probe anything if they detect that it holds
promise of a new discovery or a new way of doing things.

If this strength is not developed by constant use, the NT is ashamed of
themselves and their self-image falls. If it has fallen, the path to its
recovery is to simply use this strength. Strength is built by constant
use.

Not to know our world can be embarrassing for the NT since they
pride themselves in knowledge and understanding. This drive to know
is fueled by their sense of who they are.

You remember the adage "curiosity killed the cat"? The main weakness
that can develop from this strength is the overuse of curiosity.
Overuse can not only kill, but it can destroy one's project, lead to
endless investigation with no profitability, and can become an end in
itself. Remember the cat!

Curiosity is a fabulous tool, but like all other tools it has a limited use
and purpose. The NT will find it hard to accept that curiosity can be
overused.

(NFs are also very curious. Their focus is on the future and its possibilities and on people and their complex functioning. Nearly all I have written here can be said of the NF as well, particularly the INF.)

The sense of fulfillment that the use of this strength brings to the NT is very rewarding. They feel they are being useful when they are seeking answers. The world would still be in the dark ages if it weren't for NTs being released to use their curiosity and being appreciated for it.

It starts early for most. Ron had been very curious as long his parents could remember. Everything from the light socket, the stove, the washing machine and to the TV, of course, had been investigated. To visit his room and find the computer in pieces all over the floor was hard to take calmly.

Ron's room was full of rocks. Yes, rocks. All were lined up according to some system that was mysterious to his parents. His teachers in high school loved his curiosity but were threatened by his astute questions that often left them without a good answer. He sometimes attempted to embarrass them whenever they stalled as a bid for time to find an answer. Science classes were his love, from biology with its dissecting of frogs to the mysteries of chemistry.

Strangely (to his parents) he had no interest in girls. He was far too focused on his research to be much concerned. That would come later. When an interest in girls did surface, it seemed like he married quickly because it supported his need for someone to take care of all the things he had no time for.

All this early curiosity paid off. Now he is trying to design better and more functional streets and public places for the enjoyment of all, and he has an impressive portfolio of his successes. The NT is born to be curious and to make a better world for society. Curiosity can lead us on a wild ride, from dismantling computers to rocks, frogs, chemicals, streets, and structures. Where it will lead one can never tell.

Success is in the continued use of this strength and to following where it leads.

How Do I Develop this Strength?

- Be curious. Ask questions of everyone. Don't settle for lame answers.

- Follow your urges to discover.

- Build your knowledge. The more you learn, the more questions you will have. Knowledge does not lead to a mental file of facts, but to questions and more questions that lead to more knowledge. We learn to learn more.

- Link your curiosity to your ingenuity. Play with answers and create ingenious inventions. That way you will feed your curiosity with success.

Caution:

All temperaments lapse into weaknesses when they don't use their strengths, overuse them, or use them for destructive purposes such as damaging themselves or others. Here are further cautions for this strength.

- Remember the cat! Curiosity can lead us into danger, loss, and frustration. Beware.

- We can become so focused that we disrupt or destroy our human relationships. We need to cultivate relationships or we won't benefit from the wisdom, knowledge, love, and strength of others.

- Hypersensitivity in the pursuit of anything can lead to burnout.

- For the human system to operate at its maximum we need to feed all of its demands, not just one overpowering urge.

Questioning — Skeptical

A fact is a simple statement that everyone believes. It is innocent, unless found guilty. A hypothesis is a novel suggestion that no one wants to believe. It is guilty, until found effective.
~ Edward Teller

Skepticism is a negative pursuit for most people and, therefore, not a strength. Strengths are positive, not negative, drives. Questions can be positive or negative too.

Being skeptical has a positive orientation for the NT. Its purpose is not to break down or destroy but to find truth and to prove its positive findings. (Philosophically speaking, we can't prove a negative anyhow.) In this sense it is a great strength and blesses humanity.

NTs, with their conviction of the power of logic, find questioning that is guided by logical reasoning to be a handy tool. The truth must be found. Questions can lead to truth, and logical skepticism that is aimed at the discovery of truth (not the defense of a damaging theory) can be that tool.

They do not trust the past. Whatever was thought back then could be wrong now, and some even feel it is wrong simply because it belongs to the "ignorant" (in their minds) past. So all past ways of doing things, which means all traditions as well, must not be petrified or held precious, but challenged and replaced with new and better ways or dispensed with altogether. The SJ, with their desire to protect tradition, clashes head-on with this way of thinking.

NTs wish for the future to be better and to change. They also believe they have the mental equipment to do this, and some appoint themselves the apostles of a new and better world.

This strength gives the NT great confidence and a belief in their abilities because they feel they are the ones who logically probe and dissect everything, finding the hidden elements and the better way of doing things. NTs are not usually shy about being called arrogant since they feel they possess hard-earned knowledge and have come about it honestly.

At best, the past is only of historical interest to them, and it is not needed to guide the future. They believe their ingenuity and their use of reason are their only needed guides.

This attitude disturbs the SJ terribly because the past, to them, holds many lessons for the future, and we don't throw away what has proved useful and needed. "Change is risky," they say, "and is not always good."

The future is not trusted either, so the skeptical element in the NT tries to control it and mold it to their theoretical fancies. When taken to the extreme, this amounts to a mental power grab that sets the NT up as the only authority and the sage of all things. Skeptical attitudes can, in a strange way, lead to confidence.

Obviously, this extreme is a display of arrogance and ignorance. Skepticism, curiosity, and ingenuity are not the only tools for the making of a better world; love, faith, trust, and the traits of the SP, SJ and NF are also much needed and equally efficacious.

The other side of this dispute is the great value that careful, honest, and appropriate skepticism can bring to our world and our beliefs. Nothing is sacred to the NT. All must undergo constant scrutiny with the purpose of finding new ways of understanding it, or using it, or of making a better "mouse trap."

To find new ways and use new concepts, one must possess a natural degree of doubt. Doubt should lead to questioning with a positive purpose: a search for solutions. Skepticism, to the contrary, when negative in purpose, tears everything apart, except for the skeptic's own cherished beliefs.

Questioning is a strength. Skepticism can quickly become a weakness. Skepticism often leads to premature abandonment of an idea or a project. It can also develop a harmful tenacity to continue when the exit has long been passed. So this strength must be used constructively or it can be damaging and ineffective.

The proof of the positive effects of questioning is immortalized in the story of Doubting Thomas, John 20. Thomas wouldn't believe without the evidence that he finds necessary. His purpose is not to destroy but to be convinced.

In the story, it is instructive to note that he is not condemned for his search for evidence or his skeptical attitude. He is granted his evidence and then warned of the lesser glory for those who must have evidence before they believe. The NT needs to understand the role of purpose in being skeptical.

Weaknesses abound in the overuse and wrong use of this strength.
The fulfillment the NT feels from ardent questioning feeds on its own successes. The NT feels justified in questioning and adopting a skeptical attitude, and they feel empowered by their success to a

significant degree. To be the best that they can be, NTs must question with positive purpose. It characterizes the NT's road to success.

How Do I Develop this Strength?

• Question!

• Do so with a positive purpose in mind.

• It is a means to an end, not an end in itself. Therefore, don't consider it a goal for your life.

• Questions open up possibilities. Statements close a subject and end debate. Favor questions.

Caution:

All temperaments lapse into weaknesses when they don't use their strengths, overuse them, or use them for destructive purposes such as damaging themselves or others. Here are further cautions for this strength.

• Watch out for skepticism in its negative, destructive form.

• If we are going to destroy we must somehow know beforehand that what we would destroy has no purpose in this universe. Limited as we are, we can hardly assume that kind of knowledge.

Independent – Self-Reliant

It is not wealth one asks for, but just enough to preserve one's dignity, to work unhampered, to be generous, frank and independent.
~ W. Somerset Maugham

Independence in an NT is a very strong drive. If things go wrong, they will show you that the NT must find a way to fix it. They will often refuse help and struggle excessively in the belief that they must not fail. Only with independent effort can they feel proud of their accomplishments. "Going it alone" is the definition of independence for the NT. If they don't singlehandedly do it, they have proved to themselves that they are lacking in ingenuity and mental acuity.

We want people to be independent and self-reliant, but we are social beings, dependent on each other to be able to live in our complex world. We depend on others for our food, water, shelter, and a thousand other things. Total independence is not an achievable goal, since male depends on female and vice versa to begin with! NTs must teach themselves the limits of independence. Others usually can't teach them since that amounts to being dependent on the teacher.

Their self-image drops dramatically when they fail to be self-reliant. To have to depend on anyone else for life's necessities is failure for them of a devastating nature.

These are seldom the ones that stay at home and rely on the support of parents, unless it is an INTP who has lost direction and is circling without a strong motivation. This condition is, of course, an NT living in his weaknesses. They need to return to their independence and carve their own path if they are to succeed.

Reliance was not what Shirley would admit was her problem. True, she was still at home at age 30 and financially dependent on her parents' care. However, some things are too hurtful to admit.

She played sports, worked on her theoretical business, which would (in her estimation) provide for a rich future. To fill the rest of the time she drenched her lack of fulfillment at the bar in the company of her friends. They were thinning out. She had no job and hadn't been employed for more than two years.

Her strength was independence, but here she was, as dependent as one can be. The only way out of her weakness was to exert her strength and lay plans for immediate change, and then with determination to pursue them. The way out of weaknesses is the reverse of how we got there in the first place.

Refusal to admit our condition and exercise our strengths always leads to behavior that is frustrating to ourselves and others. There is hope for Shirley. She is contemplating help at last. For an NT, this is a tall hurdle to jump.

Independence can feed self-approval to the point of pride. Pride is defined as "thinking more of yourself than the facts justify." The facts show that the NT is a dependent being as well as one who must exercise an appropriate amount of independence. The weakness of independence is in overuse of this self-reliant attitude in the NT — or in anyone.

Healthy use of independence supports the ingenious, creative, questioning powers of the NT.

Self-reliance is self-fulfilling. The strength pays us back. Success is often a matter of balance. Keep this strength within its healthy parameters to be the best that you can be.

How Do I Develop this Strength?
• Strengthen your beliefs in your abilities.

• Remove the obstacles that are standing in the way to independence.

• Plan for independence and pursue your plans.

Caution:
All temperaments lapse into weaknesses when they don't use their strengths, overuse them, or use them for destructive purposes such as damaging themselves or others. Here are further cautions for this strength.

• This is a limited strength and can hurt you too.

• Practice it with caution.

• Balance your independence with acceptable dependence.

Calm — Cool — Collected

Nothing is so bitter that a calm mind cannot find comfort in it.
~ Seneca (5 BC-65 AD)

Never be in a hurry; do everything in a quiet calm spirit.
~ St Francis de Sales

NTs have been accused of having ice in their veins. However, calmness of spirit can be a very necessary strength, since a calm spirit often handles the pressures of life best.

Keeping emotions in control removes (for NTs) the possibility of interference that can disrupt their thoughts and confuse the results. They can face extreme criticism and pressure without flinching or panic. Most of us would wish for more of this natural NT ability — especially the NFs. We have already met this strength when we considered the NT's strong will and determination and their use of calmness to aid their determination.

Passion and excitement are kept inside the NT most of the time because both of these display emotion and must be kept in control.

NTs appear to have no emotions until someone tries to inhibit their freedom to explore or make them conform when they don't think it makes sense. They can resist with stubborn determination. Resistance can be a refusal to communicate or outright anger vented at you for limiting their drives.

The cool calm exterior is a control on emotional engagement with a purpose to further enable a pure rational process of the mind.

If they are ruffled, you can be sure they are living in their weaknesses and this strength is simply not being used. Teach them to use it. Without it, they fail themselves. They are also the ones with a strong willpower who can be told "Use your strength" or "Be calm and think clearly," and they can.

To some they appear rude and self-centered in their cool responses and calm resistance. It can be used by them as a mask or a defense or a weapon to keep distractions at bay.

In its own way it deeply fulfills them to be calm and keep their cool. They see this as an expression of proud superiority to be able to do it in the face of attack or pressure.

How Do I Develop this Strength?

• Keep believing in the positive benefits of rational responses.

• Savor your calm spirit when it shows itself. Appreciation of a strength directs attention to its value.

• Keep developing control over your emotions.

Caution:

All temperaments lapse into weaknesses when they don't use their strengths, overuse them, or use them for destructive purposes such as damaging themselves or others. Here are further cautions for this strength.

• Don't discount the value of emotion altogether. You are using emotional powers to be calm and cool.

• Overuse of it can lead to disconnectedness with your world.

• Wrong use can lead to disrespect of others, among other things.

Logical — Reasonable — Must Make Sense

NTs, in their consistent use of logic, should not forget...

If scientific reasoning were limited to the logical processes of arithmetic, we should not get very far in our understanding of the physical world. One might as well attempt to grasp the game of poker entirely by the use of the mathematics of probability.
~ Vannevar Bush (US electrical engineer)

Logic is a function of our minds. Thinking logically is a way to control our thinking. Greek philosophers have thought of logic as having a spiritual content since thoughts belong to our spirit — the things that happen inside us that can't be seen, the spiritual world. The NT and NF are people who live their lives in this so-called spiritual world more than in the real world. Being all about your mind feels comfortable to the NT and the NF.

If they are anything, NTs are logical — children of the Sophists. Almost everything in this temperament supports the common goal of ingenious discovery by the use of logic. Logic, analysis, reason, and the drive to do nothing that does not make sense convene an atmosphere of discovery.

This temperament is not in sole possession of logic, but they are unique in that their logic is usually devoid of emotional disturbance. They might even feel emotions have no place in intelligence, which is of course not true. Emotions discover and verify things just like logic does. Logic provides a guide to the thinking process. Emotions also guide thinking and are simply a different way of thinking, a different guide.

If it makes sense, is reasonable or is approved by them as logical, NTs can be easily persuaded to do it. They will normally do it without much consideration.   Reason and logic are their ultimate standards of judgment.

They like to argue and are true followers of Protagoras, seeing two sides to every issue and arguing the superiority of one. (Cannot two sides of an issue be equally true?) When logic is used alone in the field of human relationships, much can be missed and misinterpreted. Overuse of logic to the exclusion of emotions is a common mistake of the NT.

An NT father attended a parenting seminar designed to help people understand their children. He was supplied with an assessment intended to help him define the temperament of his children. Studiously he examined each question. The answers are a choice between A and B. He was told that he would most likely find a little of each answer in his child and must settle on which he felt was the most dominant.

He struggled with the answers endlessly, coming to no firm decision. Likelihood is not conclusive; nor is a leaning one way or another to the NT. He wanted conclusive proof of his son's tendencies. Logic itself often does not provide conclusive proof, only probability, which fact he appeared to have forgotten. When asked "What do you feel is the best answer?" he felt that he was being asked to judge based on emotions. That didn't help; it only confused him more.

When the NT is looking in pure black and white, all shades of gray are lost. He was lost in logic and preciseness and couldn't decide on A or B. To help him be satisfied with a dominant tendency proved very difficult. He needed to see that the shades of gray, which most of us display in our personalities, were as important as black and white in determining who we are.

Then he turned to his own assessment. Now more trouble faced him. How could he be a little of both A and B? And why the vague request to answer based on an estimate of his preferences.

I use this experience to point out that few things in life are solved with pure logic or black and white thinking. Logical people find preferences dubious elements. Logic, while a valuable tool, has its limitations in an emotion-packed world.

A few moments later a question was asked, "Does this make sense to you?" and his answer was instantaneous.

To talk and reason logically gratifies the NT. They feel as though they have control and are being honest to themselves and with others. To ask them to decide based on feelings is another story. We must be who we are and follow the road to success written into our *innerkinetics*. So the NT must make maximum, but accurate, use of logic to be the best that they can be. They can enhance their decisions at times by including the logic of emotions.

How Do I Develop this Strength?

- Train your mind with logical exercises (mathematics, for example, or chess).

- Study logic.

- Practice analyzing statements, because it opens up the meaning so you can more easily see what is logical.

- Take a statement to its logical conclusions and the rationality of it will become apparent.

- Keep emotions controlled, but don't eliminate them from the discussion as they hold truth of their own.

- Learn and use the guidelines of probability, presumption, and burden of proof.

Caution:

All temperaments lapse into weaknesses when they don't use their strengths, overuse them, or use them for destructive purposes such as damaging themselves or others.   Here are further cautions for this strength.

- Remember the limitations of logic in all informal discussions.

- Settle for probability in most human matters.

- Live life with more than logic.

Ingenious

It will be found, in fact, that the ingenious are always fanciful, and the truly imaginative never otherwise than analytical.
~ *Edgar Allen Poe*

Originally the word *ingenious* meant "gifted with genius."   A genius is one who has great mental ability in some area of the brain, usually not in all mental skills.   Geniuses are exceptions to the norm.   No temperament can claim sole rights to producing geniuses.

The word ingenious in modern usage means clever, original, inventive, resourceful, and this is the sense in which we use it of the NT.

Ingeniousness appears most often in the NT's inventions, strategies, and theorizing.   Therefore, this strength frequently appears as a major drive that pulls them toward discovery.

The NT is the intuitive mind with a compulsion to create a better world.   Their intuition is, however, governed and limited by reason and, therefore, their ingenuity is confined more to the cerebral than the emotional insight and prescience displayed by the NF.

NTs can take longer to come to their ingenious discoveries than the NF because reason is a slower process than the lightening speed of emotionally driven insight. The NT majors on the analytical approach, and the NF, using both reason with emotion, majors on insights that see things in a flash of inspiration and then, after the fact, analyzes them. Speed, however, is not everything.

To be ingenious, NTs generate and organize ideas and concepts in their minds in resourceful, insightful, and clever ways. This has led to many discoveries and inventions that have improved our way of life.

It is hard to see how overuse of ingenuity is possible. Nonuse and wrong use are the likely causes of weakness. Creativity in the theoretical world brings great satisfaction and the NT is truly fulfilled when their ingenuity has been accepted and successfully used.

An ingenious discovery or invention can mean instant success. This is a certain path for the NT to find and reach their potential greatness. So develop ingenuity in all its forms.

How Do I Develop this Strength?
• Think outside the box.

• Bring together ideas that have not been previously associated for an ingenious result.

• Organize and reorganize your ideas. New concepts may develop.

• Use the greatest mental power, imagination, to give you new insights.

• Logic, determination, questioning, the use of curiosity, and strategy aid the ingenious discovery or design.

• Pursue the inspiration of your intuition.

• Perspiration sometimes surpasses inspiration.

Caution:
All temperaments lapse into weaknesses when they don't use their strengths, overuse them, or use them for destructive purposes such as

damaging themselves or others.   Here are further cautions for this strength.

• Remember, ingenuity is a result of the use of several strengths, so develop all the related strengths for the best chance at being ingenious, but avoid dispersing your energy and weakening it. Weakness is found in focus that is too widely dispersed.

• Avoid a focus that narrows your vision and excludes the unexpected.

• Don't waste too much time at finding an "ingenious way of being ingenious!"

Efficient — Effective
Competent — Achieve

The efficient man is the man that thinks for himself.
~ *Charles W. Eliot*

The self-image of the NT depends on achieving and acting with competence! Without effective results they feel they have proved to themselves that their drives are retarded.   That hurts!   NTs must succeed.

Being *efficient* means to produce a desired effect with a minimum of effort and with the least waste and expense. NTs are always trying to achieve this goal and feel rewarded with success when they do.

Every temperament can be *effective* with their own strengths.   We call effectiveness a strength of the NT because they must be effective or they will fall into a demeaning self-image.   It is critical to them. Theories must be effective or they end up on the scrap heap. They see logic as effective and that's why they value it.   Their desire to be mentally superior also demands that they be effective. If not effective, they are not who they are.

With the NT, their theorizing is all for the practical purpose of being competent. What works really matters to them. They are in all things stubbornly pragmatic. They focus on the relationship between the means and the end and press toward their goals, trying to anticipate the complex results of their actions. It must work.

The word "chief" means a leader. Placing the letter "a" in front (a-chief) is the way we got our word *achieve*. Therefore, when we achieve we become the chief. That's interesting since the NT always wants to be the chief. Again, it is the demand of their self-image.

To achieve, they set goals and create expectations and are driven in their desire to reach them, and even exceed them. Everything about their temperament is designed to succeed in discovery and ingenuity. When expectations are not met and must be dismissed the NT suffers the pain of defeat.

In their drive to efficiently achieve their goals, if they get bogged down in logistics, they usually do not equal the skills of the SJ (who plans the efficient movement of goods and people with unmatched success) and they feel failures. Their pride is affected. Efficiency of thought and strategy is more the skill of the NT, not logistics. It is not easy to observe the difference in practical matters since strategies are usually logistically implemented.

A man in his twenties (NT) came to me to sharpen his skills at leadership. He expressed this overpowering desire to be successful. He saw himself as ingenious, logical, and determined, but he could not settle for that knowledge of himself without proving that he was effective. This is typical in my experience of all NTs. Failure to get results crushes their self-esteem.

He was the leader of a church youth group and was looking for this position to springboard him to something else. He told me he would do anything to achieve his goal and his determination was obvious.

After some extensive examination of his leadership, it was apparent that the youth liked him but had disconnected from him. He was not paying attention to their powerful, emotional experiences and was all about what makes sense, not what their feelings were doing to them. So he ingeniously used several of the youth to first educate him on what they really felt and where in life they really were. Then he co-opted them to be his mouthpiece to the group.

He reasoned his faith, and they applied it with the emotive content the other youth could relate to. He was soon successful in regaining the youth and increasing the size of the group significantly.

Most often, it is the emotional disconnect that makes the NT ineffective in human relations.

Weaknesses are formed when these strengths become an end in themselves. Overuse can lead to obsession with details. However, to achieve is a real fulfillment and brings a sense of personal worth with it.

Success is defined as effective achievement. Therefore, the NT must achieve this goal and use this drive to give thrust to their attempts at being all that they can be.

How Do I Develop this Strength?

• By setting effectiveness and competence as your intermediate goal.

• By careful examination of all your methods, excluding all that are ineffective and focusing on those that achieve results.

• By determining whether you have developed mental blocks or mental sets that make it difficult to achieve results.

• By feedback. Feedback is the champion's breakfast.

• By using another's "eyes" to improve your vision.

Caution:

All temperaments lapse into weaknesses when they don't use their strengths, overuse them, or use them for destructive purposes such as damaging themselves or others. Here are further cautions for this strength.

• Results are not everything; quality of experience is important too.

• An overemphasis on results can defeat you.

• Place major emphasis on who you are, not just on how effective you are.

Abstract in Speech

If you are an SP or SJ there will be a communication barrier with NTs. You will find NTs difficult to follow at times. Abstract conversation does not focus on concrete facts and details but uses the language of concepts, ideas, and theoretical abstractions. You will find yourself saying, "Tell me plainly," or "Put that in real details."

NTs think like they talk: theoretically. A concrete, real-life example may be difficult for them, at times, to supply, since it causes them to think of the various possibilities. Possibilities lead to the creation of theories, and it can distract them from finding a real-life example, or even from wanting to find one. Making sure you understand what they are trying to say is the way to solve most communication problems between Ss and Ns.

Just thinking abstractly and dreaming up theories is a reward in itself to both the NT and the NF.

These NTs, though rare, will open up a new world to the SP and the SJ, and their strengths will enrich life for all of us. Like any temperament, their weaknesses are not helpful.

If you are an NT, I hope you have chosen a strength and determined to develop it. Even if you are not an NT, you will have sharpened your understanding of your own temperament by the study of the NT temperament.

A Convenient List of the NT Temperament's Strengths

Here is a convenient list of the NT temperament's main strengths that we dealt with.

Keep a list with you and develop them one at a time.

- First focus on being aware of when you are using your strengths.
- Then, with practice and persistence, you will develop them.
- Training develops them even more and will help you understand them as you discover ways to further their use.

NT Strengths Featuring Independence

Time is relevant to the task

Strong will — determined

Strategic — theoretical systems

Intense curiosity

Questioning — skeptical

Independent — self reliant

Calm — cool — collected

Logical — reasonable — must make sense

Ingenious

Efficient — effective — competent — achieve

Abstract in speech

NF Strengths — Featuring Idealism and Sensitivity

All strengths may be found in any temperament to some degree. The following strengths are native to the NF and are found with greater intensity in the NF temperament. These are the core strengths at which an NF naturally excels if they take the time and effort to develop them.

The path to success for each of us is written in our strengths. Here you will find that path for the NF.

The strengths are not set out in any particular order, nor do they have to be understood or practiced in a set order.

Take any of the strengths of your temperament one at a time and develop it until you are:
- Aware of when you use it and when you don't
- Have developed it as best you can
- Feel ready to go on to the next

To help you develop your strengths, a convenient "how to" list is at the end of the discussion of each strength. You might copy it and take it with you as you get used to operating your strengths.

NF strengths can be divided into two main categories: those that relate to the future and those that relate to sensitivity. Some have a relevancy to both. This is the super sensitive temperament. Before we deal with the strengths, we will examine the nature of the NF mind because it can be a puzzle.

The NF Mind (Complex)

Note these differences. The SP is tactical and practical; the SJ is logistical and practical; the NT is strategic and pragmatic (as Keirsey and others would designate them), and the NF is complex and conceptual, blending a number of elements from the complexity of their *innerkinetics.*

My observations and understanding of the NF **mind** is that it is fashioned by idealism (it seems to be always ideologically influenced), intuition, imagination, and the emotions, which are used together with reason but sometimes predominate. That's a complex bundle.

To the NF, emotions are facts of life and reason should include emotion in its calculations. This results in a mind that thinks in symbol, metaphor, and the broad, holistic patterns of "the big picture."

These powerful drives work together to fashion the NF's mental landscape. There is a constant interaction of elements. Emotional content is affected by idealistic dreams, imagination, and by the insistence that everything has significance. Intuition appears by way of the path of feelings and spiritual insights and is not limited by the rules of reason. They all influence each other. It is "seeing the big picture" (in idealistic colors, perhaps) that characterizes the NF mind most. Diplomatic, yes, but it is much more. I have not found one word that includes all these elements and still does justice to them all.

Whereas the NT is reductionist in thinking (examining the details to form a theory of the whole), the NF is expansionist and holistic, scanning the whole for consistency of patterns, connections, and generalities that reveal the characteristics of the whole and the meaning of the details. NFs know that the forest will reveal its nature, not by the study of the individual trees but by the patterns that pertain to the forest as an ecosystem. Therefore, the NF mind does not determine the meaning of the whole by the make up of its parts. Like the NT mind, the NF mind works conceptually and, of course, abstractly. As a result, the NF tends to be the philosopher who examines the big picture of the meaning of life and the universe. The NT, in contrast, is often the scientist who pursues a reductionist's path to understanding and suggests the meaning of the whole by the characteristics of the parts. We need both mental disciplines.

For the NF, logic as a tool for understanding and accurate communication and it must concern itself, not simply with a mathematical form of logic but with the less measurable emotional facts because truth lies hidden in emotions as well as the external facts.

The spiritual content of human nature is usually recognized by the NF and their intuitive insights have often been proved to be highly accurate along with premonitions and inspirational discernment. To the NF, beauty, love, hope, joy, peace, and other ethereal values contain the truth of the human experience along with all the physical factors of our make up. As a result, all the functions of the NF mind are an expression of art as well as reason, of emotion as well as logic.

Now to the strengths of the NF.

Strengths Related to Future Time

The NF strengths that relate to the future appear as lives in the future: idealistic, imaginative, passionate, trusting, and concerned with personal growth.

Lives In and For the Future
(Orientation to Time)

Look not mournfully into the past. It comes not back again. Wisely improve the present. It is thine. Go forth to meet the shadowy future, without fear.
~ Henry Wadsworth Longfellow (NF)

Hope deferred makes the heart sick, but a longing fulfilled is a tree of life.
~ Proverbs 13:12 (Truly an NF's experience)

Anyone who is among the living has hope.
~ Ecclesiastes 9:4

Is it possible to live in the future? Not in the same way we live in the present moment of the real world. You can live in the future only if you do so in your mind!

NFs live in their minds more than they live in the physical world. Their sixth sense, together with their imagination, enables them to find real fulfillment in the virtual world of their minds and it is very rewarding for them.

Defined for the NF, living in and for the future means: constantly scanning the future for possibilities and ideas, penetrating its mists with imagination and a high degree of expectation, always surveying the big picture to spot connections and patterns, creating a dream, and finding the meaning and significance (without which they cannot happily live). They do this in abstract ideas in their virtual world. Let's look more deeply into these futuristic dreamers.

As they walk through the real world they are living in the imaginations and realities that they create in their minds. Some bump into things and some forget where they are. Driving down the freeway they pass the exit and wonder, "Why did I do that?" They were paying attention to what was being created in their minds. That's why. Everyone does a little of this, but NFs do it frequently and for the real imaginative NFs, constantly.

A parent reported concern to me. "My son is always bumping into things. We have had him checked out for sight problems and brain abnormalities and our doctors say all is normal." Sounded typical to me. We assessed their son and he turned out to be an NF and old enough to tell me what was going on in his mind. He verified that he was indeed walking around so mentally busy that he just was not paying attention. It can scare a parent who has never imagined how intense inner communications can be.

NFs use this mental world to help them search the future for its promises and opportunities. Then they choose the ideas their imagination can make a reality and, filled with expectations and hopes, they trust their intuition and surge forward. This is why when they lose hope their whole world crumbles. The NF has imaginatively fashioned the future to (among other things) refresh their spirits. It often happens when they are creating and enjoying idealistic dreams and hopeful aspirations. Loss of all refreshment causes a serious malnutrition in their spirit. The future is often their resource.

Their relation to the future is also a searching of its possibilities, not just its opportunities: what could be, might be, should be. Some possibilities are predictable and others are not. Some turn out to be real opportunities. NFs can see so many possibilities that they often spin in circles, going from one good idea to another.

Most of their strengths are related to a pleasurable, idealistic search for meaning and fulfillment that is held and hidden in those future possibilities. These possibilities are often experienced by them a second time in the realities of the present moment if the opportunity becomes reality, and again for a third time in their memory. In the world of ideas, possibilities, dreams, fantasies, opportunities, and imaginations they find most of their happiness.

Whereas the SP squeezes every ounce of pleasure out of the present moment, the NF gets the most pleasure out of the future and wrings out the rest of their refreshment from the present and the past. They see the value of all three, but they walk with their eyes fixed on the future.

Everyone *can* do as the NF does: enjoy everything three times — in expectation, in actual experience, and in memory. However, the SJs are not so happy when facing the future since it often suggests change, and that's scary. The NTs are too busy creating ingenious projects to bother with too much dreaming about emotionally charged possibilities. The SPs are fixed on the present. Some consider this NF's world too fanciful. So the NFs are left to explore their fanciful world's emotional wonders and become the experienced experts of turning the future into present enjoyment, even before it arrives. The art of living can be, for some NFs, the art of dreaming.

Because the NF stands facing the future, searching and evaluating its opportunities, they walk passionately into its possibilities. This can create a very optimistic attitude if the possibilities look bright. Depression ensues, however, if the possibilities are dark or don't generate the pleasure of positive passions.

The future turned black for Lisa, an NF. She lost her job, blamed herself, and watched her husband fall into an addiction. She was, in her mind, to blame for the latter too. Her mother was none to happy when she found that Lisa was also imbibing at an alarming rate.

Depression followed fast and deep. She now knew she was no good. She said later, "I saw nothing to give me hope. The future looked awful for me, and I couldn't face the emptiness any longer."

We worked on understanding how and why she had arrived at her present condition of mind and how she must concentrate on finding hope on the horizon by finding new possibilities. When they surfaced in her mind she made a fast recovery and found her optimism and her balance again. Recovery of this nature is not always fast.

Like the SP, whose optimism is hard to dampen, the NF can display some Epicurean pleasure, too. However, the NF's pleasure must be meaningful or it feels empty and too shallow to be indulged.

Success is all about possibilities for the NF and the seizing of them with purpose and vivid expectations. An imagined possibility that they passionately embrace as an opportunity can start a successful venture. Then, with more imagination and intuitive insights they can easily develop ideas creatively and brilliantly. They need the help of others to manage all the details of their ideas, but they must believe that, as people-people, they can always find partners. This is a clear path to success that is written into the NF's *innerkinetics*.

It will be interesting to discover how many of the drives that propel the life of an NF are related to this future-time orientation. In the terminology of Disneyland, they live in Tomorrow Land.

How Do I Develop this Strength?

- Search for the possibilities that the future holds. You will come alive.

- Keep that optimism that sees a silver lining in the dark cloud and stars in the darkness of night. Cling to future hopes. Hope will not leave you.

- Schedule some special time each day to examine possibilities. You can do this as you do other mundane tasks.

- Keep fashioning your virtual world the way you want it to be.

- If faith, hope, and love, fill your world. You will keep negativism away and stay on top.

Caution:

All temperaments lapse into weaknesses when they don't use their strengths, overuse them, or use them for destructive purposes such as damaging themselves or others. Here are further cautions for this strength.

- There is an over use of this strength that can cause a person to lose touch with reality. Beware.

- All of us must live in the real world, so coming down out of the clouds of the future to live in the present is very necessary.

Idealists — Dreamers

Change is the law of life. And those who look only to the past or present are certain to miss the future.
~ John F. Kennedy (An SP expressing an NF's viewpoint)

The future belongs to those who believe in the beauty of their dreams.
~ Eleanor Roosevelt (NF)

An optimist is a person who sees only the lights in the picture, whereas a pessimist sees only the shadows. An idealist, however, is one who sees the light and the shadows, but in addition sees something else: the possibility of changing the picture, of making the lights prevail over the shadows.
~ Unknown

An idealist is one whose behavior and thoughts are motivated by their ideas. Nine centuries BC, a Greek poet, Homer, used the word *idealist* in his great epics, and it has continued in several languages to this day. It must be a word that some people need! They do. The idealists (as Keirsey calls them) or the NFs (as I refer to them) insist on the need for this word and the life of idealism it displays because it motivates them so strongly.

For the NF, an idealist is one who sees the ideal as though it were real, lives by idealizing all hopes and loves, and examines their own performances (as well as those of others) by the standard of the ideal.

Before Kelly got married he talked in otherworldly terms of the amazing traits of his fiancé. It was the first sign of his idealism. She was "perfect"! Then they married, and before long he was shocked and rocked to the core. His inner world of idealism had been shattered.

She had gotten angry over his insistence at trying to please her (a crushing blow to an NF). She didn't want what he was suggesting and he was oblivious to her strong feelings or their reasons, aware only of his desire to please her and shine in her eyes. It was a little thing: nothing more than her distaste for a restaurant that he thought was romantically perfect for her. Some time before she had had a bad experience at this place and had vowed never to patronize them again, but she had not communicated her feelings.

His devastation was not about the restaurant or her choice not to go. It was her anger. He hadn't seen her mad (seemingly without reason) before and the harmony between them had been lost. All he could see was a cracked image of a perfect lover. She wasn't perfect any longer! He even had thoughts of whether this marriage was worth it, but that passed quickly and he looked with sadness at a dashed image.

Adjusting to loving an imperfect person can be a stretch for some NFs. It usually devastates them and can ruin a wonderful relationship. Kelly learned that it was his idealism, not his wonderful wife, that was to blame for his feelings. He soon let it pass but was warned of the result of idealizing one's partner. None are perfect.

"An idea," says the first usage of the word in Homer's epics, "is a sight, a seeing or an ability to see things." Idealism is simply seeing things as they should be or as we would like to see them rather than as they are.

NFs see things as they would like to have them and live in hopes that their ideals will come to fruition. There is a school of artistic expression called *idealism*. It paints the world as the artist prefers to see it: the artist's idealism, if you like, which turns out to be not exactly as things are. Idealists often see things differently from reality — and they want to!

NFs are very inwardly focused. Jen was living a successful life as a sales person. She dreamed of great success and each day kept her dream in the front of her mind. She would look at a completed sale and dream of what the commission was doing for her dreams.

Her positive frame of mind and the constant motivating power of her thoughts made each lost opportunity or failure seem small. She had learned to dream with positive thinking and action. A failure was an opportunity. Both her parents were concerned about her upbeat spirit. Did she really get it? Were her feet on the ground or in the clouds? Perhaps she was mentally incapable of realizing the meaning of a failure. Her inward focus was transforming failure into opportunities to learn more and be better. Her parents could not see this.

She didn't have much in the way of material possessions, but her dream account in the bank was growing fast. She was focused and inwardly enjoying the journey.

Why do people think there is something wrong with a person who is positively oriented to possibilities? Because it isn't their normality, I guess. Pessimistic people often feel a dreamer is mentally "light."

Wow! Different from pessimistic reality? Yes, and this is the NF's strength that helps people see a bad circumstance as bringing some good or a dark future as glimmering with the possibility that things could be better. To always see the world as it is can be boring and defeating. At least for the NF it is. Hope is all about seeing the world differently from what it is. NFs, being very sensitive, can't live without seeing things as they should be or could be or might be, rather than how things are.

No temperament is so affected by ideals as the NF. They see almost every possibility with the optimism of the idealist. They create visions of the ideal, strive for the ideal, imagine the ideal, and live in the ideal creations of their minds. They should, for their sake and the world's sake, develop this strength to be all that it can be. It is one of their paths to success. When they do develop it, the lives they touch sparkle with a million flashes of light.

It was a sad day for John. His wife was wrapped up in finishing her urgent projects and he felt separated from her love. His ideal of what their loving relationship would be like just wasn't happening. He hurt on the inside over his feeling of disconnectedness and, until his ideal was regained, he would mull over his hurt and life would become sadder.

"Join her!" was the advice of a friend and, for an idealist, it was the answer. Now he was near her, involved, helping her with her projects. Nearness alone can warm an NF's heart and can magically defeat the over-demanding feelings of idealism. Other temperaments can't fathom the feelings of the NF. They are so tender, yet so pressing, strong, and powerful.

This is why, when the ideal image they have created and set on their pedestal of hope falls, they are so desperately devastated and shocked. They have already lived it in their minds and walked its golden streets in their imagination, so to see their vivid versions that were displayed in living color in their virtual worlds smashed is like losing reality. It was real to them! Powerfully real! And now they face a void that others can overlook, but they can't, and they wilt in the desert of loss!

They are the masters of trusting relationships and everyone they trust or love becomes an ideal in their minds. Idealists can be called the optimists of the "not yet." As long as they see the future in this hopeful mold, they are happy and above despair.

Idealism is the world of imagination, hope, creativeness, and the magnetic pull of the perfect. It is a form of perfectionism, a strength we will meet later in the list of NF strengths. Their worlds and all others are bettered for the idealistic drive of these upbeat dreamers.

Often, the word idealist is seen as overestimation, exaggeration, rashness, or miscalculation, and sometimes it is. However, there is a more sober, needed meaning to their idealistic dreams. To see the future through the eyes of hope and to hope for the ideal conclusion to something is better than to look dismally and negatively, doubting the good and magnifying the bad. So it is that there is health and happiness reserved for the hopeful optimist. Their idealism never dies, resurrecting itself endlessly.

The NF enjoys the idealistic dream while it lasts. Isn't it better than looking at the equally unpredictable pessimist's projections of the future? The SP's optimism and the NF's idealism and hope see eye-to-eye on the value of this cheerful approach to life.

A considerable number of the NF's ideals are actualized — more than they remember, unfortunately. They count their disappointments religiously because of a typical low sense of worth (introverts in particular) and they tend to forget their realized dreams and hopes. What a pity. It is true of all of us for whom trouble registers in not-to-be-forgotten colors that our realized dreams pass unfulfilled at times and we move on, depressed and anxious. NFs cannot afford to let this happen.

Idealists can be and have been the visionaries and world leaders of new beginnings and humanistic ideas. Gandhi is a powerful reminder. Gandhi was an NF.

The most common negative reflection of this strength is its nonuse. Without it, weakness in the NF character is rife. Idealism, like sensitivity and living in the future, is a condition the NF can't and must not live without.

Fulfillment for the NF is often defined as idealism, but this is in making the ideal happen in realistic form for themselves and others. They must chase the ideal. Many other strengths of the NF combine to achieve this end.

How Do I Develop this Strength?

- Idealists develop a healthy idealism by *using* and *enjoying* their strength and in making a significant difference.

- Dream when your spirit needs refreshment.

- Treasure and keep an optimistic attitude of hope.

- Believe fervently that optimism is better than pessimism.

- Practice using your mind's eye, since it sees with equal clarity to your physical eye and at times refashions what your physical eye sees.

- Develop related strengths, such as imagination, trust, optimism, and sensitivity.

- Always try to see the world as it can be, not as it is.

- See the good in everything — the stars in the blackness of night.

- Let the pull of the perfect always call you to things much greater.

- Remember your actualized dreams and write them down. Keep a visible display of them where you will notice them often and benefit from their advice.

Caution:

All temperaments lapse into weaknesses when they don't use their strengths, overuse them, or use them for destructive purposes such as damaging themselves or others. Here are further cautions for this strength.

- Prepare for the letdowns when your ideals crash, and simply face them with renewed optimism. A smashed image is the material from which you can build another.

- Too much dreaming without enough determined effort to make dreams come true removes people from the responsibilities of the present.

Imaginative

The future belongs to those who can rise above the confines of the earth.
~ Alfred North Whitehead

Imagination belongs to everyone, of course, but some have sharpened its use, and none more than the NT and NF because they live primarily in their inner world: their minds. It is here that imagination flourishes and grows.

Defined for the NF, imagination means: creating in their virtual world (the world they want to live in), exploring fantasy and the impossible to enrich the possible, and discovering new and wonderful concepts and ideas that stimulate dreams and that beckon the NF to turn them into reality. It is mixing the powers of reason and emotion with a strong dose of intuition. The NT is imaginative too, but the NF takes it and enriches it even more with their emotional sensitivity.

Little Kenneth worried his mother. He would sit outside, staring into space and in his daydreams imagine creatures and events that were unreal and scary to a realistic SJ mother. When she disturbed him, he would tell her with pleasure of these fictional, vivid, creations of his fertile imagination.

"This is not good," she told me. "He seems to be mentally lost or missing something." I assured her this was not unusual in a little NF, and she needed to understand that her knowledge of the power and purpose of imagination was missing. Medical examinations had indicated everything was normal. She did learn to understand and avoid damaging the growth of a tender NF mind.

Never crush the imagination of a child or an adult. Gently guide the child to notice reality as well and preserve what will be a great blessing to the world. Imagination is the vehicle that takes us to potential worlds beyond the reach of our knowledge.

Einstein's words will help us all understand the importance of this strength that can lead the NF to the refreshment of fantasy and the creativeness of a fertile imagination.

*When I examine myself and my methods of thought, I come to the conclusion that
the gift of fantasy has meant more to me than any talent for abstract, positive
thinking.*
~ *Albert Einstein*

Unlike experience that exists only in the real world, imagination creates
its wonders in the virtual world. It leads to all kinds of discoveries. In
the NF, since the imagination is fueled by their very sensitive emotions
as well as their reason, imagination is used for more than innovative
purposes. It lifts spirits, warms hearts, and fashions minds for all the
creative and inspirational human purposes. It is most prevalent in the
NF. As children, they may have imaginary friends and their rooms and
toys may all be a part of a fantastic imaginary creation. The NF is the
master of rich, emotionally rewarding imagination. Imagination helps
the NF live life as a story.

*Roger's mother was amused and puzzled by his behavior. He would come home
from school and, after his chores were done, would go out into the field by his home
and play football. The only evidence of his game being football was a stuffed sock
his mother had sewn up to resemble a football, and both knew of the identity of this
otherwise doubtful toy. They were poor and he didn't mind the substitute.*

*She would watch out the window at this strange display that she did not understand
until one day he explained. He would kick the ball in one direction (the start of a
football game) and then run to catch it (he was now the opposing team). He then
took off in the opposite direction only to fall down (tackled). This went on for half
and hour or so until one team emerged victorious in his mind. He had imagined the
plays of a whole football game, with rewarding stimulation to his creative powers.*

Imagination forms mental images of what is not present in reality, what
has not been experienced, or what has not been combined in reality
before. It can be a fantasy, unreal — even foolish, creative or
ingenious. Imagination is the cradle of all creative efforts. The NTs
show this in their ingenuity, and the NFs, in their visionary
resourcefulness and insight-driven creativity.

Imagination appears as a strength of the NF when their rich emotions
stimulate what reason cannot. Imagination goes beyond reason to
probe the possibilities of the unseen. It often discovers what reason
cannot. It drives passion and makes the future much more exciting.
An NF cannot imagine what it would be like to live without

imagination lighting up the path and dancing like fireworks on the future's horizon.

The world of literature and legend is filled with imagination. Consider: Jonathan Swift's Lilliput, southeast of Sumatra, where the inhabitants are six inches tall; Ponce de Leon's fountain of youth that he sought in Florida and the Bahamas; Edwin A. Abbot's two dimensional land; places and creatures like Camelot, the Abominable Snowman, Leprechauns, Hobbits, and Bigfoot. Lewis Carroll's "Looking Glass Land" (populated by chess pieces and other creatures); Robert Louis Stevenson's Treasure Island, and J. R. R. Tolkein's Middle Earth, for examples.

How poor we would be without novels and imaginary places to fuel our minds with this special kind of refreshment. What would we read to our children?

Imagination fuels pristine visions, illumines perception, fashions insights, guides in solutions to complex problems, and develops creative passions. The mind is the home of imagination and the headquarters of inventiveness, dreams, concepts, and pretense in the NF.

Discoveries, both scientific and geographical, have been actualized by first using imagination. Medical advances are, to a large part, due to imagination and without it, these wonders would not have eventuated. Speaking of imagination's treasures, Marianne Moore exclaims,

Nor till the poets among us can be "literalists of the imagination" and can present for inspection, ... "imaginary gardens with real toads in them," shall we have it.

Much imaginary work still remains to be done.

The main weakness related to this strength is its nonuse. It can be overused and wrongly used, but its nonuse cripples the world of possibilities for the NF. NFs who don't develop this strength rob themselves of much of the richness that their *innerkinetics* offer.

This is a certain path to success and, for the NF, holds many hopes. Never let a day pass without setting a moment aside to imagine something. Keep a journal of your ideas, both realistic and unrealistic. Daydream. It's healthy.

Imagination has a payback or satisfaction unrelated to achievements or reality. We simply feel its worth and its wonder. It takes us to worlds where experience cannot enter and we feel the ecstasy of the mind's powers — reward indeed.

How Do I Develop this Strength?
- To develop this strength we must listen to our thoughts and follow their mental paths.

- Turn your mind into a world of adventure.

- Living in the realities of life can blunt the creative thoughts of our imaginations, so take time to imagine.

- Dreaming is a positive way to awaken the imagination and develop its marvels.

- Imagination's utopia of wonders calls the NF and they ponder with Helen Keller how to reconcile this world of fact with the bright world of our imaginings. Ponder!

Caution:
All temperaments lapse into weaknesses when they don't use their strengths, overuse them, or use them for destructive purposes such as damaging themselves or others. Here are further cautions for this strength.

- Sometimes their imagining can be so real that the NF mistakes it for reality.

- When reality is suspended for too long, the NF can lose their footing on this earth and feel disconnected and disoriented.

Passionate — Enthusiastic
Value-Based Decisions

*The happiness of a man in this life does not consist in the absence but in the
mastery of his passions.*
~ Alfred Lord Tennyson
Success in not the result of spontaneous combustion. You must set yourself on fire.
~ Reggie Leach

If NFs are anything, they are passionate. Now, of course, you may not
see the passion very easily at times, and that confuses some. Surely
passion can be seen, you may argue. Not always — especially in the
introverted NFs. In the NF, passion is being experienced at a high level
of intensity within themselves and not always shared. Therefore, it is
mostly not seen. Often, all you will see is the intensity in their
demeanor and nothing more.

To the NF, passion and enthusiasm mean an inner fire, usually burning
over some value that they hold dear. It often accompanies imagination,
idealism, or a dream. It grips their soul and motivates with inner
emotions that are second to none and takes up all the conscious space
in their minds.

*They had a fight over next to nothing, and that bothered Jane (the NF) even more.
First she had felt hurt by his remark as he came in the door.*

"Why is this house such a mess," he barked?

She swallowed hard and said nothing.

Then he went on and on with his cutting remarks. "What do you do all day long?"

She was silent, but wounded. It turned out to be a quiet evening at home for Bud.

*For Jane, this was the beginning of a buildup of intense emotions, all locked up
inside her heart, and she did not understand what was happening inside her.*

*He was still mad the next morning and she was the target of a couple more blows
as he left. Days went by, and now the argument was over his socks not being folded
the way he thought was correct. It started small, just an accusation, and then before*

he knew it she had blown up in his face with such fury he was stunned. What he did not understand was that it was not about the socks. It was about his lack of appreciation and mainly about the effect of his remarks some days ago.

Jane had suppressed the pressure of her passion and now it had finally blown. She could not understand why she became so angry — and over the folding of socks, at that. Bud made a strategic retreat to think things over.

The suppressed passion of an NF can surprise all concerned, including the NF. However, the pain was the real issue and it had built until it exploded. Hurt that leads to anger (and it always does), if internalized, will soon build internal pressures, ferment, and erupt. For Jane, understanding why she erupted was very helpful. For Bud, understanding helped him to relate better to his wife and realize the damage negative remarks can have on a sensitive temperament. Both learned other valuable lessons as well.

Passion comes from the Greek word *pathos*, which means suffering. Passion is a form of suffering. It revs up the senses and the inner intensity it causes can be stressful, even ultimately damaging to the system.

Passion and intensity are constant companions. To be impassioned is to be intense. Among passion's synonyms are a horde of revved up feelings that our language has named ardent, fervent, obsessed, fanatical, inflamed, volatile, mercurial. Be passionate! For the NF, when they do, they access their vast memory bank of emotions; they encounter feelings waiting all too often to be triggered.

Passion inspires because it persuades with the power of emotion. Emotional passion persuades more reliably than reason. As a speaker, if I persuade with a touching story as opposed to convincing logic, I change more people's perceptions. Emotions are a power in the human system that nothing can better. Lacking a reference to any other emotion, passion can then generate an emotion of its own.

An NF's passion can express itself in anger or love, in hurt or happiness. Anything can become a passion, and its command of their system means it is essential that some form of control over it be learned to avoid the malfunctioning of the human system. All NFs face the need to learn the self control of their passions. When under control, passion is a creative power for good and can bring much joy and reward to the NFs' lives and to others.

Enthusiasm is a form of passion. The word comes from two Greek words meaning "in" and "God." Many will say their enthusiasm is fired by their belief in a superior being. If we understand that belief is the prime motivator of our human systems, this is no surprise and points to the added power generated by trusting a higher being. It can be a positive or negative force.

You have probably heard someone exclaim, "I believe that passionately." The combination of a strong belief and intense passion will drive a human to amazing feats or fears.

Those who have studied the life of Abraham Lincoln have remarked on the quiet passion that kept driving him through defeat, depression, and doubt to become one of the great achievers and Presidents of American history. The intense fire inside of him would not be put out.

The passions of an NF are chosen more on the values that the NF treasures than on what makes sense or what the facts might indicate. To the NF, there are hidden facts in values. When they make decisions, they must consult their feelings because values often inform their feelings. So what they value is what they choose to support and give themselves to without reserve.

To succeed requires power. There is no greater inner force than passion at its peek. Passion drives and fashions our success or failure. The NFs must plug into passion's energy to reach their potential. They are always at their maximum power when fully passionate.

Passion is not an unmixed blessing. Choices about our passions and wisdom in their execution is mandatory because they can do harm. The wrong use of passion is its greatest potential weakness.

How Do I Develop this Strength?
- Light a fire in your heart. Find your passion.

- Fan it until it glows with intensity.

- Focus is the key to lighting a fire and intensifying it. Focus on your passion or your key idea.

- Passion burns brightest when beliefs are strong. Strengthen your beliefs.

- Emotions can be called in to fuel the fire.

- A single passion is more intense than several passions.

- Watch for passions to increase with age. If we keep focusing on our passions, the longer we live, the stronger they get.

Caution:

All temperaments lapse into weaknesses when they don't use their strengths, overuse them, or use them for destructive purposes such as damaging themselves or others. Here are further cautions for this strength.

- Master your passions or they will master you.

- Chose your passions carefully. Negative passions can quickly ruin us.

Trusting

The key is to get to know people and trust them to be who they are. Instead, we trust people to be who we want them to be — and when they are not, we cry.
~ Unknown

Love knows no limit to its endurance, no end to its trust.
~ Unknown

The tendency of the NFs to trust others increases their ability to influence and motivate people. People like to be trusted. They sense those who will trust them and confide in them. But when thoughtlessly used, trust can become a weakness. The weakness appears as misplaced trust and an unwillingness or an inability to disconnect when trust has been violated. This strength has two images that are easily recognized: helpful or harmful (when misused).

To the NF, trusting means: willingly including others and always giving them the benefit of the doubt (unless an intuitive voice has warned otherwise). It means trying to please, treating others with the respect all people inherently deserve, and creating and maintaining harmonious relationships.

Most NFs will tend to trust everyone. Because they feel trust brings out the best in people, they want to give it liberally. Pleasing someone and creating a harmonious relationship is a motivation to trust, and trust becomes the inspiration and opportunity to please. Trust is the basis of all relationships, of course. Without it, no love can be authentic nor any relationship stable. This means that this strength of trusting is more important to them than the surface impression indicates, giving NFs important reasons to trust.

NFs have more reasons to trust. When smooth and effective relationships are the goal in their interactions with people, trust is seen as an essential strength. People skills are also markedly improved with trust. If helping people realize their potential is an NF's main goal, then again, the NF needs to develop trust to better develop people.

In intimate relationships, NFs trust readily and will often not disconnect — even if abused — since they feel there still are possibilities for change and the ideal may return. This is yet another reason.

For those who trust, relationships can be almost sacred — a bond hard to break. People are first attracted to each other, and then they trust each other and start a firm relationship built on trust. Trust is a commitment. Often, they commit and then find out afterwards who each other wants to be. The discovery is not always exciting news.

The NF falls harder than other temperaments in this game of trust when things turn out unexpectedly. Initially, that may not a bad thing.

Once the relationship deepens and the stresses of a commitment are tested, they sometimes find their trust has been seriously misplaced. The SP will typically hang on for a while until their freedoms are being restricted and their passions unfulfilled, and then they will face the exit door with determination. Only a strong belief system will help the SP hang on and recreate their relationship. The SJ usually holds on longer and the NT will also. The NF, on the other hand, can stay in an abusive relationship and suffer great hurt, both physical and psychological, since they still want to believe the other person. Even when they can't take it any longer, they will, if asked, reconsider and try to rebuild it.

NFs are the trusting optimists. Understanding themselves and this excessive urge to trust will help them be better equipped to manage an overuse of this strength.

Trust is also related to possibilities. The NF finds possibilities in everyone. For all those who have low self-esteems, an NF's instinctive trust in them is therapeutic. Their natural role as coaches and counselors, advisors and teachers is supported by this tendency.

Because, to the NF, everyone can be trusted, any divine authority figure can be easily trusted, too. Their spiritual nature encourages this. Any metaphysical belief can extract a complete commitment from them. However, if they believe they have been jilted or unjustly treated by the divine, trust can turn to bitter resentment and outright opposition.

Another element of this strength is that conflict can be avoided when we trust people up front. Avoiding conflict is attractive to the NF. However, trust can be taken advantage of by the less scrupulous, and this is a practical issue NFs wrestle with.

The feelings of reward when they trust are largely their feelings of harmony, peace, and acceptance that a trusting attitude can generate. Trust is a powerful strength and fulfills the NF by encouraging hope, faith, and love.

This is a strength that can support other strengths on the road to success. It cannot be overlooked without possible trouble. Develop it, but keep it under your mastery.

How Do I Develop this Strength?
• Trust, where it improves your relationships. Use the strength.

• Believe in others.

• See the good in others.

- See the possibilities in others.

Caution:
All temperaments lapse into weaknesses when they don't use their strengths, overuse them, or use them for destructive purposes such as damaging themselves or others. Here are further cautions for this strength.

- Disconnect when the evidence is clear that you must.

- Remember, when you disconnect you often give a friendship the best chance to remake itself.

- Danger awaits those who won't exit a friendship when the other person has lost all concern.

- Don't allow yourself to be disrespected.

Personal Growth — Meaning — Significance

Rebellion against your handicaps gets you nowhere.
Self-pity gets you nowhere.
One must have the adventurous daring to accept oneself as a bundle of possibilities and undertake the most interesting game in the world — making the most of one's best.
~ Harry Emerson Fosdick

The meeting of two personalities is like the contact of two chemical substances: if there is any reaction, both are transformed.
~ Carl Jung

Personal growth, for the NF, is making improvements to their inner life: harnessing and mastering their inner powers, mind, attitudes, mental skills, emotional self management, imagination, etc., that make them the best they can be.

Personal growth has only one goal: experiencing all the NFs were made for. It is not competition with others, rather it is competing against themselves and achieving their own greatness. Ethically, emotionally, mentally, spiritually, relationally, it is an attempt to rise to satisfy their own standards.

The goal is seen clearly in the INFJ (who seeks to lead other people to realize their highest potential) and in the INFP (whose goal is to heal the wounds and bring wholeness to others as they struggle to do the same in themselves). This, to both types, is the fullness of life.

Both the ENFJ, who teaches and exhorts, and the ENFP, who champions a cause, are focused on the personal growth of others as well as their own. The theme of helping others turns them outward, a direction that is healthy for them since they focus inwardly most of the time.

When they fail to achieve this goal in themselves and in everyone they struggle to help, they feel like failures and question their abilities to influence and cause vibrant growth.   They chastise themselves mercilessly at times for not being able to lift others.   When they have such a drive inside that calls them to attempt a goal, they accept only success. Failure is depressing. Here again is the idealist.

Listen to Sid. "I wanted to feel significant, to feel I was someone, not nothing. It was not fame I wanted. In fact, at times I avoided it. A life that helped others and at the same time made me feel as though I had reached my potential seemed to be the only thing that would satisfy me."

"I worked hard trying to better myself. I studied to learn and always felt I hadn't learned enough. Books about personal development fascinated me, and I read avidly to find some secret to help me get better and better."

"I would set goals for myself, and when I had finally reached them I can remember the sense of failure I felt because I would feel that I hadn't achieved much after all. I would sink again, depressed for a short time, and then set another goal. There was always another mountain behind the one I had climbed, but none satisfied. Sometimes I wondered if anyone else was like me: always, to themselves, falling short.   One day it dawned on me that I was feeling anxious because I might die without reaching all I could be and that would be the ultimate failure."

"I refused to share most of this with anyone, but when I did offer someone a glimpse into my aspirations, they would tell me I was a perfectionist and needed to settle for

lesser things. I felt misunderstood and as though no one would really want to take the effort to know me. Life for me was trying to understand why I was like this."
"Do you still feel this way," I asked?

"Yes."

"Do you know you are driven by a strength, not a weakness — one that I call 'longing for meaning and significance through personal growth'?" I asked. "This urge inside you can be captured and used to help you reach your aspirations rather than used to cripple them with personal disappointment and self condemnations?"

What followed was a personal growth journey into understanding and self confidence for Sid. He could follow his drives and celebrate every victory without pride or arrogance and be motivated with satisfaction and a real feeling of self worth. Life only has meaning for the NF when they use this urge to achieve and celebrate each advance along the way.

Weaknesses develop mainly when NFs don't use this strength. The NF then wanders aimlessly through life. That can mean trouble: addictions, and being captured by damaging urges that lead to disappointment with themselves and even aberrant behavior.

Deep indeed is satisfaction when personal growth takes place in them and in others they are helping. To the NF, it feels as though they were born for this. They were. No temperament is more clearly purposed than the NF and none loses their way because of low self-esteem more than they.

If an NF would be successful, they must develop and feel the satisfaction of passing the milestones of growth along the way, celebrating each. They must learn, struggle, develop, and reach their personal goals. Success for the NF is, above all, their own personal achievement of meaningful growth. Success is the expanding of their knowledge and control of themselves so that their giftedness can be released without imploding and crushing their motivations.

How Do I Develop this Strength?

• Remember, personal growth is a drive inside of you. It is there to call you to better and higher things. It is like the mountaineer who climbs the mountain and says, "I did it just because it was there." He is wrong, of course. He climbs because of what drives him inside, just like the NF must reach his own potential.

• Believe in the way you have been created. Accept your finely tuned nature with its sensitivity.

• Follow your drives.

• Read good books that help you train and develop.

• Understand your own temperament because, if you don't, this will hold you back more than anything else.

• Study, learn, and pursue your goals.

Caution:

All temperaments lapse into weaknesses when they don't use their strengths, overuse them, or use them for destructive purposes such as damaging themselves or others. Here are further cautions for this strength.

• Don't wrongly use this drive to achieve things that damage yourself and others — like trying to be perfect. You will self-destruct if you do.

• Avoid turning failure on yourself and crushing your self-esteem. Failure is an opportunity to move up, not a trap door through which you fall to lesser things.

Strengths Related to Sensitivity

In the NF there is a very noticeable second pole around which the strengths can be grouped. Time is the first one and, to me, sensitivity is the second.

Others who study temperament psychology may see the groupings of strengths differently. The important thing is to discover your strengths and develop them.

The first cousins of sensitivity are intuition, emotion, empathy, caring, kindheartedness, people skills, reality and authenticity, romanticism, introspection, and perfectionism.

Sensitive

Beauty of whatever kind, in its supreme development, invariably excites the sensitive soul to tears.
~ Edgar Allen Poe

A light, tender, sensitive touch is worth a ton of brawn.
~ Peter Thomson (British motivator)

She wanted to scream, "Don't touch me!" Even in bed at night, it was more than she could comfortably take to have her husband touch her. Of course she let him, but she slept on her side of the bed and her husband ached, wondering why their marriage was so disconnected, why she would cringe at his touch. Was she rejecting him? Was the marriage on the rocks? It wasn't. That's the strange thing.

The tender stimulation of a breeze also made her feel on edge. Clothes would irritate her and raise her level of nervous activity. She could remember that as a child there were times she couldn't bear the rub of brand tags and certain textured materials. She still had trouble with wearing some materials.

It was not only things that touched her body, it was the edginess of her spirit as well — a kind of side effect of the physical sensitivity, she thought. She felt all things with a sensitivity that others didn't. She was an ENFJ. She could have been any NF.

Once she discovered her tendency to sensitivity, she followed the simple instruction to try to pay no attention to it and after several weeks she was asked, "Did you notice the wind as you came inside?" To her surprise, she had to admit she didn't. She thought back over the past week and realized her awareness had diminished greatly and it was (in her words) "great to feel normal." Her husband was quietly delighted!

Sensitivity can become a real problem for some NFs. The more they pay attention to it, the more it takes over their consciousness. It is real and can be a physical, as well as an emotional, edginess.

Sensitivity is a finely tuned response to stimuli, both outside of us and inside of us. The word comes from the Latin word family for *sense* or *senses*. Sense impressions are received physically through the five senses and in the human spirit through inner mechanisms, one of which is intuition. Imagination, thoughts, and emotions can emit sensations too, just as truly as touch, taste, and smell. Whatever we vividly create on the screen of our virtual world exudes sensations that we feel.

When we say the NF displays the strength of sensitivity, we mean they are sensitive to all external sensory input, but particularly to the inner senses. Therefore, unseen, inner experiences suddenly affect them, create anxiety, and engage their complete attention. This feeling for the NF can be very forceful. It can overpower them at times.

Many have described the NF as being over-sensitive. So watch for the NF to be sensitive to even the slightest thing: to what you say and do, to what you don't say and do, and to things that don't affect you at all.

Just to make it difficult, they will often show no signs of being affected by outside or inside stimuli because they often internalize all they sense and feel and do not feel the need to let you know what is going on inside of them. This makes knowing them fully almost impossible. "Now you see it, now you don't" is what you will have to get used to with the NF.

Sensitivity alerts us to danger and opportunities. Both are helpful flags. Therefore, we should not see this strength of the NF as unnecessary or harmful, and certainly not because we consider their sensitivity to be over reactive. Only the nonuse, overuse, or wrong use of a strength is damaging. Because it is seen as the cause of their emotional volatility, people (including the NF, at times) want to eradicate it. What a mistake!

They need to be very sensitive for their intuition to function well and for their creativity, love, empathy, and people skills to flourish. Artists, of which there are quite a few NFs, rely on it to create their masterpieces. Many more create masterful relationships from the same strength. Sensitivity is a necessary element of genius and the possessor pays the price of its discomfort.

People skills rely on sensitivity. How can we know people by a predetermined set of rules? People are moved by emotion and feelings that are hidden and most of the time only the slightest twitch reveals some mysterious response. Intuition detects the unobserved. Being super sensitive to people and their inner responses aids the NF (who has been named for the role of diplomat) in bringing people together. NFs can be very intuitive and instinctive diplomats.

Managing their own responses to sensitivity helps them master its insights and reduce the damage caused by overuse and misuse. It also improves their ability to be positively sensitive to others. If they over internalize things, sensitivity turns out to be more of a curse than a blessing. Nonuse of the strength makes an NF hard and harsh in their interactions with people — the opposite of what they were born to be.

On the positive side, they feel very much in touch with people and, when others respond with gratitude that someone understands them, they simmer with pleasure and that unmistakable feeling we all have when we are living in our strengths.

Since this strength undergirds many other strengths, an NF should seek to encourage it, develop its powers, and master its many faces. The interplay of one strength with another develops both strengths because both are being used. Therefore, it can be strengthened along with any of the strengths in this section.

When sensitivity is a key factor in achieving the NF's goals (such as in artistic work and in all work involving the management and development of people) its powers and idiosyncrasies must be mastered. The writer reaches people's emotions and sensitizes them. The artist creates out of their own sensitivity. The teacher maximizes their skills when they are sensitive to the student's needs. The spouse creates a rewarding relationship with the positive use of sensitivity and so on.

Whatever strength you use, along with it develop your positive sensitivity.

How Do I Develop this Strength?

- Become aware of your use of and degree of sensitivity. The more aware you are of when you use or don't use it, the more you can improve your use of it.

- Notice your sensitivity to all things such as nature, art, impressions, people and their behavior, your own feelings, the feelings your thoughts generate, etc.

- Pause and focus on what is around you. Focus magnifies any strength.

- Choose any of the strengths that relate to sensitivity in this section on NF strengths and strengthen it.

- Become more aware of your surroundings.

- Become more aware of your inner feelings and thoughts.

Caution:

All temperaments lapse into weaknesses when they don't use their strengths, overuse them, or use them for destructive purposes such as damaging themselves or others. Here are further cautions for this strength.

- NFs become harsh and hard when they are insensitive to others.

- Overuse can not only increase your sensitivity to what you are focused on, but it can also desensitize you to other things. Develop your sensitivity wisely.

Intuitive — Insightful

For whereas the mind works in possibilities, the intuitions work in actualities, and what you intuitively desire, that is possible to you. Whereas what you mentally or "consciously" desire is nine times out of ten impossible; hitch your wagon to a star, or you will just stay where you are.
~ D. H. Lawrence

> *The only real valuable thing is intuition.*
> ~ *Albert Einstein*

> *Intuition comes very close to clairvoyance: it appears to be the extrasensory perception of reality.*
> ~ *Alexis Carrel*

Intuition is the knowing of something without the use of the five physical senses or the powers of reason. A nonphysical, sixth sense is employed. Intuition finds its full expression in the NF because they welcome the wonders of emotion through which intuitive insights are often conveyed. The NT is also intuitive but tends to limit it with their focus on reason. Intuition cannot be limited by reason because it goes where reason cannot go. In the NF, intuition is concerned with human interactions and introspections, personal sensitivity, projects, and (particularly) with future events.

I have encountered some astounding examples of intuition in NFs. Often it surprises the NF and, as a result, they keep it to themselves because they do not want other people to think they are strange. To be thought strange happens too often for the NF, anyhow.

This intuitive knowledge can cause them to be able to look at someone and perceive their thoughts, feelings, and attitudes, but not at will. It isn't a tap that can be turned off and on. When it happens, it happens. It operates as a mysterious force whose plans remain top secret.

It can be "creepy." How do we know things that our five physical senses can't tell us? Obviously, some other dimension is involved. We can deny this, but if we do we must have a reasonable explanation for the experiences of intuition and what used to be descriptively named Extra Sensory Perception. The person who lives across the country, yet knows by intuition alone that his father has just died, is an example of raw intuition or at least of something, whatever we want to call it, that has the same characteristics.

"I was asleep and suddenly I awoke and looked at the clock. It was 3:00 AM, and a disturbing feeling made me feel almost sick," a client told me. "I didn't know what it was. I must have dozed off and fallen into a dream. Something in the dream woke me; I remember it clearly, and I looked at the clock. It was, as I said, 3:00 AM"

"In my dream, an old man was lying on a stretcher beside my bed. He turned and looked at me. I found myself turning over and hugging him as my tears gushed, but his body was stiff and cold in death, and that frightened me. In my dream he had just looked at me! I couldn't understand what it meant or why I was having a dream like this. The shock of it all must have awakened me."

"At 3:30AM. the phone rang, and my sister's sad voice said, 'Your dad passed away about 30 minutes ago.' I was in the Midwest, and my dad was on the East Coast. How could I have known this in a dream? I haven't told anyone until now. People would think I was crazy or something. I now know that in the dream I was being told of my dad's passing. Am I psychic or something? Or is this what you mean by intuition?" he asked.

I explained how intuition can result in premonitions and that this was one of those experiences.

Coincidence does not explain these things adequately, unless we give to coincidence the same powers we have given to intuition. Then all we have done is change the name. There is a spiritual explanation that involves a spirit world. Others see it as a gift, but from where they don't know. Is it ESP? Is it a heightened sensitivity to a world beyond our physical world? Since this is not the place to discuss intuition's rationale or spiritual basis, we will simply accept its reality in our human experience and realize it is a power that can help us understand ourselves, others, and their problems. It does much more than that, of course, and remains a mystery, defying logical analysis.

NFs are especially given to visions, dreams, and extra sensory experiences. They live in the world of their complex minds day and night. When we refer to these things as real experiences we are acknowledging the reality of something, even if we know little about it.

Intuition is most commonly experienced as knowing what another person is thinking or feeling or that something is wrong with someone when no indication of it has been observed by our five senses. Counselors, mentors, and coaches with a high degree of intuition frequently intuit their client's inner condition and needs. Often, intuition and empathy work together to touch and encourage a hurting spirit.

Children often intuit their parent's feelings and tell their parent what the parent is feeling. A child will also have striking experiences with perception, like little Ben who was an NF and who knew someone was at the front door — even though he was in a room at the other end of the house. His mother insisted there was no way for him to have heard or to have detected someone's presence.

Sitting on the floor, playing with his toys, Ben quietly announced, "Someone is at the front door." His mother thought he was playing with her, but she decided to check it out. As she was on the way to the front door, he called out to her, "He's gone now." She didn't respond. She felt stunned and angry at him for playing games with her like this, but she kept going and, as she peeked out of the window, she saw a man just leaving and going down the path to the front gate.

Surprised and a little unnerved, she raced back to her son and asked, "How did you know?" He quietly muttered, "I don't know." She picked up the phone and called me in desperation. "What was wrong with her son?" was her first response. Intuition can be unnerving, particularly to someone of a less connected temperament.

I'm not presenting you with scientific evidence, simply reporting the experiences of people as they report them. Intuition has long been acknowledged and used for good purposes.

Temperament keys that are built on the Myers-Briggs and Keirsey models accept that intuition is a way of gathering information from the world around us by a method distinct from the use of the five physical senses. This appears as either an S (sensing) or an N (intuition) in the temperament profiles. It is no surprise that the Ns (NTs and NFs) are the masters of this inner world and use intuition to get added information about their world.

Intuition can easily be misinterpreted, misunderstood, or even inaccurately recognized. Given all this lack of knowledge about intuition, it is still a reality and a force in our human experiences. Weaknesses develop in us all when we try to force our *innerkinetics*. Intuition is an inner strength and all our inner strengths play by rules of their own — at times, beyond our understanding.

Reward from the use of intuition comes as a feeling of satisfaction at being able to "see" and understand the issues that concern us or someone else. The satisfaction of seeing with our physical eyes is the same satisfaction the eye of our mind feels when it perceives.

Sometimes an intuitive dream or insight has been used to create sudden success for the recipient. Most often, intuition gives insights that can hasten our success along the way to our goal. We surmise that intuition, in itself, is little-concerned with the effects. Perhaps we could call intuition a passive participant in reaching our potential. However, don't regard it as insignificant.

Until we know more of this inner power we can simply be thankful for its help.

How Do I Develop this Strength?
• Intuition is something that happens or doesn't happen. Accept what you receive with gratitude.

• When we pay attention to our insights we tend to increase their occurrences.

• Intuiting the feelings of others, however, seems to clearly be strengthened by use.

Caution:
All temperaments lapse into weaknesses when they don't use their strengths, overuse them, or use them for destructive purposes such as damaging themselves or others. Here are further cautions for this strength.

• Caution must be exercised because intuition can be misused for harmful purposes. Hold yourself to high ethical standards.

• All strengths can be abused.

• All strengths should be used for positive purposes only.

Emotional — From Love to Hate

Affection is responsible for nine-tenths of whatever is solid and durable happiness in our lives.
~ C. S. Lewis

The hunger for love is more difficult to remove than the hunger for bread.
~ Mother Teresa

Emotions can trouble an NF and stir the wish to be rid of them, but the emotional power of both love and hate is undisputed in the NF and is one of their potent strengths.

The NF is capable of extremes in both emotional directions. At one extreme they can love with unbelievable passion and commitment. At the other extreme they can hate with a bitter vengeance. This wide swing in their emotional makeup can often get them labeled as bipolar. At least it appears that way to many diagnosticians. The extremes are native to their temperament and not a mental imbalance. Bipolar is more than just swinging to extremes of love and hate. We call these swings in the NF "emotional volatility," and they must learn to control it.

Anger the NF, and they may release a verbal broadside of gigantic proportions or keep an equally forceful reaction locked up inside themselves. Love them, and you can be the recipient of overwhelming expressions of affection. Hurt them, and they will withdraw and cut you out of their lives, erupt, inwardly blame themselves, seek to make amends with a passion, or defend themselves with determination in an attempt to free themselves from more hurt. When the emotions of an NF are aroused anything can happen. This is why they can seem to be hard to manage as children and difficult to control as adults.

"My NF was the most difficult child for me to parent," reported one father.

A friend of an adult NF comments, "It's hard for me to understand his bursts of upset and the more frequent withdrawals."

"Jannelle is such a loving person, and she tries to please so hard. Why does she show such swings in her feelings, and why does she apologize so often after she has been upset with me? Its all a mystery to me."

A manager says, "I can't complain about Jack. He is a model employee, but he is so easily hurt and when he is hurt, he can be very emotional. I never know which Jack is on duty each day until the day is over. Usually both turn up."

Hurt and anger go together. When hurt, we are automatically angry. When an NF is hurt, their emotions flare in a flash. Then they are sorry and try to regain the harmony that they believe they have disrupted. "In reality, it's often my fault, not theirs," said the manager. That only adds to the puzzle.

The control of emotions is hard for NFs or anyone to accomplish. EQ (emotional quotient) depends on the control of these powerful emotions, so it is worth much effort to help all NFs, in particular, to self-control early in life. It is best for an NF to learn the rudiments of emotional control before their teenage years. If they don't, it can be a trying time for both parents and child to have to deal with emotional intelligence in those turbulent teenage years and beyond.

Emotions are such a complex drive that it is impossible to do justice to their importance and their unpredictable appearances within the scope of this book. We all find them difficult to manage when they are stirred. They can interrupt the briefest of encounters and change a relationship in seconds. However, we would live a sterile life without them. When their negative powers are in full flight, however, we often wish we did.

Parents sometimes pay more attention to developing a child's IQ when their EQ will have more to do with their success or failure in life. To create a mature and successful adult, give most of your time to teaching your child emotional control and the positive use of their emotions. For the adult NF, success is spelled the same way: emotional control. That control can offset depression and raise an otherwise low self-image to healthy levels.

Weaknesses are many from the overuse of this strength (which is most common), but don't forget those created by the nonuse and the wrong use of emotion. The most common problem is an angry outburst and a long cool down period.

Since emotions get such a bad rap, let me sing their praises. Emotions fulfill like no other human response. They are a rich mine, producing precious treasures for the human spirit and genuine gold for all relationships. Emotional richness makes the most commonplace experiences of life reward us deeply. Emotions warm us and cool us, excite us and calm us. They sparkle when touched with the sunshine of love. They intrigue and they play in our minds, creating worlds of imaginative wonder. We love them and hate them. They can drive us to success and throw us into the pit of despair. If we can be objective, we would never choose a life without them.

Tap into your emotions and develop their positive powers. They are one of the most powerful tools to make you reach your goal. Never be without their power and drive in the use of any strength. The more the better if they are positive and healthy.

How Do I Develop this Strength?

- Enjoy your emotions. Become a friend and heed their messages. That way you can easily become aware of how they are influencing you.

- Give your positive emotions away to others. They strengthen and multiply when given away. All temperaments should do this.

- Make love, faith, joy, and hope your key emotions, and keep them pure in motive and plentiful in your heart.

- Learn to control your emotions. They are a selfless servant, but an ugly master.

- Developing healthy emotions should be your goal. Healthy emotions are positive emotions.

- Control of healthy emotions is as necessary as the control of negative emotions. NFs have an abundance of emotions. It's the control factor that worries them most.

Caution:

All temperaments lapse into weaknesses when they don't use their strengths, overuse them, or use them for destructive purposes such as damaging themselves or others. Here are further cautions for this strength.

- Learn how to manage your emotions. Some control factors will be used before the emotions erupt; others afterwards.

- Coping mechanisms can help.

- Prayer and meditation can help.

- Damaging, negative emotions will destroy any of us.

- Once we are able to control our emotions we can learn to keep the negative ones from hurting us.

Much more needs to be said about emotional control. Our purpose here is to highlight it as a strength and introduce you to its issues.

Empathetic — Caring

Love is the only sane and satisfactory answer to the problem of human existence.
~ Eric Fromm

I have been watching an empathetic NF mother. Her child has just been hurt — not seriously, but the mother is obviously drawn into the hurt of the child and hurts with the child. She seems more concerned and emotionally involved than the child. It's called empathy and it is found in its most intense expression in the NF. This mother is extremely caring and very loving. I detect she is concerned with what is going on inside her child as much as she is concerned with what happened to the child's body. She is reluctantly leaving now and her child is returning to play with the other children. Clearly, it is hard for her to step away and disconnect. Empathy bonds an NF to another in a way that sympathy doesn't.

She joins us as we are talking about the values she wants Emily (her child) to have. They are all the inner values of spirit. Empathy is one personality merging with another, and these values of an NF mother are projected into her dreams for her child. This is all internal, very "spiritual." These feelings are introjected into her own spirit as though she carries her child inside her mind and heart. This mother displays true empathy.

The ability to feel another's pain and empathize is an NF's native strength. SPs, SJs, and NTs find themselves more comfortable with sympathy even though some do empathize, and those who do are usually the ones with a strong "F" in their profile. Sympathy is feeling sorry for someone. It generates concern and offers of help. Empathy goes deeper and feels the pain with the other person who has been hurt. It takes real effort and a special quality of the human spirit to empathize as opposed to sympathize. Empathy drains a person faster than sympathy.

Here is a further insight into empathy for those who want to understand it better. The English word comes from the Greek word *empatheia*, which conveys the idea of passion, affection, and concern. It suggests our emotions are passionately involved in positive affection and concern for another person. This can't be true if we don't feel the pain of the other. The insight of the ancient Greeks is again right on target.

Sympathy falls short of feeling the pain. Empathy takes sympathy a step further. Empathy is one personality blending with the concern of another personality and feeling the pain. Empathy has also been described as projecting our personality into the other person's personality. Usually the purpose is to share the burden of their feelings and concerns at a deeply personal level of involvement. This ability to sense the feelings of others, know what is felt or thought, and share their pain is what distinguishes empathy from sympathy. Sometimes it will be just a knowing, sometimes a feeling, often both, and always with deep concern.

Some people are so empathetic that they find it hard to function when experiencing the pain that others feel. Sharing the pain of another, even to the point of becoming sick, is not uncommon for the sensitive NF temperament.

Most of us would agree that empathy is a wonderful gift and does much good in any society, particularly the small society of a home where the issue of feelings can be paramount. It is hard for NFs not to be empathetic, so they usually only develop a weakness from this strength by overuse.

Sharing another's concerns is fulfilling to the caring spirit of the NF. We are humans who will risk our lives to save others, and though to some philosophies that seems a foolish commitment, it will always be to the NF a law of life. To be sacrificial satisfies.

Empathy is a strength that supports the bonding so typical of the NF. It is then a supportive strength and enhances several of the others.

Develop it to elevate and intensify another related strength. You may ask, "Will empathy help me achieve my goal?"

How Do I Develop this Strength?
- If you would empathize, you will have to care. People can often sense your care, and that's why they are drawn into its comfort. Empathy is not possible if you don't care, so develop your caring spirit by using it often.

- Sympathize with all since sympathy can awaken empathy in an NF.

- Words that indicate you understand their suffering usually ignite feelings of empathy in you. If you truly understand someone's suffering, start sharing your feelings with them and your empathy will deepen as you reach out to help them.

Caution:
All temperaments lapse into weaknesses when they don't use their strengths, overuse them, or use them for destructive purposes such as damaging themselves or others. Here are further cautions for this strength.

- Caution: Some NFs get so involved with feeling the other person's pain that they cease to be objective enough to help in a practical way.

- Some get involved to the point that they become sick, as we have noted. Such depth of empathy is laudable, but it is not helpful to either patient or care giver.

Humanitarian

There is one word that may serve as a rule of practice for all one's life -- reciprocity.
~ Confucius

Humanitarianism surely is expected in a temperament that majors on empathy, concern for others, love, kindness, and emotional sensitivity. A humanitarian is one who promotes the welfare of our human race by their gifts and actions. Put simply, it is one who helps humanity by seeking to eliminate pain and suffering.

Some NFs extend this humanitarian concern to all animals. If they inadvertently squash a bug they become upset and feel guilty. Others are selective. They show concern for all animals except snakes or spiders!

Animals, at times, show care for other animals, but human animals seem to be more dependent on each other's care. The protection of others is ultimately the protection of ourselves. Therefore, humans fight for other humans and their freedom. Freedom itself must ultimately be based on the understanding that we stand or fall together. Again, as in empathy, the rewards of sacrificial service go to the one whose humanitarian heart gives of itself. The ethical nature of the NF calls them to humanitarianism.

Again, this is a supportive strength on the way to being our best. Develop it as with other supportive strengths to augment the powers of another strength.

How Do I Develop this Strength?
• Become familiar with the needs of people.

• Determine how you can help and build your resources to be able to be active as a humanitarian.

• Dream big and involve others in helping.

• Be all you can be for others. This strength needs to create a vision and belief that supports its growth.

Caution:
All temperaments lapse into weaknesses when they don't use their strengths, overuse them, or use them for destructive purposes such as damaging themselves or others. Here are further cautions for this strength.

• Don't neglect your own family to help others.

- Don't neglect your own spiritual and personal needs to help others. If you do, you will soon be unable to be effective in your help.

- Always plan and carry out your own personal growth so that, in helping others, your help can increase together with the quality of your help as the years go by.

Seekers of Harmony — Haters of Discord

Always aim at complete harmony of thought and word and deed. Always aim at purifying your thoughts and everything will be well.
~ Mahatma Gandhi
Live in harmony with one another ... be careful to do what is right in the eyes of others. If it is possible, as far as it depends on you, live at peace with everyone.
~ St Paul (INFJ)

Because the NF is all about relationships, any lack of harmony registers sharply on their radar.

It is not so much the verbal agreement that they seek, but the harmony of feelings. Harmony, for the NF, is a wholeness, a oneness that creates the secure feeling of spirits being united. This strength fears the cracks and divisions that weaken a society. Therefore, the NF is cautious not to disturb peace and harmony where it exists and to seek it where it doesn't. The exception to this is the NF who is passionately promoting a cause without concern for the ethical boundaries of how their actions affect others. This is an NF denying his own strength of personal integrity and ethical fairness.

NFs will resist the harshness that demands truth without love. "It doesn't matter how you tell them, just tell them!" may fall from an SJ's lips, but it shocks the NF who can't stand a rough, don't-care-about-your-feelings attitude.

Unless April was angered, she couldn't bear the harshness of some of her fellow workers. She had to admit that when she was angered she could become as harsh as they were, but to hear them talk to each other in tones that must damage the harmony of the workplace demotivated her and left her feeling alienated and lonely.

They were putting each other down and speaking with cutting sarcasm, even when they weren't apparently angry with each other. It tore at her sense of human decency and concern.

With a goal to bring a sense of togetherness, she spoke with her supervisor about it. He told her with a laugh that is was all right and they meant no harm. "Don't be so sensitive," he said.

"I hated that remark," she said. "How could people talk to each other that way?" She had been told she was too tender and sensitive by many people and, since she didn't know who she was without an understanding of herself, she felt disturbed that an urge inside her was deemed so wrong when it felt like it was so right. She had tried to be unconcerned, but the waves of bad-will the course comments of her coworkers had created still affected her.

She finally erupted in anger at one of them one day. That set off a chain of reactions. Laughter and scorn, angry retorts, a reproof from the boss, and efforts to toughen her up the rough way.

NFs are haters of discord and, when pressed too far with disharmony, they will, without thinking, add to the disharmony by exploding in anger in return. They are deeply hurt by this inconsiderate behavior and it is their method of defense to explode, which usually doesn't work. It left April with no alternative in her mind. She gave her notice and left, feeling guilty, angry, unjustly treated, and quite demotivated by such an atmosphere.

Some NFs have learned to be hard and rigid because they have been walked on, put down, and their sacrifices disrespected, but the harshness they have adopted is only to their own harm. It strips the tenderness from their love and makes them fight with an SJ's weapons in an SJ's world where they are not likely to win. They are more likely to do what April did: leave.

Love is the NF's ultimate weapon. They must not let others walk all over them. They must speak up in a way that wins, not in an angry outburst that only leaves them the loser. Love is what they breathe and give and love always wins in the long run. They must believe in their ultimate power and learn how to use it effectively.

When damaged by hurt and when the NF takes up the weapons of revenge and reprise and fights with passion, their own emotions dismantle their effectiveness. They lose the effectiveness of their most potent weapon, love, and that assures their rejection and defeat. A harsh NF is an emotionally angry NF. We must be what we were created to be to maintain the balance of our powers and the effectiveness of the combination of our strengths.

Grace was another NF, a gifted leader with passion and determination enhanced by a training in administration and organization. Her distaste of unfairness made her react sharply to the efforts of her working companions to question her leadership and get rid of her. She had been too demanding of her vision for the organization and her fellow workers felt they were being railroaded into changes they were not willing to make. To them she was a threat. Instead of addressing the threat she had created to their comfort level, she felt abused and rejected. She insisted on her program for the improvement of the department, and they dug their toes in.

A leader whose followers stop following is not a leader any longer. Her removal was a simple matter: just refuse to cooperate and blame her for their reactions and her superiors may well get another, more effective leader.

She was devastated by the unfairness of it all since she had sacrificed for each of these workers and could not understand their rebuttal of her leadership. The power to fix this withdrawal of support lay in her ability to reunite and diplomatically meet each person's perceived needs. She didn't and she bled with hurt, carrying her own pain into the next leadership position. You can predict the result of that one too. This happens all too often to NFs who become obsessed with their hurt.

Here is a rewritten conclusion. When challenged, she could have welcomed their challenge with the comment, "We are a team, and a team listens to each other. What is it that concerns you? Let us find a way to reach our vision." Her leadership would then have been solidified and, for her, her emotions that had been stirred by her hurt would now have been controlled, using her gifts, her people skills, intuition that something was amiss, logical analysis, trust, and imagination. NFs have the strengths to solve discords. Allowing their emotions to divert them is their nemesis.

In Greek mythology, the goddess of vengeance and retribution repays us for our mistakes, and Grace was her target in this instance.

So strong is the NF's love of unity that, when disturbed, it can turn them negative and incapacitate them like it did Grace. This complicates their ability to use the strengths they are endowed with to solve their relationship problems. Remember that they are very complicated with their emotion and their reason vying for dominancy in their actions.

Discord is hated with a passion. In turn, the anger that their hatred of discord creates exacerbates the problem. Hatred is a negative force and does not engender the positive atmosphere that they need in their minds to pursue pure harmony. Of course, to solve personnel problems they must prevent their negative passions from drawing them into escalating discord.

Harmony calms them and they can then become productive. To the NF, harmony is the sign of health in relationships. All workplaces and homes benefit from this oneness. Please remember, harmony is not the same as agreement. It can exist where disagreement is accepted and respected.

I have pointed out some of the ways weaknesses develop in the use of this strength. It can lead to reducing other strengths to weakness or to giving up the responsibilities of leadership just to maintain harmony. The problem is not new, as this quotation indicates...

The thing that impresses me the most about America is the way parents obey their children.
~ King Edward VIII (1894-1972)

Just the presence of harmony brings reward to the NF. It is an important strength because only in harmony does anything in this universe operate smoothly. Discord causes friction and the friction of human spirits takes the meaning of the word discord to new heights. NFs would always "like to teach the world to sing in perfect harmony."

Harmony or its absence can affect reaching our goals. It is, again, a supportive strength.

How Do I Develop this Strength?
• First, establish a firm belief that harmony is superior to discord in home, work, and play. If you don't believe it, you won't tend to use it.

- Dislodge the belief that force, authority, and brutality are the greater and more effective ways of handling disputes. They may result in immediate change, but not acceptable change, and usually for only a short term.

- Write the word harmony on your mind and, also, where you can see it and profit from the reminder. Always try peaceful means to resolve problems first. Harmony is unity and unity is strength.

- Increase your awareness of when and where you could use attempts at harmony in the home, at work, and in play environments.

- Live with people in harmony yourself.

Caution:
All temperaments lapse into weaknesses when they don't use their strengths, overuse them, or use them for destructive purposes such as damaging themselves or others. Here are further cautions for this strength.

- Don't attempt to bring harmony about by forceful methods. Oil is not water.

- Don't attempt to achieve harmony with more disharmony (anger).

- Harmony is achieved with love and respect for all.

Kindhearted

A kind word is like a spring day.
~ Russian proverb

Kindness is the language that the deaf can hear and the blind can see.
~ Mark Twain

With all this sensitivity and emotional concern for others, kindness seems to be an essential medication for an NF to have in their "relationship first aid kit." It is!

W. E. Sangster, in his book *The Pure in Heart,* tells an amazing story of kindness.

> "It is any time between 1616 and 1654 at Cartagena. A slave ship is soon to arrive. The port is busy and expectant at the prospect of another rich cargo of black ivory. A good sale means prosperity all around."

> "The ship appears in sight and, with it, the most appalling stench that can assail the nostrils of man. It comes in firm and solid like a wall. Strong men vomit as it hits them and the crowded quay is cleared in a moment as people run from this awful breath of corruption. One man remains at the quayside — one man and his blanched assistant. Serene of countenance and aching with love for the suffering, Peter Claver is at his post. Hardly before the ship has tied up, he hurries aboard. Is he human? Does he not see and smell what coarse men cannot stand? Straight for the dying he goes ... He whispers words of love to them. They do not understand his words but they see his blazing eyes. He puts his arms around their putrid bodies and kisses them into eternity."

> "He turns next to those who yet may live. A bit of tobacco for this one to chew: it will dull the unbearable pain. A sip of brandy there. He will wash those festering wounds. Put the dead aside for decent burial ... In a few days the ship is "cleared." Peter Claver is shepherding the new arrivals and waiting for the next boat."

He is human, and kindness was never better among this human race.

All people can be kind, but some are noted for it. The SP and the SJ are very kindhearted. Differentiate between the SJ's kindness as helpfulness, the SP's kind generosity, and the NF's touching attempts at creating a world of love.

Kindness has been with us from the beginning of human existence. Plato believed the idea of the good (*agathos*) is all embracing — the highest most dominant idea or thought for us humans — and he equated this goodness with kindness. Kindness, then, is a great thought and most noble when it is translated into an action.

Aristotle, in his *Ethics*, also defines it as the goal of all action! The Greeks believed that to be kind we need to free ourselves from material ties, and the NF is the spiritual temperament who can so easily embrace this ancient and still valid idea of kindness being goodness.

The Greeks had several words for it, including *Chrestos*. Just like all the ancient understandings of this strength, this word links goodness and kindness, too. A "kind" wine was a "good" wine to the Greeks. Kindness was seen by them as someone having a friendly nature and a mildness about them that shunned roughness. The NF who is living in their strengths exemplifies this!

Perhaps of interest is that *Chrestos* was, on one known occasion in ancient literature, mistakenly used for *Christos*, the Greek word for Christ. He was, in effect, being named "Kind" instead of Christ. It is a happy mistake as the core of his teaching is love, practically expressed in kindness — a love that would eventually give birth to mercy missions and spur the spread of kindness in our world. Kindness is love in action. Kindness has been emphasized by all leaders who view goodness as important to social welfare.

It expresses love practically and effectively. That is what the NF who is living in this strength is doing: expressing and showing love. They long for a world where everyone is kind since that would bring harmony with it. Kindness is strengthened by caring, humanitarian concerns, empathy, the quest for harmony, and other strengths of the NF temperament.

The most common weakness that relates to this strength is their nonuse of it when they have withdrawn due to anger. When this happens kindness is not in sight.

All the ethical strengths of the NF reward them in the same way: inwardly. That deep-seated feeling that "I am being true to all that is good in me" is the way we were meant to feel and the payback is immediate.

How Do I Develop this Strength?

- Kindness is an action. Act kindly if you would develop this strength.

- Become aware of opportunities to be kind and take them wherever possible.

- Believe in its superior power to change society and people.

Caution:

All temperaments lapse into weaknesses when they don't use their strengths, overuse them, or use them for destructive purposes such as damaging themselves or others. Here are further cautions for this strength.

Nonuse is the path to most weaknesses for this strength.

People Skills — Diplomatic

Effective people skills begin with changing ourselves rather than trying to change others.
~ Ray W. Lincoln

If you can't go around it, over it, or through it, you'd better negotiate with it.
~ Ashleigh (English author)

Diplomacy is the ability to bring opposing parties together, to work with people in difficult circumstances, and to respectfully merge opposite agendas. It does not, in my opinion, describe the complex intellect of an NF fully enough. See: "The NF Mind (Complex)" at the opening of this chapter.

Keirsey, who coined the use of the phrase "diplomatic intelligence" for the NF way of thinking, has pointed us in the right direction though. He calls the SP the "tactical intelligence;" the SJ, the "logistical intelligence;" the NT, the "strategic intelligence," and the NF, the "diplomatic intelligence."

Think of diplomacy, not in the limited terms of politics and mediation but as the interpersonal skills of the NF in building all relationships. It brings us close to an understanding of their nature.

They seek to bring people together everywhere, but they do so idealistically and only where fairness, truth, and love meet. They believe that emotions (love), not just logic, lead to truth and love should be the motivation or goal of all honest efforts at reconciliation. Where these are absent in a dispute, the NF's efforts at diplomacy usually center on creating a need for it.

In their diplomatic efforts they display their people skills, tact, and perseverance to accomplish their goals. Diplomacy also describes the NF's ability to use intuition, sensitivity, emotion, and rationality to find solutions to complex problems. They certainly think relationally, even when solving what seems to be a purely logical issue between people.

NFs purposefully use people skills to maintain relationships and morale. They are the masters of people skills and will often sacrifice personally just to maintain morale in the workplace. The urge for creating harmony among people is what drives them to intervene and attempt reconciliation. At this, they are very skilled.

People skills can be abused. The wily con artist who knows how to rip someone off, the flatterer, the sham, the artful dodger, and the self-serving politician use people skills to accomplish their goals. All strengths can be misused and when they are, weaknesses are created that can harm others and the perpetrators themselves.

People skills lead NFs into occupations where the management of people and the powers of persuasion are paramount. As sales people they will show a strong desire to please the customer and sell only what they believe will be for the customer's good. To sell the customer something they do not need leaves them feeling guilty.

The nonuse of this strength is seen most often in the NF when they are upset or disturbed.

The fulfillment they feel when people are brought together or to inner harmony and relational health is the same sense of fulfillment Hillary must have felt when he conquered Mt Everest: that of achievement.

People skills and diplomacy can lead an NF to achieve their goals. It is a basic strength, and developing it is very helpful. The NF can't afford to be without its assistance on the way to their ultimate goal.

How Do I Develop this Strength?
• People skills can be learned, but the NFs may have an edge due to their native drives.

• Dale Carnegie's book, *How to Win Friends and Influence People*, is still a handy tool for people skills.

• Study people and their complexities.

Caution:
All temperaments lapse into weaknesses when they don't use their strengths, overuse them, or use them for destructive purposes such as damaging themselves or others. Here are further cautions for this strength.

• Avoid the temptation to use this strength for harmful purposes since it offers that possibility.

• Check your use of this strength with the question, "Am I bringing harm to others or to myself by using my people skills in this way?"

Real and Authentic ——Ethical

Ours is a world of nuclear giants and ethical infants.
~ Omar Bradley

We have focused so intently on the tangible that we have, to our human loss,
displaced the intangible.
~ Ray W. Lincoln

As champions of causes, NFs (led by the ENFP) exert their influence often. Mother Theresa, Gandhi, the Dalai Lama, and many sages have left their mark on history through their zealousness at being always authentic and ethical. As NFs, they sought not only to better the world but to find purity in themselves and to live at peace with themselves. Wanting to be real, authentic, and ethical, these NFs go down in history as the champions of just and merciful causes.

Being false or unauthentic eats away at NFs (as it does with all the temperaments) and causes real guilt, but this feeling seems more prevalent and persistent in an NF, driving them with a passion to be real. Being a real, genuine, ethical, person is so important to them that they will often sacrifice their goals and comfort just to be seen as authentic. This is the ethical temperament who feels a strong urge to follow the standards they have adopted for themselves.

Ethical inconsistency in their virtual worlds (minds), where they live most of the time, amounts to war with themselves. They can be slow to see that their anger is, at times, a loss of personal integrity, since they are not being true to their desire to love and bring harmony. They sometimes adopt harmful methods to bring their causes to triumph and this denies their true nature as we have noted under other strengths.

They are very sensitive to any disturbance inside themselves. They are the judges of their inner purity and they can judge themselves harshly, often establishing exaggerated guilt. Every failure or lack of integrity is internalized and, unfortunately in most, is mulled over and becomes their focus. Their self-esteem suffers. This strength can turn quickly to the weakness of self condemnation. When they don't have a guide to what is right and wrong, it can disorient them and leave them without motivation for their actions. However, the sense of fulfillment that being real brings is the feeling all sages have experienced and the one that drives them onward. Don't run with the impression that all NFs are sages or holy people. Far from it. But they do find reward in being full of inner integrity.

This is a supportive strength on the NF's road to being their best.

How Do I Develop this Strength?
- Be real. Whenever you feel discomfort, challenge your actions and your thoughts and find the authentic you.

- Choose your cause with great care because your passions will bind it to you, and you will find it hard to change.

- Examine the ethics of your cause before you adopt it.

- Once you have built your ethical standards, you will have built the foundations for this strength.

- Then light up the cause with your life and commitment. Every NF should have a cause to feed their passion.

Caution:
All temperaments lapse into weaknesses when they don't use their strengths, overuse them, or use them for destructive purposes such as damaging themselves or others. Here are further cautions for this strength. Halfheartedness is not the way to build this strength.

- Halfheartedness, in an NF, causes weakness.

- Keeping it real means being consistent.

Romantic

The most effective kind of education is that a child should play amongst lovely things.
~ Plato

As I gaze upon the sea! All the old romantic legends, all my dreams, come back to me.
~ Henry Wadsworth Longfellow

Two days ago (at the time of writing) as I was conducting a seminar, and an NF known to everyone present described himself as incurably romantic. The chuckles of agreement collapsed the whole group into understanding laughter. Everyone knew this "romantic" had correctly identified himself. Scan the list of NF strengths again and I think you will see many strengths that contribute to NFs being known as romantics, including idealist, passionate, sensitive, and emotional.

To the NF, romantic means: beautiful, idyllic, picturesque, fairytale, idealistic, utopian, dreamy, a refreshing mood, sex without the dirt, Eros without the distortion, the passionate awakening of their warm emotions. It is found in music, nature, dance, film, poetry, and anywhere love and the love of things is found.

A security officer came to me with what was, for him, an embarrassing problem. His wife had left and he wanted to get her back. He had tried, and his efforts to that point had not succeeded. She had told him that he was cold and remote. What should he do? She was an NF, so I knew that, being an NF, she liked romantic things.

Sometimes a man who is all about rules and regulations, duty and responsibility (SJ) does not know how to be romantic. He was willing to learn to meet her needs. Since she was coming back home after a short vacation, he prepared a meal. His skills as a chef were seriously limited, so he decided to emphasize a warm welcoming atmosphere. He put a special, clean table cloth on the dining room table, set out the best china, lit candles, arranged a centerpiece of flowers, turned on soft music that she loved, and met her at the door with more flowers and a welcoming smile.

For a tough security officer, this was a feat! I don't know how many calls for instructions he made, but he got it all done with style. The food wasn't great, but the effort was superb.

She nearly fainted at the door when presented with flowers. When she saw everything he had done and sat down for a meal in a romantic setting, she was overcome. Her only question was, "Will he treat me as special all my life?" That was still to be answered, but he had made a good start. NFs can be deeply affected by the warmth of romantic environments.

For the NF, romance extends beyond people and relationships. The atmosphere of a favored restaurant can romantically touch them. A sunset can stir their romanticism — and nearly always does. All temperaments can wax romantic, but the NF is richly endowed with sensitive feelings. Therefore, they become known as the romantic temperament.

Is it surprising that the word *romantic* came to us from the French? An exciting way of life, liberally sprinkled with love and adventure, can induce romantic feelings, as can the fanciful and imaginative in literature. Amorous behavior, dreams, vision, tenderness, and affection stimulate this strength.

An NF is deeply stirred by the power love has to penetrate their spirit. Weaknesses enter when the NF doesn't welcome their romantic feelings and life then becomes prosaic, featureless, and bland. NFs don't believe that they can ever overuse this strength.

The reward is obvious. A flat battery can be recharged and the NF's spirit refreshed by a simple romantic environment. This strength of the NF, whose self-judgment and feelings of worthlessness often afflict them, is bliss.

On the road to their goals, romanticism refreshes the NF. Therefore, it is a supportive strength.

How Do I Develop this Strength?

- Romanticism is an attitude as much as it is a pleasure in things, places, and surroundings. Develop your love of all things beautiful into an habitual way of seeing things.

- Look for the good and the wonderful everywhere.

- Quieten the noise and clamor of your mind.

- Develop a deeper appreciation for art, beauty, the finer things of pleasure. We must have pleasure and we must thrill to the beauty of our universe.

- Open up your feelings to all things romantic around you and become aware of your inner pleasure-meter rising. Romanticism can elevate the normal and climb into the rarefied air of intensely stimulating emotions.

Caution:

All temperaments lapse into weaknesses when they don't use their strengths, overuse them, or use them for destructive purposes such as damaging themselves or others. Here are further cautions for this strength.

- Be real and authentic, and the empty meaningless comment or thought will not easily disturb you and rob you of the true awe of all things wonderful.

- Romanticism is empty if it is not filled with genuine love.

Introspective

Who am I ... How can I become my true self?
~ Stephen Montgomery (spoken of the introspective)

NFs tend to internalize everything. They compare themselves to others and to their own inner standards constantly. Introspection is the internalizing of feelings, thoughts, events, and reactions that they have observed or imagined. It is a fierce self examination. In this they stand opposite of the SPs and SJs, who content themselves with extrospection — the examination of things outside of themselves.

Is self-examination a strength or a weakness? It is a strength if it cleanses and empowers the person who uses it. If the NFs use it to better themselves and do not condemn themselves, it becomes a valuable tool for personal growth.

Creativity can be the result of internalizing things and sensing their affect on the human mind and spirit. It may play a part in the NF's intuitive strengths. Most masterpieces have been processed internally in the light of personally held standards before they find their final form.

It is a weakness if the NFs use it to punish themselves and drag down their self-image and if negative introspection destroys human potential. It also saps the energy from relationships. Our self-image is the ceiling for our performance and, therefore, we need it to be as high as it can be supported by reality. Self examinations either increase or decrease our sense of self worth. Therefore, introspection must be used for positive uplift, not negative lashings.

Negative self-talk multiplies the damage done by negative introspection. Use introspection to clean house and create a positive confidence and an atmosphere for success.

How Do I Develop this Strength?
• Keep self-examination positive.

• Create a positive understanding of yourself.

• Look for its lessons of improvement and you will learn not to fear it.

• Have specified quiet times to help you examine your inner life, your motives, and thoughts.

• Expect creative results from introspection.

Caution:
All temperaments lapse into weaknesses when they don't use their strengths, overuse them, or use them for destructive purposes such as damaging themselves or others. Here are further cautions for this strength.

• Outlaw self condemnation, and all condemnation for that matter.

• Create an awareness of negative self thoughts that lead to disapproval of yourself.

• Avoid all negative self talk.

Perfectionists — Must Do and Be Right

Every time, all the time, I am a perfectionist. I feel I should never lose.
~ Chris Evert, Tennis player

It is not too great a leap from the high self demands of the NF to the desire to be perfect. Every perfectionist is a perfectionist in some, not all, of the things that they do, and they are happy to be selective. A perfectionist must do and be right in all areas that matter to them. Hence the drive is intensified.

Attempting to be perfect, for the NF, is a strength when it motivates them to high achievement. It is a curse when it is overdone or wrongly applied to beat themselves up for a failure. Notice how this strength and the last teeter on the edge of being weaknesses because of their potential for extreme damage to our spirits.

There is a difference between being a healthy perfectionist and succumbing to perfectionism. Perfectionism is the demand that we be perfect. Being perfect — without error, faultless, without defect or omission — is not achievable in this life. All perfectionists must modify or limit true perfectionism or face constant predictable failure! They defeat themselves. Perfectionism can create an aversion to wanting to succeed. It can be counterproductive to personal growth and reaching our goals.

Perfectionism is aligned with the NF's idealism. It drives the NF to even greater efforts to reach an unreachable standard.

Positive perfectionists, on the other hand, are people who aim at perfection and celebrate their near miss. They use the drive to be better, not to create an impossible hope. Perfectionists know they are imperfect and are happily related to being the best that they can be.

Again we face a strength that needs careful application. We are limited beings, as evidenced by our need to go to bed every night for the rebuilding of our bodies' strength. Therefore, we cannot be perfect in the absolute sense. A perfectionism that condemns us should be avoided with passion. It dismantles our inner strengths and keeps us from achieving the true goal of all true perfectionists: namely, calling us to be the best, not simply to be better.

The weaknesses that the overuse and wrong use of this strength can create are only too clear. Watch for the NF's perennial habit of setting high standards and (whether they are reached or not) raising the bar constantly, knowing they cannot clear it, and then sinking in self condemnation and defeat as they fail. Introspection and perfectionism combine in the NF to create a dangerous climate for the building and maintenance of a healthy self-esteem. Living positively with these strengths is living on the edge.

Keeping the standards for our performance realistic allows the perfectionist the thrill of reaching their goals and reaping the benefit of success.

How Do I Develop this Strength?

- Go ahead. Try to jump over the moon if you are happily related to not clearing it unaided.

- View being a perfectionist as a call to be your best, not a call to being faultless.

- Reward all your efforts that show improvement, not just those that reach your goal.

- Keep a list of your achievements for motivation and for appreciating improvements.

Caution:

All temperaments lapse into weaknesses when they don't use their strengths, overuse them, or use them for destructive purposes such as damaging themselves or others. Here are further cautions for this strength.

- When you fall short, repeat to yourself the correct definition of failure: Failure is opportunity and hope, not defeat that leads to despair.

- Refer to your list of improvements often.

Abstract in Speech

NFs prefer to speak abstractly, talking about concepts, ideas, and possibilities: what if, what should be, what could be, what might be.

They often don't finish their statements as their minds race on to the next thought. The SJ can't follow such fast-paced, abstract thinking without anchoring to some detail. "Details!" cries the NF, "We'll deal with them later. Let's get the big picture in place first."

If you are an NT, communication with an NF should be no problem since both talk abstractly. All Ss will feel NFs are in the clouds much of the time and not grounded in the real world. They mean "not grounded in the details." Don't worry. Just ask for the NF to say it again, slowly, and with some details, if they can do that. Then you will understand them.

Their vocabulary will enrich yours if you are an S, since they are the masters of the superlative, graphic, poetic, expression, and they talk in metaphore and simile. "Plain Jane" language is not their best performance. Encourage their metaphoric style, since this is their best contribution (unless they are writing a scholarly paper).

NFs and NTs will benefit from including a little concrete reporting at times to keep them rooted in the reality of details.

If you are an NF, I hope you have chosen a strength and determined to develop it. Even if you are not an NF you will have sharpened your understanding of your own temperament by the study of the NF.

A Convenient List of the NF Temperament's Strengths

Here is a convenient list of the NF temperament's main strengths that we dealt with.

Keep a list with you and develop them one at a time.
- First, focus on being aware of when you are using your strengths.
- Then, with practice and persistence, you will develop them.
- Training develops them even more and will help you understand them as you discover ways to further their use.

NF Strengths Featuring Idealism and Sensitivity

Strengths that Relate to Future Time

Lives in and for the future

Idealists — dreamers

Imaginative

Passionate — enthusiastic — value based decisions — eager to learn

Trusting

Personal growth — meaning — significance

Strengths that Relate to Sensitivity

Sensitive

Intuitive — insightful

Emotional — from love to hate

331

Empathetic — caring

Humanitarian

Seekers of harmony — haters of discord

Kindhearted

People skills — diplomatic

Real and authentic — ethical

Romantic

Introspective

Perfectionists, must do and be right

Abstract in speech

Section 5

Releasing and Developing Your Innerkinetics

Taking the First Steps

The future is purchased by the present.
~ Samuel Johnson

Fortitude is the marshal of thought, the armor of will, and the fort of reason.
~ Francis Bacon

For four days they had replenished their strength with a mere one ounce of dried meat per day. Dehydrated and sapped of all energy, they struggled to put one foot in front of another. Through the parched deserts of Nevada and now across the arid wastes of the Great Salt Lake Desert, they inched their way forward. That night had been like so many over the past days. Dreams of lush pastures, cool waterfalls, simple luxuries like a decent meal had kept them from the refreshment of urgently needed sleep. One can't sleep when physical cravings are so intense. The feeling of utter relief from the thought of just lying down, giving up, and dying tore mercilessly at their minds. The pain of standing up again and lifting one foot after the other wracked their bodies and destabilized their sanity. Only a tenacious human spirit, stronger than all the pain and one that faced the impossible with undying hope, was driving them to keep up the struggle.

These early explorers under the leadership of Jedediah Smith ("Old Jed" they called this 28-year-old Mountain Man) were demonstrating that the greatest power we possess is the inner drive of an indestructible human spirit that can conquer untold mountains of hardship and impossibility. When all else says stop, our spirit can raise a determination from somewhere in its nonphysical depths that qualifies us as creatures of immense potential and energy. Even though "Old Jed" died at 32, he reached his highest plain of success.

Tenacious devotion to a thought, a hope, a cause, an idea or a person can generate great power, as history has lavishly documented. Luther, Gandhi, Emerson, Shackleton, Livingston, Mother Theresa, Hillary, and all the countless reformers, saints, explorers, and leaders have displayed the human mind's capabilities. These people lived to be the best they could be.

The human spirit can drive the human body and scoff in the face of torture and even death. Of all our human "parts," it fires us with an energy that seems akin to the Divine. So let's travel deep into this mysterious territory inside us and ask, "How can I develop its amazing potential? How can I, if I follow my *innerkinetics*, release its powers?" Three inner forces will yield the secret.

The Simple Formula

Here is a simple formula to develop and release the powers of any strength of any temperament. It's simple because we all can do it and we don't have to get a PhD in human functioning to understand and use it. It's called a "formula" because these three powers of the human spirit must work together to release our strengths. Follow these preparatory steps to ready you for the successful use of the formula.

Choose One Strength
To develop and release a strength, we first need to know on which strength to focus our energies. Choose one, *only one*, to begin with. Struggling to develop all our strengths at once spells failure. Diversifying our energy with multiple goals weakens its effects. We want all the power we can muster aimed at developing one strength. Then we can focus on another.

We can find the inner powers that Jedediah's party found only in a pinpoint mental focus. So, select the one core strength in your temperament that you need to develop most. (You may have already done this.)

Begin a Simple Log
For some temperaments (SJ, NT, and NF), recording our efforts can be a big help. Record the strength you have chosen and the day you

started developing its potential. Make brief notes of your reactions and results from day to day. Writing these things down strengthens your resolve and informs you of your progress as well as any needed changes. Don't make it a laborious chore. It is an aid, not another unwelcome job.

Remember, we can make big changes in 40 days. If you have the persistence to work at developing a strength for 40 days, you will not only see great progress but you will increase your happiness from the fulfillment you feel. In one year, you can develop nine of your major strengths! Of course, you will choose the nine that best equip you to reach the goal of your personalized definition of success.

Visualize the Change
Go back and reread the comments on the strength you have selected from the chapter on your temperament's strengths (chapter 12, 13, 14, or 15). Make a note for yourself of the benefits you will receive from maximizing this strength and write them in your log.

You can also benefit from rereading the comments on your temperament under the section "Keys to Developing an [SPs, SJs, NTs, NFs] Potential" in chapters 7, 8, 9 or 10 (whichever is your temperament). These comments can help you understand issues that need your attention in developing your strength. If you identify any, write them in your log as well.

Now you are ready to visualize the results of a developed strength. You may see yourself with a higher self-image, a clearer focus, a strength that makes you feel the satisfaction you were intended to experience, a crystal clear goal for life, and a well-defined path to being the best this strength can make you be — whatever.

Example: (I have chosen a more difficult strength to work with since you may have chosen a difficult one too.)

Suppose you are an NF and have selected *"imaginative"* as the strength you wish to develop. You should go first to the section, "Keys to Developing an NF's Potential," and list these issues as ones you might need to pay attention to:

337

- I need to repeat often, "Imagination is more important than reason." A stronger belief in the power and purpose of imagination will help me.

- I need to search for possibilities more than I do and not settle for the status quo with that horrible feeling of surrender. Finding possibilities is what I am supposed to be about.

- When I am successful in using imagination to solve a problem, mine or someone else's, I feel significant. More of this!

- I must start helping people to realize their potential as I work on my own. This will help me work on my own strength. It's harder to work on my own potential, easier to work on someone else's.

- I will need to develop empathy, intuition, spirituality, sensitivity, and passion since they strengthen each other. I'll attack them next, one-by-one.

- Meditating will help me develop imagination. I will learn how.

- I must keep harmful stress low. I need to develop coping measures. High stress demotivates me.

Next, you should turn to "Imaginative" in the chapter, "Introduce Yourself to Your Strengths — NF." You should make notes similar to the following ones from the section "How Can I Develop this Strength?"

- I must listen to my thoughts more. I often don't listen when ideas come. I discount too many of them before I have really given them a chance.

- I must expect my mental paths to lead me to fruitful imaginings.

- I must spend time refreshing my spirit by dreaming of my future and of solutions to problems for myself and others.

- Perhaps I could set aside three uninterrupted minutes a day to pursue solutions and exercise my imagination.

As a result of these steps you may be able to say, "I can see myself feeling like I am important to others. I have a clearer focus on what to do with my life. I can imagine the feeling of satisfaction I have always wanted to feel. I think I can see my goal for life and a well-defined path to being significant beginning to take shape for me."

Now, fire your spirit with this vision of what you can become and the steps to its accomplishment. Do this by imagining all these things as true and actual in you. Imagine what this strength, when made remarkable, can produce. See the new you in your mind and what being empowered in this way will do for you. If you imagine it and focus on it, it becomes reality to your mind. When your mind gets comfortable with this new you, you will automatically act this way and the power will have been released in your life.

So, go ahead and picture the change and the possible results in you and your world that the maximizing of this strength will create. Do this imaging exercise daily for 40 days as you work on faith, force, and focus. By doing this you will become who you really are!

Faith, Force, and Focus
The Three Generators and Releasers of
Fantastic Inner Power

What Are Faith, Force, and Focus?
(Definitions)

To make sure we are communicating, here are the definitions I will be using for faith, force, and focus.

Definition — Faith Is a Belief.
Faith is a belief, not just a thought or a wish. A belief is a thought that we accept and act on. It doesn't have to be an overwhelming conviction, although the stronger it is the more power it generates.

It can be felt as a real conviction or just a necessity. I shower because it's both a conviction and a necessity! Upon examination it is my belief that motivates me to shower. Even a necessity is only a necessity to me if I *believe* it is. We are all motivated by our beliefs ultimately.

We may also find ourselves questioning a belief even after we have accepted it and acted on it. Or we may continue to wonder about its value even while we have incorporated it as a working belief for our lives. It may grow in importance or wane as we live under its influence, but it is, at the moment, our belief and motivates our actions to the degree of its intensity.

No strength in our temperament can be exercised without some kind of belief in it, and the first secret to maximizing the strengths of our *innerkinetics* is to strengthen our beliefs about the value and importance of the strength we have selected to develop. This is why faith or belief is number one on this list.

Definition — Force Is the Mental Energy that Produces a Decision.

The old term for making ourselves come to a decision was willpower. Jeffery M. Schwartz renames it "mental force." So the second factor in releasing our powers is the strength to make a clear-cut decision (mental force) and act on our belief. We all have the ability, but we must use it and maximize it where needed.

Acting on a belief is the test of whether we have made a decision and have used mental force. Just getting around to making a decision is the trial of their lives for some of the types. The four letters of your personality profile ended in either a J or a P. Those with a J usually have little difficulty with making and acting on their decisions, unless they fear something. Most of those with a P can find it very hard to make a decision and find themselves always waiting for more evidence or for some event that may make the decision for them. For the P, mental force is a real test of their determination.

Acting on a decision can also cause the P concern and stress. They are the ones that need to modify this preference (the P preference) to dismiss their fears and force a decision where it is necessary. Modifying our preferences under certain conditions is not "changing" our temperament; it is adding flex to their functions.

Mental force, if not present, can halt any desire to improve. It seems as though we would all use the force necessary to make decisions, but remember, fear can foul us all.

Definition — Focus Is Creating an Intense "Attention Center"

The finer the focus, the greater the power that is generated. Focus depends on faith and force. Without a belief and a decision to act on our belief, we have nothing to focus on intensely.

At times, our focus is instantly created, as when a bear rushes at us or the news reports a market crash (interestingly called a bear market). At times, focus grows slowly as our belief and conviction grows. Then, intense and demanding, it can become a sharp pinpointed obsession.

When we focus, we center our attention on one thing. The activity of the brain intensifies the more we focus. Also the more intense our focus becomes, the more centralized the activity becomes.

Focus magnifies whatever it is asked to concentrate on. It grabs and holds our attention; our inner tension rises as other interests along with distractions disappear and yield to the attention center. The tension caused by our focus can be positive and healthy or negative and damaging.

I am writing this at the time of the great Haiti earthquake of January 2010. People and governments around the world responded with massive gifts of money, prayer, time, and effort. The mental journey everyone took was positive. An intense, positive focus creates positive results for all concerned.

A criminal who robs a bank takes the same journey, but it is negative, and negative results occur for all concerned. The criminal may, at first, believe the results for him are positive, but in the long run, when everything is taken into account, they are profoundly negative.

To determine whether we are using faith, force, and focus correctly and effectively, we will discuss them one at a time.

341

Here's What Motivates and Drives You

Faith (Belief)

Faithless is he who says farewell when the road darkens.
~ J. R. R. Tolkien

According to your faith it will be done to you.
~ Jesus

The Path to Belief

As we have said, we don't do anything without believing we should do it. Therefore, everything must have some value to us for it to become a belief. We have thoughts all day long. Some we dismiss without another thought, and some we rehash in our minds for good or ill. The ones we mull over hold some potential value to us, good or bad. Unless our thoughts are promoted to become a belief of some sort, they quickly become history and vanish.

A thought forms into a belief by first having some value to us. It must then be accepted as worthy of promotion to the status of a helpful belief. This often means we turn it over in our minds, examining it and thinking it through, wondering about it and evaluating it. Are we going to accept this thought? To what extent — wholeheartedly or casually occur will we accept it? We may take days, months.

Although we don't do this consciously step-by-step, this is the path that a thought travels to become a belief. If we consciously went through this process of evaluation every time we believed something, we would not have time to think of how good the ice cream was. Therefore, only if the belief calls for an important change do we take our time and process it with conscious thoroughness.

Intensity Really Matters

We perform according to the intensity of our beliefs. "According to your faith it will be done to you," is one of the most crucial reminders of how life works. These words of Jesus are pragmatic to the core. Only when we realize that our belief and the intensity with which we hold it is the measure of our success or failure can we be released from all the thoughts and fears that limit us.

There is no strong action without strong belief either. The stronger the belief, the more power our faith generates. Our minds are made to operate according to the strength of our belief. We have always known this, but we seldom live as though we understand it. Strong belief produces strong action.

Intensity motivates. Believe that you *might* succeed and the pressure to succeed is slight. Believe that you *will* succeed and you feel an instant step up in intensity inside of you. There's a big difference between "might" and "will" in the way these words motivate us. It's no longer, "Let me wait and see what might happen." It's the challenge of having to act on our belief (which said "I will succeed") that increases the tension and the motivation.

The increase in tension is all about what happens if our belief is challenged in any way by fear. For example, it may become known to others that we believe we will succeed. Then the fear of not succeeding in the eyes of others increases the inner tension. Now we must perform and it's over to us to make it happen. Fear increases tension.

344

If you can feel the difference inside of you between a casual belief and one that is intensified with determination and commitment, you know that how intensely you believe makes a big difference to the grasp that either fear or hope has on you.

Fears and hopes will sap your faith or energize your faith. The only thing that overcomes a debilitating fear is a faith that is stronger than the fear. The intensity of our faith really matters. It will be done to us according to our faith!

The Content of Belief Matters
What we believe about our strengths and ourselves is, of course, extremely important too. Because we are interested in how to release our strengths and empower them, we must first know that what we believe about our strength will release it or imprison it. A negative belief about it will do the opposite of a positive belief. Equally, what we believe about ourselves will either release it or imprison it.

Do I find people have negative attitudes toward their strengths? All the time! They don't understand their strengths and wonder if they are strengths or weaknesses. What they are confusing is the overuse or misuse of a strength, which gives a strength a bad name or causes the thought of it to promote fear. Take the strength of sensitivity in an NF for example. Over sensitivity is a harmful thing. It encourages paranoia and a self-hate, to name just two results of overuse. The wrong use of sensitivity in constantly comparing ourselves to others is also very damaging, but the right use of sensitivity is essential to intuition and creativity. Without sensitivity we are robbed of all the benefits for ourselves and others of intuition and creative genius.

Some have never used their strength and are afraid to do so. They even feel more comfortable denying they have a strength that others clearly observe because denying it means they have no responsibility to use it, or so they think. What we believe about our strengths is the first thing to check if we would release them.

For example, if you are an NT, perhaps the strength you have selected to develop is ingenuity. If you believe it is not very important for you to be ingenious and if you believe that ingenuity is an overrated and useless strength, you will not release its powers. You will lock your ingenuity up in your own private jail and weaken it for lack of exercise.

Your negative thoughts will also take away any motivation to use it. What you believe about your strength is then self-limiting. To be the best that you can be, you can't afford to limit your strengths or yourself.

In this case, you must believe that ingenuity is very important, is what the world needs, and is what you can give the world. You must also have faith that it will be effective and that it will give you the ability to discover new and exciting things. You must thankfully believe you are endowed with ingenuity and are fulfilled by its use. With this kind of belief, you open the gates for the powerful release of your ingenuity. The more intensely you believe this, the more power you infuse into it.

False humility is another damaging attitude. It is not personal pride to believe that you have been given worthwhile and important gifts. Rather, disapproval of ourselves and our gifts is an illness. It leads to our being nothing.

Some people just feel too uncomfortable or too humble (it's a spurious humility) to own their strength with openness and pride. "Oh, I'm really not ingenious," they condescendingly confess. (The gift of ingenuity being an NT strength and NTs being not too bashful about their gifts, they are not often subject to this fate, thankfully. SJs and NFs are more given to false humility.) It is not motivating to confess you are not gifted; nor is it honest. You might be surprised to know that believing and admitting you have a gift is more often denied than it is humbly owned. Your belief in your giftedness will either free your strengths for use or keep them tightly locked up in your self-destructive unbelief.

Keep developing your belief. Nurturing and growing your belief should be a daily pleasure. Keep asking yourself, "How important is this strength to me? How will it enrich my life and the lives of others if I believe in it and own it?" Visualize what its results can be when you use it to its maximum. The stronger the belief you have in your inner strength's ability, the greater your motivation to use it and develop it. I can't say it enough! Increase your faith in and your ownership of your strengths daily to keep increasing their power.

Action Must Follow

Remember our definition: A belief is a thought that we accept *and act on*. Without acting according to our beliefs, we simply file them away.

They are then lost to our consciousness and are powerless to release our strength. What a tragedy to have a strong faith in your given strengths and then not act on your belief. At the very least, plan the next small step you need to take; act on your belief and do something to give your faith legs.

Using our strength ever so little develops it. Therefore, at the very least, use it. Keep using it at every opportunity of which you are conscious. If your strength is kindness, be kind at every opportunity. Train yourself to become more aware of opportunities to be kind, large and small. Mental awareness of your situation presents you with opportunities to act. See every attempt to upset you or please you as opportunities to be kind and grow your kindness.

Actions have a cyclical effect. When you use your strength, it bolsters your belief in that strength (which motivated you in the first place) and strengthens your resolve to use it again. Faith feeds force, which feeds focus, which promotes actions, which feed faith. Round and round it goes, building your strength.

Beliefs Can Be Long Term Principles or Instant Impulses
It doesn't matter whether beliefs are long term principles or instant impulses. They function in the same way. The SP who acts on impulse (a short-term belief) is not circumnavigating faith, force, and focus. They simply have the gift of processing it all in an instant. If you are hiking in the Rockies, the appearance at high altitudes of a late afternoon thunderstorm, complete with lightning and thunder, will encourage any temperament to act on impulse and descend quickly! The SPs respond to impulse best, but we can all produce a respectable replica when needed. So we all have short-term beliefs and most of us have long-term beliefs too.

Long-term beliefs are the principles and values we adopt. They affect and underwrite all our decisions. They motivate with the feel of a constant nagging urge to act a certain way. Life is fashioned by these long-term principles and values and the beliefs they support. We all need them. Our temperament's preferences may be the source of some long-term beliefs. If we don't have them, our lives drift with the winds of circumstance or peer influence. No predetermined direction means no goal and no purpose. Hence the importance to attain the very best beliefs, principles, and values we can or we will never achieve our potential.   A mixture of negative and positive values, for example, counter and destroy each other.   Our negative beliefs take away the power our positive beliefs give us.   Result?   No power or forward motion toward our goal.

Faith Grows Strongest in a Climate of Optimism

All our strengths are called upon to operate in whatever the current climate of our mind happens to be.   Think of your mental attitude as the weather forecast for your mind.   This "weather" either warms and encourages your strengths with mental force or it cools them in the frigid temperature of an icy negative blast.

Few people pay attention to the atmosphere of their minds.   It's a good thing to make a habit of checking throughout the day, asking yourself "Is my mind negative or positive?"   A mind that is happily related to its circumstances and the people in its world is a catalyst for the powerful release of its strengths.   When we are thankful and happy all bad events appear in a different light.   We challenge them and win regardless of their negative impact.   To be unhappily related to our circumstances or the people in our lives is to defeat ourselves and let them rule us.

Therefore, the mind that is filled with regret, anger, disappointment, negativity, and bitterness releases its strengths like the old black powder gun whose powder is wet: with a "poof" as the bullet barely escapes the barrel.   A strength without effective energy will raise a laugh on any late night show.

The strength of optimism in the SP is a daring, risk-taking belief in a positive, abundant world.   In the SJ, it is a calculated, serious attempt to challenge the status quo.   The NT is optimistic in a determined, non-emotional, self-reliant way.   NFs breed optimism in hope, imagination, and passionate trust, fueled by harmonious relationships.   We must all fill our minds with the power of optimism in our own ways, because we all need to fight the negativity of our circumstances or the negative people around us.

Just as the weather can affect our plans, so a negative or positive mind can seriously affect our power, our effectiveness, and our plans to succeed.   Release your strengths, whatever your temperament, in a positive, optimistic mind.   That's the key to constant empowerment.

Beliefs Can Be Stubborn

Stubbornness can have value. Stubbornness is not always a negative trait. Consider the early explorers again and the intriguing story of the Rio Buenaventura.

The United States was seeking a water passage from the Midwest to the Pacific Ocean. Lewis and Clark's passage, unfortunately, required the negotiation of difficult mountain passes and treacherous waters. The belief that a common source for all the rivers that ran either to the Atlantic or the Pacific was so ingrained in the minds of that age that the Rio Buenaventura (a name given to this fictional river) was imagined to be a large river that ran from a common source (which was thought to be the Rockies) south of the Columbia River to the Pacific.

Explorers searched in vain for it. The evidence mounted against it, but the stubborn belief stuck. It drew many to risk their lives to find it and in the process opened up the vast southwest and discovered passages that a wagon could negotiate all the way to California. The stubborn belief inspired action that resulted in a better way to the Pacific and opened up the colonization of those vast lands. Stubborn beliefs can be the parents of worthwhile children.

Used in a positive way, stubborn beliefs can unlock your future success. Just make sure they are positive beliefs that are helpful to your life's direction.

How Each Temperament Handles Faith.

Each of the temperaments handles faith differently. This is because each of them approaches the matter of faith differently. Each has different struggles, and each is equipped with different strengths with which they can activate their faith. You can read all four ways that the four temperaments handle faith or just read your own temperament's patterns of faith.

SP

Faith is a natural and frequent event for the SP. They readily believe in their own ability. Other people are also believed until it is clear to the SP that they are not to be trusted. The SP makes this transition from trusting someone to not trusting them with ease. Optimism is the default atmosphere of their minds, giving them a lightheartedness and pleasant, problem-solving attitude to life. They see the world as a place of abundance and, therefore, live and give generously. "Easy come, easy go" is their belief, which to them also means "easy go, easy come."

Optimists take the best possible view of things. They look on the bright side and expect the best outcome. With such a positive view of life, believing is easy, compared to the SJ temperament that must protect against things going wrong and must constantly be aware of the negatives.

Encouraged by optimism, SPs are bold risk takers. Whatever might go wrong can surely be fixed. (Note the dramatic difference to the belief that if it can go wrong, it will go wrong.) If it can't be fixed, their attempt to fix it is a badge of their optimism and courage and a proof that they believe in the best outcome. To the SP, faith is an essential part of enjoying life.

Faith is impulsively and spontaneously adopted wherever excitement is promised. A successful quest for excitement requires that they take this attitude and when things turn out well, their faith is strengthened. It's not reason and logic that buoy their faith, but the good experiences they have. If they have more bad experiences than good, they believe they were simply looking in the wrong places. That their luck will change is their optimistic attitude.

A call to believe in abstract ideas or beliefs can be a problem for them. For the SP, life is not abstract. It is made up of the real, concrete experiences of life. They believe in things they can see and touch — in things, rather than concepts or values. In contrast, the NF is abstract: trusting people, experiences, and ideas because of the abstract values that drive their beliefs.

SPs don't often halt between two opinions. Decisive and impulsive, they make up their minds in a flash when needed or simply decide to move on to more exciting things and forget what bores them.

If you are an SP, work on believing in values and building guiding principles into your life.

SJ

Faith is entered into with caution for the SJ. They are naturally cautious and careful. Faith has an element of trust, and trust does not live with ease in a world of caution. A sudden move or change in beliefs is unnerving to the SJ. When they trust or are called upon to exercise faith, they insist on taking calculated risks only!

Therefore, it is better to work hard and store goods for the rainy day, rather than enjoying the present and believing their needs will all be taken care of in a way they can't yet see will happen. SJs must see! Instead of believing in an abundant universe, SJs believe in one you must control or it may let you down. "Optimistic attitudes" they sometimes refer to as "irresponsible attitudes." "How can you trust in something you can't be sure of?" they ask. Since things go wrong all the time, how can you trust what you can't control? And when they carry their cautious beliefs too far, they become the pessimist.

Pessimism comes from the Latin meaning "worst." In street philosophy, pessimism is the belief that the world is never the best it can be. It is much nearer to being the worst it can be. In this world, there is more evil than good in the pessimist's belief. Therefore, they expect the worst to happen because it supports this philosophy. Not all SJs go to this length. If they have adopted a philosophy of hope and follow it, they live where faith and trust is the safe air to breathe.

In rationalizing a pessimistic leaning, they point out it is best to believe that the worst will happen because you then prepare for the worst. When and if the best happens, or something a little better than the worst, you have cause for celebration. This is a tortured way of being happy. "Mind you," they say, "make it a short celebration," for pessimism instructs the reveler that the worst will happen again and soon. Beware!

This negative thread that runs through the overuse of the SJs' strengths surely makes it harder for them to believe in something new, in some change, or even in the best outcome.

Faith is easier for them if the belief is a traditional belief. Anything supported by experiences, and anything accepted as part of what their culture or religion teaches, is believed strongly. Once accepted, a belief is often immortalized in their minds. So all traditional or tested beliefs are clung to. The SJ has abundant faith in these. What a difference from their polar opposite, the SP, who believes spontaneously in things that haven't been proven.

New beliefs have a hard time establishing root in the SJ. To do so they must be examined and pass the test of sound common sense, which means to the SJ, they must not be risky. Likewise, if they are still unproven or examples of their safe use cannot be cited, they are suspect.

Beliefs are carefully thought out, mainly for their practicality, and checked for detailed consistency. "You can't be too sure!" is another SJ motto. Likewise, "Better safe than sorry." In other words, "Don't consider it if you don't know it really works!"

Decisions come easy though. They hate to live with the uncertainty of not knowing what they are doing. A belief that is not yet proven and that suggests change or calls for a leap in the dark is left in the dark.

When trying to build their strengths, faith can be a real obstacle, except for the building of strengths like caution, which SJs usually overbuild in fear of failure. Pessimism, which is an ever-present problem, must give way to at least a cautious optimism for the strengths of the SJ to develop. If you are an SJ, work on developing beliefs and values that inspire hope and trust.

NT

The NT is not known for faith, but look more closely and you will see that they do believe. Remember, everyone is motivated by what they believe and NTs are strongly motivated. They firmly believe in their own intellectual adeptness, their ingenuity, and their need to be self reliant. Like the SP, the NT usually has no problem believing in their own abilities.

If it also has to do with new theories and new ways of doing things, faith is a given for the NT. To put the time and effort into constructing a theory requires at least a belief in it being worth the effort and struggle. The discovery of something new is worth any amount of effort to an NT. It is impossible to proceed with any scientific or pragmatic idea without at least some faith. NTs often lost sight of this since faith is not seen as a useful "scientific" tool, even though scientists use it all the time and cannot proceed without it.

The NT does have a problem with faith, however. Faith can't be seen or examined with any preciseness. It is ethereal, nonphysical, even metaphysical in the sense of being beyond the physical. NTs are soundly pragmatic and intangible things that smack of being supernatural are hard for them to accept, so most NTs surge ahead in faith while turning a blind eye to faith being a reality.

Another hesitancy to accept faith is that unless a belief is pragmatic it is of no use to the NT. This belief in the pragmatic (something that works) comes from a word meaning "skilled in business or law." Now business is pragmatic! It has to work. Believing in what works is like believing in what you can see and what has been proven. It is not a great faith, a trust, or a leap in the dark to believe in what has been proved. So the NT's faith is rooted, like the SJ's, in proof — either the proof of experience or an applied test. What the NT must be led to understand is that before anything was proved, they trusted in the procedure or the idea and that is where their faith came into play. Although the NT is intuitive, they are soundly rooted in this practical, pragmatic world.

Faith must also be shown to be reasonable for the NT to embrace it. Of course, if it works it is reasonable. To the NT, faith must pass an abstract skeptical and practical review. Anything that cannot be rationally explained is suspect. To my knowledge, it was only the Greeks who gave us the following meaning for the word skeptic: one who is thoughtful and inquiring. Faith can live with being thoughtful and inquiring, but it cannot live easily with rank skepticism.

Some NTs pride themselves on doubting everything and believing nothing. That is a contradiction of reality that apparently they haven't noticed. It is impossible to believe nothing, and they don't doubt everything or, for example, they wouldn't eat. How does anyone know that the apple they are eating has not been injected with some poison? Faith can't be proved, but it is reasonable. Therefore, because it is reasonable the NT can believe it is worthwhile to use a strong faith to develop their strengths. An NT's beliefs must also support their independent spirit. Any dependence on others in the forming of their beliefs is an admission of inadequacy to them.

When an NT works their way through these mental abstractions, they can believe naturally and with ease. It must seem reasonable (not necessarily proved beyond doubt), useful, and pragmatic, and it must be understood as the starting fuel of any theoretical undertaking. With these understandings, faith is released as a power in the life of the NT.

Ask the hard-core SP to take a leap in the dark and he or she will want to oblige. Ask an SJ or an NT and they will look at you and wonder if you are not somehow missing important gray matter. But explain the above understandings to an SJ or an NT, and they will not want to leap. They will examine the leap and propose — which is, for the SJ, a cautious way to proceed, or for the NT, a reasonable way to approach taking the leap.

NF

Faith is a necessity for the NF. As children, they fed on fantasy and make-believe. The NF must believe. Imagination and intuition feed their faith. When they imagine, they feel in touch with a world as real and fulfilling as the real world of the SP, SJ, and NT.

They are the idealists. Idealism requires having faith in something or someone and idealistic beliefs are sometimes even worshipped. The important people in an NF's life are idealized and they can pin their future and all of its hopes on just one person. Believing in people can be even easier for them than believing in ideas, although the distinction is fine. There is danger to face in their readiness to believe, just as there is in the impulsive faith of the SP or the cautiousness and pragmatism of the SJ and NT respectively.

The future is believed in too, if it has viable possibilities. However, we all know that the future is unknown, and this can thwart the NF's faith with unexpected disappointments. On the other hand, faith in the future is another term for hope and without hope people perish inside. NFs live on hope and happy expectations.

If some idea has a spiritual, ethical or mysterious overtone, it is treated as a serious candidate for faith. To the NF, faith is the mental and spiritual quality that does not dismiss the unknown and the mysterious just because there is no rational explanation. The NF does not dismiss faith without serious consideration of the values that underlie that faith or what reasonableness there is to be found in that faith. For the NF, emotions, values, and mystery have an important part to play in this universe, and they see the world of ideas as pregnant with ethereal worth.

Intuition is unexplainable by reason alone and they welcome the mystery that it, too, presents them. They tend to trust their intuitions readily. This perceptiveness is just another factor in the world beyond reason that they cannot dismiss. They are not necessarily gullible, but can be if they don't call their rational abilities into play. Credulous, perhaps, is a better word to describe them. They are easily persuaded and, at times, a little too quick to believe something, but they are usually not stupid enough to act on it. They often ponder their readily-trusting conclusions and, unless naive, will proceed with an unexpected caution. The healthy NF is a blend of people skills, reason, and trust.

Beliefs that produce harmony are treasured. NFs have a robust faith in harmony. It is the state of relationship that best nurtures the closeness and comfort of love. Therefore, they are nervous when conflict appears because it threatens the harmony and their trust. Confrontation is disliked chiefly because to them it destroys the emotional equilibrium of love and trust and because they have such a strong need for love that they feel they are in danger of being robbed when love is disturbed.

They have a strong faith in the ability of people to reach their potential and to experience the fulfillment of personal growth. Faith in ideas and people always beckons them. It is very hard for them to give up trying to help someone because there is always hope for everyone.

For the Js among them, deciding to believe is easier than it is for the Ps. Therefore, the Ps can also have trouble trusting when a major decision has to be made. A decision and a faith calls for action and at times they are not ready to act.

Their focus on what they believe is intense and constantly examined, especially for the introverts. Like reason (which NFs value, but don't worship) what they believe is not beyond evaluation. The overall good and the personal good are the standards for much of their evaluations. Ethics, especially justice and love, are at the center of what motivates their inspection of all they believe. Justice and love must not be threatened by what they believe.

Faith in oneself is their greatest challenge! We might expect that such free use of faith in others would mean a high self-esteem and confidence. Not so. Their sense of self worth probably fluctuates more than any other temperament. Often you will see them exercising faith in others while they feel worthless themselves.

Depression, for the NF, is most often associated, not with insecurity as it is for the SJ or failure to succeed as it is for the SP, but with a low self-esteem and an inability to see something encouraging on their future horizons. In short, these NFs, who live on faith and trust, can teeter at the edge of despair because of a recurring feeling of low self-worth.

If you are an NF, work on adding to your faith in abstract principles, values, and the world of the unseen a vibrant faith in yourself.

If your understanding of how faith works for you is clearer now, you will be more effective in using its amazing power in driving you toward your goal. The best that you can be is only achieved with faith. According to your faith it will be done to you.

Here's What Kickstarts Your Future

Force (Decision Making)

Always bear in mind that your resolution to succeed is more important than any one thing.
~ Abraham Lincoln

Faith alone is not enough. We must act on our faith. Remember these three — faith, force, and focus — are the ingredients of the mix to release and empower your strengths. We will now add the second ingredient.

A Decision Identifies a Direction.
The mind flounders and stutters without direction. All movement calls for a direction, a purpose, or it can be meaningless. The mind asks, "What am I doing? For what? Where am I going? Are you going to give me any directions?" Directionless is decision-less, purposeless, and powerless.

Schwartz (to whom I have already referred), in his book that I recommend (a true tour de force), *The Mind and the Brain*, explores how the mind shapes the brain. A decision to focus the mind's attention away from negative behaviors and toward positive ones is a mental step necessary to rewire the brain for positive behavior. We have the power to shape our brains and the mental force of a decision can change an obsessive behavior or direction on which the mind is fixed to a healthy one, he successfully argues.

Both children and adults can rebuild their minds with mental force. It empowers them when they learn that they have their life in their control. They can turn their lives around instead of living by some doctrine of fate. They can make a choice that leads them in another direction. Direction is a start.

Building Our Strengths Requires Several Decisions.
Which strength will I develop? For what purpose? When? With what intensity? Together these decisions fire the starter's gun. The motivation that our beliefs produce is waiting for a decision that produces action. Then our life is off and running, heading for some goal.

Building our strengths will help us fine-tune the direction our life is intended to go. Our life's purpose is written in our strengths. Again, let me say it: the blueprint for our happiness and the road to the best that we can be is found in our strengths.

Mental Force Motivates
Decisions also end the constant ruminating of depressed minds. Depressed minds are negative minds. Our regurgitating of negative thoughts leads to increasing concern and mental panic. Self-pity is another of its poisonous fruits. We build our own weaknesses when we negatively ruminate and only a decision (mental force) can break the cycle. Faith motivates; mental force motivates, and together they multiply the power we generate.

To exit the negative world, we will need (at some crucial point) the power of a decision. Our decision to change course can be a decision to simply distract ourselves from our negative grind, to accept a distraction that presents itself, to force a change of direction, or to leap to the safety of positive thoughts.

When decisions fire the neurons in the brain, the process of physical and mental change is activated. The brain sends messages to support the decision and prepares the body for action accordingly. Direction for what to do and how to do it and the energy to perform the act are all wrapped up in that decision. Destiny is unleashed by decisions! We are what we decide. "As a man thinks, so is he," says the proverb.

A 'J' in Your Personality Profile Means...
Those with a J in their personality profile prefer to make decisions. They sweat through the decision-making process, wanting to get it over with. Therefore, they can often make premature decisions due to the tension inside that says "I have to come to a decision quickly." The understanding of our *innerkinetics* comes to our aid at this point.

Js are uncomfortable and uneasy until the decision is made. Life is, as a result, lived with a sense of urgency. They tend to be less patient with time delays. There is also a determination and deliberateness in their style of living. Often you will find them on edge and acting nervously. Therefore, heed the trouble signs that an overuse of this strength can so easily produce: premature decisions, impatience, stressful lifestyle, nervousness, and uncalled for anxiety.

The upside of this lifestyle preference is that they seldom miss opportunities and tend to get things done. The development of their strengths usually progresses at full speed also and, apart from the misjudgments or lack of waiting for a better opportunity, they can have it all in their control.

Let's look a little closer though. The SJ temperament (all SJs have a J in their profile) displays two styles of decision making. Those SJs with a "T" in their profile tend to always be in a hurry or appear pressured and time is of the essence. Of course, they may not see it that way since they prefer to feel they have perfect timing and adequate patience. (We all feel that way.) They make decisions by understanding the facts and then, without delay, act on them. It is the fastest way to a decision. "Read the facts and do what they tell you to do" is the mantra of the Ts. They do not understand the delay that all Fs seem to require.

The reason they don't understand is that those with an F in their profile add a second step to making their decisions. They read the facts, see what the facts are telling them to do, and then, instead of deciding on facts alone, they consult their feelings. If their feelings agree with the decision that the facts indicate, all is well and the decision is relatively speedy. On the other hand, if their feelings don't support what the facts indicate, they must either adjust their feelings to the facts or the facts to their feelings before they proceed. This can be a lengthy process. Feelings don't change quickly at times. Therefore, the Fs can seem as though they are procrastinating when, in reality, they are not. They are simply processing the decision through their feelings and, since all SJs are Js, they make the decision quickly when both fact and feeling are accommodated.

Neither the Ts or the Fs have all the truth about decision making. The Ts fail to consult all the facts since feelings are facts too. The Fs consider both the facts and their feelings, but they often get bogged down in their feelings.

We make less than perfect decisions most of the time. Being aware of our limitations can help us greatly in the decision-making process. Both the T and the F can modify their preferences, when necessary, to their benefit.

A 'P' in Your Personality Profile Means...

"I like to keep my options open as long as possible." For some Ps, that can be almost forever. Ps know that if they wait, other facts may emerge that are relevant or even decisive so they feel justified in waiting. If they have an F in their profile, they often wait for their feelings to settle, and sometimes that can be a very long time. Feelings are thoughts that are less under our control than analytical thoughts.

Whereas the J feels uncomfortable before the decision is made, the P feels uncomfortable after the decision is made, fearing they may have made the decision too soon or may have made the wrong one. When they feel the fear of having to face more fear after a decision is made, they don't normally want to make the decision.

Both the J and the P protect valuable factors in decision-making. The J is unlikely to miss an opportunity; the P often does. The P waits and, in the process, is likely to turn up new and important facts, while the J has already decided and has to adjust their decision to accommodate the new facts. Both will argue their style is best.

The SP temperament (also all other Ps) is less affected by delay. They act impulsively most of the time and are the experts at fast tactical decisions. However, when the decision is not impulsive or tactical, they can bog down in delay just like all the other Ps.

There are no Ps in the SJ temperament. Therefore, the entire temperament has one lifestyle. In the NT temperament, the NTPs can make decisions but fail to act on them, especially the INTP. They see clearly what to do since the importance of facts is their life. However, to act on them is another matter and is determined by their P, their preferred lifestyle.

The Ps among the NFs are slowed by both the need to adjust their feelings to the facts or the facts to their feelings and the preference they have to keep the options open in case some other fact or feeling emerges to help them determine the decision.

When the impact of all the letters on each other are taken into account, of the sixteen types, the INTP and INFP can be the slowest to make a move. Whether this is a detriment depends, of course, on the issue and its demands.

Ps often need a jump start. It is always best for them to do it themselves so here is a way they can help themselves make timely decisions. First, decide on *when* you will decide. Then go about the process of gathering facts and preparing yourself for "D-day." All decisions are in two parts. The first is the decision itself and the second is when we are going to make the decision. If you are a P, simply reverse the order and make the first decision about when you will decide. This is the easier decision to make for the P. Hold yourself to it, but remember that, as you near the date of decision, you will have to contend with increased tension.

Decision gives you that powerful rush out of the gates whenever you make it. In developing your strengths, if you are not seeming to get motivated, it is either your lack of a powerful belief or you are stalling at the point of decision. The two must work together. A belief is not a matured belief unless we act on it.

The Force in Force

For all of us, a strong faith or belief or trust is essential to motivation and motivates if we act on it. However, there is one more factor worth a comment. A decision is the action of mental force. The strength and determination in that decision plays a crucial part in the success of the decision. Many decisions are not acted on or are quickly reversed or are implemented with the energy of a snowflake's fall. They hardly deserve the name "force." A decision that is devoid of force is as powerful as a tornado that spins at five miles an hour. The force that will release your strength for development and propel it to its potential is a mental determination that will not be stopped or delayed.

Determination starts with the way the decision is made. Mental force is stronger than physical force, as shown in the stories of the early explorers I related. All of us must say, "I will become all that my strengths can become." We must continue with the maximized force of an unrelenting determination to achieve this. Again, strengthen your belief in your strengths, yourself, and your faith in general to give the power of dogged determination to your decision.

Force releases the power in our strengths only if it is a determined decision.

Here's Your High-Octane Fuel

(Focus — Intense Concentration)

It is a process of diverting one's scattered forces into one powerful channel.
~ James Allen

Think of many things; do only one.
~ Proverb

With an MRI we can observe the increased activity in the brain when we focus intensely. We can remember the power of focus when, as children, we focused sunlight on a piece of tinder with a magnifying glass and watched as the tinder burst into flame. So we understand that focus multiplies things, including the powers in our mind. All of our mental resources are dedicated to the task when we focus intensely. We can only be our best when we focus with tenacious intensity.

We have no way of measuring the amount of power that is generated in our strengths when we focus on them. What the mind can achieve is yet to be known. This is why the word "possible" must remain vague and elastic in our language and a word both you and I are stretching. What is possible is dramatically affected by what we believe, the power generated by a determined decision, and the intensity with which we focus. Focus is the magic of the mind. We now add the third ingredient to the mix of mental power that will release our strengths to rocket to their potential: focus.

Natural Drive
A natural drive inside of us to get things done can intensify our focus since it adds energy to our focus. Some people have more natural drive than others. From wherever it comes, be thankful for it and feed it with your powerful beliefs.

All Js have a natural drive to get things done and this can increase their focus. It can also act in reverse if, in their desire to get things done, they skip over needed details and don't do a thorough job. They may, in the end, have to start again. The Ps, from all their pondering and waiting, can build a strong natural drive too. So, when we drive intensely toward our goals we need to create a tight focus and avoid wandering. The double-minded person is unstable and loses power. Create a single-mindedness and your natural drive will surface to aid you.

Mental Stamina
Mental stamina can improve focus. Stamina is the ability to resist distraction and disturbances. Concentration is more about not being distracted than about holding a focus. Children who display skills of concentration often develop great mental stamina.

It's easy to give in to distractions. Fight them if for no other reason than to strengthen your mental stamina. To reach the potential of your strengths you will need an intense focus.

Sometimes creativity comes in moments of relaxation and in the night hours, but it is usually preceded by some form of concentration. Focus on something and its possibilities are more easily released. That perspiration produces more creative results than inspiration may or may not be true, but the sweat of an intense focus produces impressive results. So here is your motto: Focus releases even the evasive powers of creativity.

The Negative Trap

Focus will magnify both negative and positive thought patterns. Beware of the brain lock caused by focusing on your weaknesses instead of your strengths. When our weaknesses (even our feelings of low self-worth) become obsessive, they create such negative forces in our minds that we lose all forward progress. Then we spin with the destructive force of a negative mental tornado. The wrong focus can hurt the release of our powers.

Focus on Possibilities

Focusing on possibilities and solutions ignites the positive powers of mental discovery. Intuition plays a mysterious part in this process too — a part we can't control. Very valuable, nonetheless.

NFs are always searching the future to assess the possibilities. In this they have the edge. Are they then the most creative and inventive of all the types? They wish. What dogs them is the depression and despair that overtakes them when they see a negative possibility on their horizon and they begin to focus on it. Negativity is the NF's curse when it shows up. When they focus on one of their "black clouds," their creative powers fade. Negative feelings overwhelm them and they begin to crater. Then the multiplying power of focus works to their temporary destruction. To keep the mind positive is the secret for an NF's creative brilliance.

Follow Your Imagination

Imagination also thrives on focus. It goes where reason cannot venture. It opens up new worlds. Logic is in your control, but imagination will follow your mental directions and then leap to new understandings without the aid of rational thinking. You may have noticed that your imagination links things that are not normally associated, such as in your weird dreams, which sometimes become the door to discovery.

Since imagination is a particular strength of the NF, it is instructive to all those who wish to increase their imagination that the NF's natural strengths of sensitivity, passion, emotion, and intuition are what sensitize their imagination and empower it. Increasing these strengths will increase the imagination. Imagination is more important than reason, so focus on your imaginings.

Recall Is Enhanced by Focus.

When we concentrate on a fabulous meal we enjoyed, we can recall the tastes, aromas, colors, emotions — even what was happening around us — the more we focus on the experience. The more attention we pay to our everyday experiences, the more they are remembered and the more about them we tend to recall.

SJs focus on the past. Its lessons, traditions, and confirmations are vital to their sense and need for stability. They often recall events with astounding detail because of their natural interest and focus on the past.

Repeated recall of experiences or imagined happenings will strengthen the memory and make it easier to focus on them when they are recalled for consideration.

To Focus, Chase Your Thoughts

Focus is not a stationary holding on to a single thought. That's almost impossible to do. We can only think one thought at a time and to hold on to it when our mental abilities can think up to 2500 thoughts in a single minute is fighting ourselves.

Chase your thoughts and ideas. Race for the pot of gold at the end of your mental exercise. Focus your thoughts with a goal and a direction. Don't let them wander all over the planet. That's not focusing; that's vacationing. A wandering mind will find some gold, but not as much as a purposed-directed mind. A wandering mind will mostly find fool's gold.

Meditation and prayer can be enriched with the same chasing of thoughts. Both are forms of focus. Let your imagination lead your meditation and prayer. You may discover new worlds of reward.

Split Focus

Split focus dissipates energy. Multitasking may get many jobs done at once, but it divides mental energy. When you want to magnify your mental powers, focus them; don't divide them.

Energy is not to be diversified if it is to be maximized. We diversify our finances to protect against loss. Not so our energy. Diversified mental energy increases losses.

The Three Powers
We can make permanent changes in our brain's neural pathways. So, wire your brain the way you want it! By your beliefs, decisions, and focus you can create a more effective you. Together, faith, force, and focus create immeasurable mental powers. They, in turn, release the network of strengths you have been endowed with. Think of them this way: They are three agents you can employ for both the release and development of your strengths. Make them work.

Each temperament emphasizes faith, force, and focus in different ways. Let's see these three elements at work in the early 1800s in the records of Jedediah Smith, an NF adventurer. He comes to mind again because he, no doubt, (along with many others) exemplifies all we have said in this chapter.

Jedediah was detained in San Jose by the Mexican Government and, upon release, was ordered to leave by a prescribed route directly out of Mexican California territory. He was regarded as an American spy and they wanted no more of this difficult individual or his suspicious movements.

He had only become difficult because his plans, for which he had traveled all the way from Salt Lake, Utah to fulfill, were now being jettisoned. The Mexicans were ready to threaten his life as well as his plans, but something more powerful than life itself was holding his thoughts ransom. He believed in his destiny as an explorer. He believed in his "mission," a faith that had propelled him through many a danger already. Jedediah was a driven man, compelled by his beliefs and empowered by a fearless focus.

So he left San Jose and, in direct disobedience of the orders of the Governor of the Mexican territory, he pursued his original plan of trapping in the many rivers of northern California. Faith in his "calling" and in his plans led Jedediah to follow his beliefs come what may. He did precisely what he had set out to do. Whether we feel he was right in this action or not, intense focus ignited all his human powers.

We see faith and force operating. Together, they produced a fierce focus when he encountered peril after peril: deep mud through which his horses couldn't move and were mired, rains, floods, dense forests (almost impassable), lack of food, extreme exhaustion; losses of his own traps, weapons, and even his animals to Indian poachers; bear attacks and increasingly dangerous engagements with Indians bent on his destruction (which they very nearly achieved). He never gave up. He escaped by what he called the "hand of God, providence."

However we can also see the effect of these three agents of power — faith force and focus — which he believed his God had given him and may have been just as determinative as providence. Let's review them again. A strong faith motivated him and unleashed his leadership skills and his passionate strengths. He developed a stubborn insistence on his plans. Decisiveness narrowed his vision and brought a force to his actions. A focus that multiplied his endurance and his skills in negotiating the many hardships created a man with an irresistible power.

As an NF, he also displays a dreamer's idealism, passionate concern for his men, a trust in others that often proved dangerous to his life, diplomatic skills in dealing with unknown peoples, the introspection of the introverted NF, and a searching for significance that is dogged and unquenchable. This was Smith with all of his unleashed powers maximized.

Whatever the temperament, faith, force, and focus concentrate and release its powers.

Another example comes from the 1800s down under.

A. H. Reed, in his book, The Story of New Zealand, tells of Hongi Hika, a Maori chief who sat one day on the veranda of Samuel Marsden's home in Parramatta, Sydney. He was carving out of native wood a bust of himself bearing the fine tattoo on his face. The missionary had admired the fine tattoo and jokingly told him that he ought to be taken to England as an ornament. Hongi handed his finished bust to Samuel and said, "Send this instead."

However, Hongi did go to England, an arduous and dangerous six-month journey by sea and, having sought and gained an audience with the King George, he came back with valuable presents which he exchanged for muskets in Australia. It was all part of a belief, a decision, and a focus that made him the first Maori to sail to England and accomplish his goals. He soon became the most feared chief in the northern part of New Zealand. No tiaha (combination of spear and club) or mere (greenstone club) could match the musket in battle and Hongi Hika was soon the most famous leader of the tribes.

Everywhere he went he conquered like other famous generals. However, the Te Arawa tribe did not fear him and provided him with his greatest challenge. They lived on an island in the middle of a large lake, Lake Rotorua. The ocean by which Hongi must come was 30 miles away over extremely rugged terrain. Upon word of Hongi's arrival, the Te Arawas gathered up all the canoes around the lake and hid them on their island fort. With such a large body of water between them and any invader and with no canoes to reach the island, they were safe — so they thought.

Hongi beached his canoes 30 miles away and began the Herculean task of dragging his immense war canoes over land. Maori canoes were hollowed out of giant trees and averaged about 35 feet long and 5 feet wide. They were very heavy. The warriors labored until they dropped with fatigue. Still known today as "Hongi's Track," his route wound its way over many hills and through dense forest for 30 miles to Lake Rotorua. His belief, his forceful unwavering decision, and his intense focus on the task at hand won out over impossible odds. Hongi's war canoes appeared on Lake Rotorua to the horror of the Te Arawas. The battle was brief and, after a decisive victory, they paddled back over Lake Rotorua only to haul their canoes again (this time laden with the spoils of battle) to the ocean. The warriors were promised nothing but a huge feast and honor, but they had performed the impossible. Most would have thought it the dream of a madman. The real reward for each of them was enduring respect among their people.

For respect alone people will toil to the edge of death and risk life and limb in dangerous exploits. What is it that drives people to do the impossible? What maximizes their powers for good or ill? A thought that warms our sense of self-worth? Is that all? Nothing material? Simply the way others think of us and the way we think of ourselves?

Yes, the way we think of ourselves. The powers that take us beyond our limits are the three agents of release, the generators of untold power when linked and employed in the development of our temperament's strengths. Faith heads the trio: faith in how we have been made and how we can maximize our potential — faith in others and faith in our resources.

Pushing our limits builds our strengths even stronger just as a muscle increases with exercise. We become more than we dreamed we could be when the powers of our *innerkinetics* are released and maximized with faith, force, and focus.

Conclusion

"One learns by doing a thing; for though you think you know it, you have no certainty until you try."
~ Sophocles

The good thing about the future is it comes one day at a time.
~ Abraham Lincoln

The plan inside of you, your *innerkinetics*, holds the secret to your best. Learn, follow, and develop those strengths, drives, and urges of your temperament. The agents that release their explosive powers — faith, force and focus — are simply learned. If you would be the best you can be, this is your blueprint.

It remains as Sophocles stated: that we learn by doing. Go back over the sections of this book that have helped you understand and start putting your understanding into actions. Live your learning and learn from your living. Live one day at a time, but live with never-ending hope.

Appendix

The Meaning of the Four Letters

You received four letters in your temperament profile. To what do they refer?

The four parings of letters seek to identify four areas of our makeup in which our preferences declare a leaning.

The four parings are: E or I, S or N, T or F, and J or P. All four letter codes in your profile are selected from these pairings. Sixteen parings are possible.

The first paring (E or I) seeks to find out where we get our energy or how we rebuild our energy when it is depleted. This factor has a profound effect on our choices and behavior. It identifies two opposite ways humans prefer to act. A completed temperament key will also give us an idea of how strongly we prefer to act one way or the other by how many answers we checked as A or B.

Extroverts get their energy from contact with people and things. Introverts get their energy from inside of themselves and, therefore, prefer solitude when drained. What energizes you? Things outside of yourself or thoughts and feelings inside of yourself? This is the issue being decided in this pairing.

The second paring (S or N) helps us understand how we receive our information from the world around us. Do we get it mainly from our five physical senses: sight, hearing, taste, smell, and touch? Or do we rely more on our gut feelings: intuition or inner senses — our sixth sense, if you like? On what do we rely to guide us through the world and give us meaning? The temperament key helps us discover which we use most or prefer to rely on.

The difference between these two dominant ways of gathering information creates the greatest divide in human temperament. The S lives in the real world outside of themselves predominantly and the N lives predominantly in the inner world of their mind, their virtual world.

The third pairing (T or F) takes our discoveries a step further. After we receive our information from our world, how do we make our decisions about it? Some survey the facts and promptly make their decisions based on the data they have received. Making a decision is a simple matter of factual analysis for the Ts. The Fs have a more complicated path to their decision. First, they survey the data or the facts and, seeing what this tells them, they then proceed to examine how they feel about it. They consult their feelings since they think that how they feel is important information in coming to a decision. If what they feel is the opposite of the facts, they must either follow their feelings or the facts. Mostly, they follow their feelings.

Which is the nearest to your way of making decisions? These are opposing ways of making decisions and preferences line up strongly at times on both sides.

The fourth pairing (J or P) has to do with how you live your life — your lifestyle. Are you more hurried and pressured by time? Do you favor routines? Are you decisive and determined or are you more laid back and not pressured by time? Do you like to keep your options open and dislike making decisions?

These opposite lifestyles cause a lot of friction and set people apart. Which is more typically you? It's a matter of preference. Some want to get things done now, while others can wait — prefer to, in fact.

The Words the Letters Refer To
If I gave you the words each letter refers to, they would make sense — except for the last pairing. E stands for extrovert; I, for introvert; S, for sensing; N, for intuition; T, for thinking, and F, for feeling. The J stands for the word "judging" and the P for the word "perceiving."

The problem with these last two words is: The Ps do as much judging as the Js and the Js do as much perceiving as the Ps. Unless we expect people to understand the words with a specialized technical meaning, they make no real sense. So the choice of words do not distinguish between the two lifestyles for most people. Forget the words and just use the letters, filling them with the correct meaning of each lifestyle.

The Two Letters that Determine Our Temperament

Two letters, S and N, are the basis of the four temperaments. When we add the P or the J to the S we have SP and SJ. Both start with an S; both are sensing temperaments and they form a large part of the population: approximately 86%. The two different lifestyles of the J and the P are what differentiate these two temperaments.

When we add a T or an F to the N, we get the remaining two temperaments, the NT and the NF. Both start with an N and are the intuitive temperaments. They represent approximately 14 percent of the population. Therefore, Ns often feel odd, strange, and different from other people at times. The T is somewhat calm and cool and the F is warm and can be quite emotionally reactive.

Because the purpose of this book is to focus on the four temperaments, I have not gone into the wealth of detail the four-letter code suggests. You will find more detail for the four letters in my book, *I'm a Keeper*, written for parents and descriptive of both adult's and children's *innerkinetics*.

This bibliography focuses on providing helpful resources for the reader, not sources for the student or a list of resources that were formative in the writing of this book.

Temperament (*InnerKinetics*®)
Briggs-Myers, Isabel with Myers, Peter B. *Gifts Differing: Understanding Personality Type.* Davies-Black Publishing, 1995.

Briggs-Myers, Isabel and McCaulley, Mary H. *A Guide to the Development and Use of the Myers-Briggs Type Indicator.* Consulting Psychologists Press, 1985.

Harkey, Nancy and Jourgensen, Teri. *Raising Cuddlebugs and Bravehearts, Volumes 1 and 2.* Authorhouse, 2004.

--------- *Parenting by Temperament,* (Publisher unknown) 2009

Hirsh, Sandra and Kummerow, Jean. *Life Types.* Warner Books, 1989.

Jeffries, William, C. *True to Type.* Hampton Roads Publishing Company, Inc. 1991.

Kagan, Jerome. *Galen's Prophecy: Temperament in Human Nature.* Westview Press, 1998.

Kroeger, Otto and Thuesen, Janet M. *Type Talk.* A Dell Trade Paperback, 1988.

Keirsey, David and Bates, Marilyn. *Please Understand Me: Character and Temperament Types.* Prometheus Nemesis Book Company, 1978.

Keirsey, David. *Please Understand Me II: Temperament, Character, Intelligence.* Prometheus Nemesis Books, 1998.

--------- *Portraits of Temperament,* Prometheus Nemesis Books, 1987.

Montgomery, Stephen. *People Patterns: A Modern Guide to the Temperaments.* Archer Publications, 2002.

--------- *The Pygmalion Project: Love and Coercion Among the Types. Volume One, The Artisan.* Prometheus Nemesis Books, 1989.

--------- *The Pygmalion Project: Love and Coercion Among the Types. Volume Two, The Guardian.* Prometheus Nemesis Books, 1990.

--------- *The Pygmalion Project: Love and Coercion Among the Types. Volume Three, The Idealist.* Prometheus Nemesis Books, 1993.

Faith, Force, and Focus
Maxwell, John C. *Put Your Dream To The Test.* Thomas Nelson, 2009.

Schwartz, Jeffrey M. *The Mind and The Brain.* Harper Collins, 2002.

Waitley, Denis. *Seeds of Greatness.*

Go to our website, www.raywlincoln.com, for additional helpful resources by Ray W. Lincoln.

Passionate About Potential!

You may have already begun telling others as you experienced success from the understanding and skills you have acquired here. So, if you are passionate about your new understanding, here are some ways you can help others to discover their own purpose and potential. Who knows, you might help to change the world!

1. Give the book to friends as a gift. They need a magnificent glimpse into the wonderful way they are made.
2. If you have a website or blog, consider commenting about the book and how it has helped you — and maybe how it has helped the lives of others you know.
3. Write a book review for your local paper, favorite magazine, newsletter, or a website you frequent.
4. Ask your favorite radio show or podcast host to invite Ray as a guest. (Journalists and media representatives often give attention to the requests from their watchers, readers, and listeners.)
5. If you own a shop or business, consider putting a display of the books on your counter to resell to customers. The books are available at a discounted rate for resale. For individuals, we offer a volume discount pricing for six books or more. Please contact us for details.
6. Buy several books and provide them to shelters, prisons, rehabilitation homes, and such where people may need help connecting with themselves.
7. Talk about the book in your e-mails, groups, clubs, forums you frequent, and other places where you engage in conversation, whether in person or on the internet. Share how the book has helped you and others, and offer people the link to www.RayWLincoln.com.
8. If you know of people (authors, speakers, etc.) who have websites, blogs or newsletters, ask them if they would review a copy and make some comments about it to their audience, fans, and subscribers.

We welcome your comments and success stories. You can send them to info@raywlincoln.com. Implement the power of your *innerkinetics*.

About the Author

RAY W. LINCOLN

Ray W. Lincoln is the bestselling author of *I'M A KEEPER* and is the founder of Ray W. Lincoln & Associates. Ray's is a professional life coach and an expert in human nature. His 40 plus years of experience in speaking, teaching, and counseling began in New Zealand and have carried him to Australia and the United States. He speaks with energy and enthusiasm before large and small audiences.

It was not by accident that he became the international speaker and coach that he is today and acquired the ability to guide so many to a happier, healthier, more fulfilled life. Ray has studied extensively in the fields of Philosophy, Temperament Psychology, and Personology. A member of the National Speakers Association, his expertise has been used as a lecturer and professor, teacher and keynote speaker, seminar presenter, counselor, and coach. He teaches and leads in staff trainings, university student retreats, and parents' educational classes, as well as other seminars and training events. He also trains and mentors teachers and other professionals and executives — all with the goal of understanding our own temperaments and those of others.

Ray lives with his wife, Mary Jo, in Littleton, Colorado where they enjoy hiking, snowshoeing, fly fishing, and all the beauty the Rocky Mountains offer. Both are highly involved in their work (which they feel is the most important and most fulfilling work of their entire career lives), filling the roles for which they were designed as they travel to speak to groups and to present seminars and workshops throughout the US.

www.innerkinetics.com Our website is a great place to order additional copies of
INNERKINETICS™

We also have additional FREE resources there to help you. Before you go to www.innerkinetics.com, however, go to:

www.raywlincoln.com

At this website you can:
- Sign up for our FREE monthly newsletter, which entitles you to:
- Receive 15% off all purchases at www.innerkinetics.com, www.imakeeperkid.com , and www.raywlincoln.com.
- Receive a FREE .pdf download of Ray''s article,

Leveraging the Power of Your Mind.

Find more helpful resources and information about our services.

OUR SERVICES INCLUDE Professional Life Coaching
Educational Seminars and Training Keynote Addresses
Educational Materials Free Monthly Newsletter

My Notes:

My Notes:

CPSIA information can be obtained
at www.ICGtesting.com
Printed in the USA
BVOW11s1910070817

491401BV00008B/27/P